EVOLUTION OF INTERNATIONAL AVIATION

Evolution of International Aviation
Phoenix Rising

DAWNA L. RHOADES
Embry-Riddle Aeronautical University

ASHGATE

Published by
Ashgate Publishing Limited
Gower House
Croft Road
Aldershot
Hants GU11 3HR
England

Ashgate Publishing Company
Suite 420
101 Cherry Street
Burlington, VT 05401-4405
USA

Ashgate website: http://www.ashgate.com

British Library Cataloguing in Publication Data
Rhoades, Dawna L.
    Evolution of international aviation : phoenix rising. -
    (Ashgate studies in aviation economics and management)
    1. Aeronautics, Commercial 2. Aeronautics, Commercial -
    History 3. Airlines - Economic aspects
    I. Title
    387.7'4

Library of Congress Cataloging-in-Publication Data
Rhoades, Dawna L., 1958-
    Evolution of international aviation : phoenix rising / Dawna L. Rhoades.
        p. cm. -- (Ashgate studies in aviation economics and management)
    Includes bibliographical references and index.
    ISBN 0-7546-3785-9
    1. Aeronautics, Commercial--History. 2. Aeronautics, Commercial--Law and
legislation--History. 3. Aeronautics, Commercial--Law and legislation--International
cooperation--History. 4. Airlines--United States--History. 5.
Airlines--Deregulation--United States. 6. Airlines--Finance--Case studies. 7. International
business enterprises--Case studies. 8. Aircraft industry--History. 9. Airports--Security
measures. 10. Terrorism--Prevention. 11. Strategic alliances (Business)--Case studies. I.
Title. II. Series.

HE9774.R48 2003
387.7--dc21   2003051921

ISBN 0 7546 3785 9

Reprinted 2004

Printed and bound in Great Britain by MPG Books Ltd, Bodmin, Cornwall

Contents

List of Figures

List of Tables

Acknowledgements

No book is truly the work of a single individual even though the title page may not reflect the contributions of these other individuals; this is the role of the acknowledgement section. I would like to thank my colleague, Sveinn Gudmundsson, for inspiring this book in the first place. I doubt that it would ever have been started without him. I also owe a debt of thanks to my colleagues and students at Embry-Riddle Aeronautical University for their support during the writing of this work. They not only supported me during the frantic days of writing and editing, but inspired me to write a text that would help to make aviation accessible to all interested parties. Aviation is a forward-looking industry and the aviation students of today will be the leaders of tomorrow. I hope that we have prepared them well.

My former research assistant, Laurie Goosens, was invaluable throughout the process in reading, editing, and compiling basic research. I will miss her tireless efforts. Graduating into the current aviation environment is difficult at best, but I am certain that her talents and motivation will help her to succeed whatever the odds. My newest research assistant, Miki Kasuga, has also proven equal to the task. Assisting in the editing of a book was not the easiest way to start her 'career' as a research assistant, but it should make everything seem simple.

I am indebted to the many fine scholars who have gone before me in the quest to understand and explain the aviation industry. Their work is cited throughout this book. There are three individuals who deserve special mention – Brian Graham, Nawal Taneja, and Dipendra Sinha. Their work proved to be especially valuable.

Finally, I would like to thank my husband, John, and two children, Ben and Deanna, for putting up with a mother who often went around mumbling to herself and scribbling notes on little pieces of paper. Their understanding and support has been greatly appreciated during this hectic time.

Chapter 1

Phoenix Rising

Of Phoenixes and Airlines

According to the most famous legend of the phoenix, the phoenix was a bird of brilliant red and gold plumage whose death in a fiery blaze gave rise to a new phoenix. Like the phoenix, the airline industry seems to have established its own cycle of destruction and renewal. From its very inception, the airline industry has been at the mercy of the business cycle experiencing soaring profits in the upturn and rapidly falling into losses when the market turns down. The so-called new economy that combined technological innovation, globalization, and abundant venture capital began transforming the U.S. economy and others around 1995. This new economy was predicted to end the business cycle or at least smooth it out so that the booms were not so high and the busts so low. Under this new era of prosperity, the U.S. economy grew at about 4.4% a year while unemployment dropped to near 4%. At the same time, productivity rose at an annual rate of 2.8% (Mandel, 2000). In short, growth, productivity, and employment seemed on an unstoppable path upward.

For airlines, the boom times have always meant adding capacity through new aircraft acquisitions, opening new routes, and negotiating bigger labor contracts. The bust has always been a downward ride into declining profits, falling load factors, and destructive price wars. Unfortunately, even before the events of September 11th, the U.S. airline industry was facing the return of its most dreaded foe, the business cycle and U.S. airlines were expected to post a $3 billion loss (Air Transport Association, 2002). While the rest of the airline world was not yet expecting losses of this magnitude, the U.S. downturn was expected to have an effect on those carriers with a sizable percentage of traffic to North America (Sparaco and Wall, 2001). Post 9/11, the downturn has become even steeper as many carriers struggle to avoid bankruptcy.

The airline industry is also no stranger to bankruptcy. In the United States, the first passenger on a regularly scheduled airline flew from Tampa Bay to St. Petersberg, Florida on January 1, 1914. The airline chalked up another first when it folded four months later after running into financial difficulty (Wells, 1994). Although several attempts were made after this to establish a viable commercial passenger airline in the United States, it was not until the development of the Douglas DC-3 that air travel for passengers became economical to operate. The DC-3 combined five key innovations - variable-pitch propellers, retractable landing gear, lightweight molded body construction, radial air-cooled engine, and wing flaps - to produce a plane that was aerodynamic and economical to operate (Senge,

1990). Even with the DC-3 and its successors, the airline industry has continued to experience periods of major economic loss, bankruptcy, and merger followed by all too brief periods of recovery. In Europe, war and financial crisis in the 1930s and 1940s led to the nationalization of many of the continent's premier carriers as a means of insuring their survival (Graham, 1995; Sinha, 2001). Back in the U.S., aviation continued to expand in fits and spurts aided by airmail contracts from the U.S. Postal Service, however, since the deregulation of the U.S. airline industry in 1978, the industry has experienced a financial crisis in the early years of each decade. The losses in the early 1990s were nearly $10 billion (Rosen, 1995). The losses for the industry in 2001 alone were $7.7 billion and are expected to be approximately $8 billion for 2002 (Foss, 2002).

A Special Case

The aviation industry has long been treated as a special case in international business, subject to different rules and held to different standards. In fact, international aviation has been 'a serious problem in international relations, affecting the way governments view one another, the way individual citizens view their own and foreign countries, and in a variety of direct and indirect connections the security arrangements by which we live' (Lowenfeld, 1975). There are several reasons for the special status and serious problems associated with international aviation. Originally, the most compelling was national defense. Under programs such as the U.S. Civil Reserve Air Fleet (CRAF) plan, civilian fleets could be used during times of military action to ferry troops and supplies. It was, therefore, vital to insure the existence and health of this civilian reserve. In the case of CRAF, the U.S. government gets a reserve fleet for times of emergency without the cost of maintaining it and the airlines get paid a rate that during Desert Storm was 1.75 times the seat mile or cargo mile rate (Kane, 1999). National defense was also cited as the reason for insisting on home country ownership of these airlines on the premise that home country nationals would or could be made to cooperate in the defense of their country.

The second most cited reason for special treatment has been the economic impact of airlines. According to the Air Transport Action Group, the world's airlines carried over 1,600 million passengers in 1998 and transported 40% of the world's manufactured exports. The industry provided employment for over 28 million people worldwide and was responsible for over US$1, 360 billion in annual gross output. The aviation industry is also a key component of the travel and tourism industry that supported roughly 192 million jobs in 1999 and generated an estimated US$3,550 billion (Air Transport Action Group, 2000). Passenger traffic grew on average 6% per year during the decade of the 1980s and early 1990s driven by a number of factors: falling real costs of air travel, increasing economic activity, intensifying international trade, increasing disposable incomes, political stability, relaxation of travel restrictions, expanding ethnic ties, increasing leisure time, tourism promotion, air transport liberalization, and growth in emerging regions and countries. Historically, air traffic has grown at about twice the rate of gross domestic product (GDP) and during the period 1960-1990 80% of traffic growth could be explained by growth in GDP. Beginning in the 1990's, falling real prices (fares) played a greater role in traffic growth. As air travel grows, the direct (value of airline and on-airport activities) and indirect (value of off-airport activities of passengers and shippers) economic impact grows as well. In addition, there is an induced impact from the successive spending of recipients of these direct and indirect benefits. In short, the economic impact of the air transport industry makes its health a major concern of governments, businesses, and passengers around the world and keeps it from being seen as 'just another industry'.

The third reason for aviation's special status is the link that exists in the minds of many between national airlines and national achievement and pride. International airlines 'carry the flag' around the world. This reason should not be underestimated as a driver of individual and government perception. When the bankruptcy and subsequent grounding of the Swissair fleet forced the Swiss football team to fly the Russian carrier Aeroflot to a qualifying match in Moscow, one article reported this event as a 'further humiliation for the Swiss flag carrier' (Hall, Grant, Done, Cameron, and Dombey, 2001). The uproar that occurred in Great Britain over the replacement of the Union Jack on the tail of many British Airways planes by the so-called ethnic tails intended to show British Airways as the airline of the world was motivated by similar nationalistic sentiment (BBC News, 1999). Likewise, the debate in Belgium over the bankruptcy of Sabena and the need for a national carrier to serve the interest of the people of Belgium has more to do with nationalistic pride than airline economics (BBC News, 1999; Sparaco, 2001).

Changing Times

Even without the defense, economic, and 'flag' arguments, aviation/aerospace is not likely to be seen as 'just another industry'. It is the stuff of dreams and has fired the imagination of much of the world's population. Alvin Toffler (1970) noted in his bestselling book *Future Shock* that in 6000 B.C. the fastest transportation available to mankind was the camel caravan that averaged 8 miles per hour. By 1600 B.C. the chariot had raised this speed to approximately 20 miles per hour. The first mail coach in England began operating in 1784 at an average of only 10 miles per hour and the first steam locomotive was capable of a mere 13 miles an hour. In fact, it was not until the invention of an improved steam engine that mankind was able to reach a speed of 100 miles per hour. It took almost 8,000 years to go from the 8 mile an hour camel to the 100 mile an hour train. However, in only fifty-eight years, men in aircraft were exceeding the 400-mph line. Twenty years later that limit doubled. By the 1960's aircraft were approaching speeds of 4000 mph, and space capsules were circling the earth at 18,000 mph.

The history of aviation/aerospace is filled with larger-than-life figures. These men and women were the entrepreneurs of Joseph Schumpeter who took on the thankless job of building and shaping an industry because 'there is the dream and the will to found a private kingdom, usually, although not necessarily, also a dynasty ... . Then there is the will to conquer: the impulse to fight, to prove oneself superior to others, to succeed for the sake, not of the fruits of success, but of success itself ... . Finally, there is the joy of creating, of getting things done, or simply of exercising one's energy and imagination' (93-94).

The stories of these individuals, the planes they flew, and the companies they founded still fascinate us today. Sadly, despite the glories of the past the airline industry is now in the mature stages of its lifecycle. There are four basic characteristics of such an industry. First, growth slows or diminishes. Second, key technologies no longer provide an advantage to competitors. Third, the experience (or learning) curve no longer provides an advantage to one competitor over another. Finally, there are few new forms of differentiation and competition is largely based on price. The issue of price is critical because industries in this stage find that their profits are very sensitive to price, price advantages are short-lived, customers begin to expect lower prices, and customers shop for low price rather than value or benefits (Miller, 1998). Alfred Kahn, the Father of U.S. airline deregulation, wrote about the possibility of destructive competition within an industry as a result of fixed and sunk costs that represent a high percentage of total cost and long sustained and recurrent periods of excess capacity (1988). He did not anticipate this occurring in the airline industry, but, in fact, it has come to pass.

Stephen M. Wolf, then Chairman of United Airlines, blamed the financial crisis of the early 1990s on three issues: overcapacity, international competition, and the lack of infrastructure. On the question of overcapacity, he said that in a truly free market overcapacity is temporary, but that liberal U.S. bankruptcy laws allowed carriers 'to operate literally for years without repaying their debt obligations; consequently, their capacity is retained in the system and the result is economic havoc for all' (1995: 19). While Wolf would undoubtedly blame the bankruptcy of his current airline, U.S. Airways, on the events of 9/11 and the failure of the U.S. government to approve his United-US Airways deal, his comments regarding overcapacity and bankruptcy remain true. Allowing carriers, any carrier, to continue to operate while receiving the benefits of bankruptcy protection not only fails to reduce overcapacity, but spreads the 'bankruptcy virus' to other carriers who are disadvantaged by the competition from this protected carrier.

Warren Buffet, Chairman of Berkshire Hathaway, is 'world famous as the greatest stock market investor of modern times' and a man who speaks his mind (Bianco, 1999). When he was asked several years ago about the stock market, particularly the internet stocks, he compared the internet industry to 'two other transforming industries, auto and aviation' (Loomis and Buffet, 1999). His statements on aviation presents a bitter truth. According to Buffet, the early aviation industry was full of promise and home to many young, vibrant companies, most of whom are a distant memory. Likewise, he cited some 129 airlines that have filed for bankruptcy in the last twenty years. The reason, he says, is clear; the industry as a whole has not made money overall in the long run. Buffet brutally suggested that a farsighted and public-spirited individual would have done the world's investors a favor by shooting down the Wright Flyer in 1903.

Like Joseph's Dream of Egypt, the airline industry does seem condemned to experience years of plenty followed by years of famine. Unlike the Egyptians, however, they do not save in years of plenty to survive the coming famine. Instead, they buy planes, expand route systems, and sign ever sweeter labor contracts. It is as though they are convinced that the airline that fattens up the most in the good times will simply outlast the others in bad times. In a truly free market, this strategy might work, but as Wolf and others have noted, the airlines do not operate in such a market. The events of 9/11 did not create this situation, but they have made the situation worse.

As Buffet pointed out, the aviation industry has transformed the way we live and do business. It is itself in the process of transforming; it is *becoming* something new. A debate has raged in the fields of paleontology, genetics and evolutionary biology over whether change in living organisms takes place in a gradual, step-by-step manner or in periods of rapid, major change followed by stasis. The latter theory is called punctuated equilibrium (Gould and Eldredge, 1977). This theory has been adapted and applied to the evolution of technology (Tushman and Anderson, 1986, 1988) and to the lifecycle and evolution of organizations and their industries (Hannan and Freeman, 1984). The idea of punctuated equilibrium or discontinuous change has caught on in so many areas because it 'seems to fit' the observed evidence. In other words, investigators in all of these fields have been unable to trace a slow, clear development from one form to the next. Instead, they see periods of relative stability and little change interrupted by sudden, radical alterations in form. In the evolutionary sciences, these periods of sudden change are usually connected to mass extinctions of older, existing lifeforms. In the areas of technology and organizations, startling innovations have arisen that make the technology and knowhow that came before obsolete. For organizations, these periods of rapid change have been hardest on the firms of the prior age, firms that developed, grew, and adapted to life in another time. This is the traditional stockbrokerage coping in the new world of the internet or the corner bookseller competing with Amazon.com. The question in the minds of organizational theorists is whether these old age firms can change quickly enough to survive in the new age. If not, they will become the dinosaurs of this new age, dying out to make room for the newer, faster, smaller mammals.

It is possible that the airline industry is entering just such a period of discontinuous change. In the United States since 9/11, airlines have reduced their schedule by 3.5 percent and retired some 350 aircraft. In addition, airlines have reduced the number of aircraft on order from 955 to 844. These actions have still not been able to prevent the decline of airline load factors to 71.3 percent for 2001. Load factor measures the proportion of aircraft seating capacity that is actually sold and utilized. Airlines have established breakeven load factors that indicate the point at which costs are met. As prices fall and costs rise as a result of post-9/11 factors, the breakeven load factor has risen to 77 percent (Air Transport Association, 2002). The European airline industry fared little better in the months right after September 11th. It is estimated that the U.S. airport shutdown from

September 11-15, cost European airlines US$171.4 million. Some of the hardest hit carriers, Air France, British Airways, and Lufthansa, moved quickly to cut capacity (Sparaco and Wall, 2001). The Europeans looked on as the United States passed the Air Transportation Safety and System Stabilization Act which appeared to them to smack of the kind of government subsidy that the U.S. has accused the Europeans of utilizing in the past to support faltering industries and companies.

Where Do We Go?

The introduction began with a twisted quote from Lewis Carroll's classic the Jabberwocky. This passage begins 'The time has come… to talk of many things'. Indeed, the time has come for the airline industry to reexamine itself and insure that what rises out of the ashes is better and more beautiful. In the aftermath of 9/11 it may seem callous to evoke the image of the phoenix rising from the ashes, but while this image may be one that many would like to forget, it remains a viable description for the airline industry. After all, the early international aviation system began to take shape in the time between the two world wars of the early twentieth century. The global framework that continues to govern much of system today emerged from the rubble of World War II. The aviation system was again thrown into turmoil by the deregulation of the U.S. airline industry and the growing movement toward liberalization and economic integration in Europe and Asia. While the world struggles to come to terms with the meaning and implications of 9/11, the airline industry must again find a way to cope with its losses while finding a new path for the future.

Because the airline industry is a special case for all the reasons stated earlier, it is important for the people of the world to be involved in this debate. We are the tourists that fly to our long awaited vacation, the businessmen that fly to important meetings, the shippers that send out goods around the world, the customers that buy grapes from Chile and wine from France, and the citizens that count on the airline industry and all the industries it helps support for a growing, healthy economy. The purpose of this book is twofold. First, the book will lay out the forces that shaped the international aviation industry in terms that can be understood by anyone interested in aviation. Starting with the first transborder crossing in a lighter-than-air balloon, it will trace the development of international aviation through the international conferences that attempted to shape the field of play to the deregulation of the industry that changed all the rules to the drive for liberalization in international aviation. Second, the airline industry in general and the international aviation industry in particular face many interesting and difficult choices ahead. These choices include many dichotomies: pulling back from the trend toward liberalization or embracing the liberalization trend, merging in search of profitability or fragmenting the industry in search of economies. These possible futures will be explored including the pros and cons of each future from a national, consumer, employer, and employee perspective. Because this book is intended for both the interested amateur and the more serious student, references are provided in the text and at the end of each chapter to allow for more in-depth study. Unless otherwise stated, the views expressed in this book are those of the author and do not represent those of the airline industry, any governmental organization or private institution associated with aviation.

The book has been organized into three parts. The first part will address the early development of the international aviation system. Chapter 2 will begin by discussing attempts by the world community to establish the terms and rules governing the system. This period saw the start of heavier-than-air flight and the first use of the airplane in military action. The implications and possibilities of this new technology would come to hold greater sway in the minds of individuals and governments in the years ahead. Chapter 3 will address the most significant conference on international aviation, the 1944 Chicago Conference. This conference resulted in the Chicago Convention which spells out the rights and obligations of states in international aviation, the creation of the international body responsible for establishing the rules and standards governing international aviation, and numerous technical drafts on recommended practices. Chapter 4 will examine in more detail the structure and role of this new International Civil Aviation Organization (ICAO) in developing the standards and practices of international aviation. If the world had not already learned at the Chicago Conference that aviation could not be divorced from its economic and political consequences, it came to learn these lessons over time in the operation of ICAO. In fact, any illusion that ICAO could deal with these technical problems on their own merit was quickly dispelled when accidental shootdowns of civil aircraft and a growing number of brutal hijackings and criminal attacks against civil aviation came to dominate the agenda of the ICAO council and its subordinate bodies (Sochor, 1991). This chapter will also address the development of another international organization, the International Air Transport Association, and its role in shaping the international aviation system through the setting of international fares. Chapter 5 will look at another time of dramatic change for the airline industry, domestic deregulation. Domestic deregulation changed the rules of the game allowing competition based on price as well as market-based decisions on routes served and the level of service quality provided. It also freed up the industry for greater competition through the relaxation of rules for air carrier entry. This chapter will explore the link between domestic deregulation and efforts to liberalize international aviation markets. Chapter 6 will discuss the European efforts to create a free market system of aviation among the European Union nations. While the Europeans disagreed with the pace and implementation of deregulation in the U.S. market, they have taken the concept of aviation liberalization further than their U.S. counterparts by opening up domestic markets to foreign competition. Chapter 7 will look at deregulation and liberalization in Asia. This vast geographical diverse region has witnessed substantial growth in air transportation as part of its overall economic growth. The variation in regional policies on air transportation liberalization and deregulation mirrors the general diversity of the region, making it important to understand the specific causes national differences and the special problems each area faces.

The second part of the book will examine the alliance movement among international air carriers. Chapters 8-12 will review the growth, opportunities, and challenges of alliances for international carriers. In an environment of heavy international regulation, the alliance became the airline tool of choice for serving new markets and extending the global reach of your alliance. There have been and will continue to be obstacles to the use of the alliance. In the post-9/11 world, the alliance can either become more important or more irrelevant to international aviation. Chapter 8 will present the reasons for the growth of alliances as well as the types of activities involved in airline alliances. Chapter 9 will examine the stability of international alliances using a typology classifying alliance activities by the complexity of the activities involved and the level of resource commitment required. Chapters 10 and 11 will outline several issues that have proven to be stumbling blocks on the way to alliance success such as government regulations on anti-trust or competitiveness policy and airline efforts to achieve seamless service. Chapter 12 examines the strategic behavior of alliances and outlines strategies for creating successful alliances that fulfill the promises of cost reduction, improved service, and expanded networks.

In the final part of the book, the future of international aviation will be examined in light of changes in the environment before and after 9/11. Chapter 13 will review the events of 9/11 from an aviation system perspective as well as relevant events in the year since the attacks. Chapter 14 will address the economic impact of 9/11 on the world in general and international aviation in particular. Thomas L. Friedman has said that the 'World Trade Center is not the place where our intelligence agencies failed. It is the place where our imaginations failed' (Friedman, 2002: 59). Hollywood has given us thrillers depicting many terrorist acts that could happen. It did not prepare us for the possibility that they would happen. This act has changed the way we see ourselves and the airplanes we fly. It will affect the airline industry for years to come. Chapters 15-17 will explore some of the challenges facing the industry in the post-9/11 era and discuss some of the brave new possibilities for international aviation. Chapter 15 will explore the industry's search for profitability in the midst of the worst financial crisis in recent memory. Chapter 16 will examine the trend in market liberalization that began with the 1978 deregulation of U.S. domestic markets and has continued in Europe and Asia. Chapter 17 will address the uneven development of international aviation and the regions that have yet to benefit from the economic promises of aviation.

Any discontinuous change creates both great possibilities and grave challenges to the firms populating that environment. Some firms will evolve to meet the challenges in ways that they could scarcely imagine. Other firms will fail to meet the challenge and slowly wither and die. Firms that once dominated may give way to newer, younger competitors. The challenge of this book is to trace the development of international aviation in such a way that the current crisis can be understood by all those affected by aviation, governments, consumers, airlines, and the many services that support and are supported by aviation. Chapter 18 will attempt to wrap up what we have learned about the world of international aviation and present the challenges to all those interested in creating a viable, competitive international aviation system. While it is possible to catch glimpses of the possible paths ahead of the industry, forecasting is best left to weathermen. The paths are there; only the aviation industry can choose which path to take and how quickly to travel it.

Imaging the Future

The airplane and the industry that it fostered have captured the imagination of generations around the world. It is time to apply that imagination to creating a viable, stable environment for international aviation that delivers on the great promise of air travel to link the world together in peace and prosperity. Thomas L. Friedman has said of his work that he hopes that it will evoke one of four reactions from his readers: I didn't know that, I never looked at it that way before, you said exactly what I feel, but I didn't know how to express it, or I hate you and everything you stand for (2002: xi). These reactions seem a worthy goal for any book that attempts to examine and explain complex issues. Even if the book evokes the last reaction at least it should foster a debate on the ideas. It is time to begin the debate on the future on international aviation. I believe that you will find it an exciting and challenging journey.

References

Air Transport Association (2002), *State of the Airline Industry: A Report on Recent Trends for U.S. AirCarriers*, Air Transport Association.

Air Transport Action Group (2000), 'The Economic Benefits of Air Transport', Air Transport Action Group, Switzerland.

BBC News (2001), 'Belgian National Airline Bankrupt', BCC News Online Edition, November 7, www.bbc.co.uk.

BBC News (1999), 'BA to Fly Flag Again', BBC News Online Edition, June 6, www.bbc.co.uk.

Bianco, A. (1999), 'The Warren Buffet You Don't Know: Ace Stockpicker, of course-and now, an empire-builder', *Business Week*, July 5, pp. 55-66.

Foss, B. (2002), 'Airlines Expect to Lose $8 billion', Associated Press Wire Service, September 26.

Gould, S.J. and Eldredge, N. (1977), 'Punctuated Equilibria: The Tempo and Mode of Evolution Reconsidered', *Paleobiology*, vol. 3, pp. 115-151.

Graham, B. (1995), *Geography and Air Transport*, John Wiley & Sons, New York.

Hall, W., Grant, J., Done, K. and Cameron, D. (2001), 'Swissair Grounding Causes Travel Chaos', October 2.

Hannan, M.T. and Freeman, J. (1984), 'Structural Inertia and Organizational Change', *American Sociological Review*, vol. 49, pp. 149-164.

Kahn, A.P. (1988), *Economics of Regulation*, Wiley and Sons, New York.

Kane, R.M. (1998), *Air Transportation*, Kendall/Hunt Publishing Company, Dubuque, Iowa.

Loomis, C. and Buffet, W. (1999), 'Mr Buffet on the Stock Market', *Fortune*, Special Issue, vol. 140 (10), pp. 212-220.

Lowenfeld, A. (1975), 'A New Take-off for International Air Transport', *Foreign Affairs*, vol. 54, p. 47.

Mandel, M.J. (2000), 'The Next Downturn', *Business Week*, October 9, pp.173-180.

Miller, A. (1998), *Strategic Management* (3rd ed), Irwin-McGraw-Hill, Boston, MA.

Rosen, S.D. (1995), 'Corporate Restructuring: A Labor Perspective' in Peter Cappelli (ed.), *Airline Labor Relations in the Global Era: The New Frontier*, ILR Press, Ithaca, New York, pp. 31-40.

Schumpeter, J.A. (1949), *The Theory of Economic Development*, Harvard University Press, Cambridge, MA.

Senge, P.M. (1990), *The Fifth Discipline: The Art and Practice of the Learning Organization*, Doubleday Publishing, New York.

Sinha, D. (2001), *Deregulation and Liberalization of the Airline Industry: Asia, Europe, North America, and Oceania*, Ashgate Publishing, Aldershot.

Sparaco, P. and Wall, R. (2001), 'Europeans Map Airline Survival', *Aviation Week and Space Technology*, September 24, pp. 35-36.

Sparaco, P. (2001), 'The Curtain Falls on Sabena', *Aviation Week and Space Technology*, November 12, pp. 43-44.

Toffler, A. (1970), *Future Shock*, Bantam Books, New York.

Tushman, M.L. and Anderson, P. (1986), 'Technological Discontinuities and Organizational Environments', *Administrative Science Quarterly*, vol. 31, pp. 439-465.

Wells, A.T. (1994), *Air Transportation: A Management Perspective*, Wadsworth Publishing Company, Belmont, CA.

Wolf, S.M. (1995), 'Where Do We Go from Here: A Management Perspective', in P. Cappelli (ed.), *Airline Labor Relations in the Global Era: The New Frontier*, ILR Press, Cornell.

Part I
Past Forces

Chapter 2

A Dangerous Idea?

Imagined possibilities

There are accounts dating back to the twelfth century B.C.E. of people in China riding in balloons. Leonardo Da Vinci sketched images in the sixteenth century of craft he believed capable of supporting a man in flight. However, it was not until 1783 that history has its first confirmable account of a manned lighter-than-air flight. Jean-Francois Pilatre de Rozier and Francois d'Arlandes flew over Paris for 25 minutes on November 21, 1783 while the residents of the city watched. Less than two years later on January 7, 1785, Jean-Pierre Blanchard and John Jeffries became the first individuals to cross above a national border when they flew their balloon across the English Channel to France. While the experimentation with lighter-than-air flight continued, the balloon inspired thoughts of fancy not fear. At the mercy of the winds, it did not seem to pose the threat or hold the promise of heavier-than-air travel. Although the French first used balloons in a military setting in 1793 when they provided reconnaissance during conflicts following the French Revolution, the balloons of war were quickly replaced by their heavier-than-air cousins and fancy was replaced by concern and calculation (Wirth and Young, 1980).

On December 17, 1903, Orville Wright became the first person to pilot a powered heavier-than-air craft. He remained aloft for 12 seconds and covered a distance of only 120 feet, but this single event would change the way people around the world viewed the sky. By 1908, the Wright brothers were working under a contract with the U.S. War Department to build aircraft for the Army (Tischauser, 2002). In that same year, Glenn Curtiss' White Wing became the first United States plane to take-off on wheels and use ailerons to control roll in turns. Another Curtiss aircraft, the June Bug, would set a new speed record in 1909 at the first great international air competition in Rheims, France. Curtiss would go on to become the first person to land an aircraft on the deck of a ship in 1910 and found the Curtiss Aeroplane and Motor Company. His company would become the largest U.S. aircraft manufacturer in World War I, supplying over 10,000 aircraft to the war effort. The U.S. Navy for whom Curtiss began building planes in 1911 would use the Curtiss NC-4 to make the first trans-Atlantic flight in 1919 (Roseberry, 1991). Nine years later, Charles A. Lindbergh would become the first person to solo across the Atlantic. Another decade would see the German Luftwaffe blitzkrieg the European continent and engage the British in the Battle of Britain (Pimlott, 1998).

The world's governments, however, would not wait for the aircraft to enter battle before acting. By 1910, they had already seen enough to know that the airplane was no passing fancy but a new technology with great promise and dangerous potential. New regulations were needed to insure the development of international aviation and protect the interests of nations. This was the goal of the Paris Conference.

Let the Conferences Begin

The French government convened the first ever conference on aviation in 1910 to draft a convention on air navigation. The conference was attended by the representatives of 19 European countries. It quickly became apparent that there were conflicting opinions among the delegates present over the rights and privileges of flying. The French and German delegations favored a system of extensive freedom based on the Freedom of the Seas model of Hugo Grotius. The British insisted on complete state sovereignty and control over the airspace above a country's land borders. This fundamental disagreement prevented the conference from achieving its principle goal of establishing a broad framework for international aviation, however, the convention did identify many of the key terms, concepts, and technical provisions that would become standard in later conferences. In the absence of agreement over an international framework, the British became the first nation to declare its sovereignty over the airspace above their country in 1911. The British Aerial Navigation Act gave the Home Secretary full power to regulate the entry and activities of aircraft into its airspace. The other European nations quickly followed suit in the years prior to World War I (Sochor, 1990).

The Peace Conference at the end of World War I faced two key aviation issues. The first was the disposition of the military and civilian fleets of the defeated countries. The second issue was to complete the work begun in 1910. The meeting, known as the Convention Relating to the Regulation of Aerial Navigation, accepted the U.S. position that permitted German civil aviation development within their national borders while eliminating all of the military aspects of aviation. The conference also produced the so-called Paris Convention of 1919. The first article of the Convention declared the complete and exclusive sovereignty of each nation over its airspace. It went on to call for 1) prescribed national registration of aircraft, 2) restricted the movement of military aircraft, 3) prescribed rules of airworthiness i.e. certification that an aircraft is safe to fly through a range of operations, 4) regulation of pilots, and 5) establishment of police measures. A permanent commission was established in Paris to continue the study of international aviation legal issues, the International Commission on Air Navigation or ICAN (Kane, 1998; Sochor, 1990). The Paris Convention was eventually ratified by 26 countries, the most notable exceptions being the United States and Russia who both chose to distance themselves from international affairs after the end of World War I. The U.S. did later sign the Commercial Aviation

Convention, also known as the Havana Convention, in 1928. This convention resulted from the Sixth International Conference of the American States and differed from the Paris Convention in several key respects. The Havana Convention did not seek to establish a uniform international standard on aviation for aircraft or pilot regulation nor did it contain any provision for influencing future aviation development such as ICAN (Groenewedge, 1996).

Domestic Developments

While the international aviation community remained divided on the issue of freedom versus sovereignty, the course of domestic aviation development diverged as well in the years leading up to the Second World War. Direct governmental intervention became the most frequent method of promoting the growth and development of domestic aviation. Governments either provided direct subsidies and/or assumed full or partial ownership of domestic air transport companies. British Airways and Air France are two classic examples of this strategy. A privately owned British Airways was formed in 1935 from the merger of several smaller British carriers. British Airways and Imperial Airways were merged and nationalized to form British Overseas Airways Corporation (BOAC) in 1939. BOAC and British European Airways (BEA) would be merged under the name British Airways in 1974 and remain under government ownership until 1987 (Marriott, 1998). Air France was founded in 1933 through the merger of five smaller French carriers and negotiated with the French government to become the country's national carrier. In 1948, the government assumed a 70% ownership stake in the newly reincorporated Air France. All four of the government owned airlines of France were merged in 1990 into the Air France Group (Hengi, 2000). By the mid-1950s, most of the carriers of Europe were wholly or partly owned by their respective governments (Graham, 1995). Although many of Asia's national carriers were formed after their European counterparts, the pattern of government ownership was widespread there as well (Sinha, 2001).

This direct intervention did not suit the philosophical and political tastes of U.S. lawmakers and officials. This did not mean the U.S. government did not feel it had a stake and a role to play in the development of domestic aviation. It did mean that any intervention would take a more indirect path. In 1912 the U.S Post Office asked Congress to appropriate money to launch airmail service, but no appropriation was made until 1916. Otto Praeger, the Father of Airmail and Second Assistant Postmaster General, not only wanted to create a system of safe, reliable airmail but an air commerce system that could attract private capital to continue its development. The last flight of the Post Office was conducted in 1927 (Kane, 1998). Henceforth, airmail service would be conducted by private contractors as provided for in the Airmail Act of 1925. The so-called Kelly Act, entitled An Act to Encourage Commercial Aviation and to Authorize the Postmaster General to Contract for the Mail Service, had awarded 12 airmail contracts by the beginning of 1926.   Table 2.1 lists the route number and the company receiving the award.

Table 2.1: The First Contract Airmail Routes

Route Number	Company
CAM 1	Colonial Air Lines
CAM 2	Robertson Aircraft Corp
CAM 3	National Air Transport
CAM 4	Western Air Express
CAM 5	Varney Speed Lines
CAM 6 & 7	Ford Air Transport
CAM 8	Pacific Air Transport
CAM 9	Charles Dickenson
CAM 10	Florida Airways Corp
CAM 11	Clifford Ball
CAM 12	Western Air Express

Source: Kane, R.M., *Air Transportation.*

The list of CAM awards is less significant for its historical value than its vision into the future. Most of these carriers would go on to form the nucleus of familiar U.S. major and national carriers. National Air Transport and Pacific Air Transport would combine with a later CAM awardee, Boeing Air Transport, to form United Airlines (Davies, 1998). Varney Speed Lines would go on to become Continental Airlines (Davies, 1984). Robertson Aircraft Corporation would become one of eighty carriers merged to form American Airlines (Bedwell, and Wegg, 2000). All American Aviation who would receive a CAM in 1939 would go on to become U.S. Airways (Jones and Jones, 1999). This consolidation would not occur by accident.

In 1929, Walter Folger Brown was appointed postmaster general. Brown would work diligently for the passage of the Air Mail Act of 1930, also known as the McNary-Watres Airmail Act, which gave the postmaster total control over the airmail bidding process. According to Brown, the aviation industry suffered from four problems: '1) being unwilling to invest in new equipment, 2) operating obsolete aircraft, 3) demonstrating questionable safety performance from cost cutting, and 4) maintaining marginal operations with no growth' (Kane, 1998: 107). To remedy this situation, Brown eliminated the competitive bidding process for contract air mail routes in favor of a system that granted awards to large, well financed operators. Only these large operators were invited to attend the so-called spoils conferences that were held in Washington, D.C. to award contracts.   In essence, the U.S. government through the postmaster forced small carriers to merge in order to obtain the lucrative airmail contracts (Glines, 1968).

By 1932, charges of graft and collision led U.S. President Franklin Roosevelt to cancel all contracts and return responsibility for the airmail to the U.S. Army. However, a series of accidents resulted in the return of airmail service to private operators by June 1, 1934. The Airmail Act of 1934, also known as the Black-McKellar Act provided for a return to the competitive bidding process of the past and prohibited awards to carriers involved in the supposed collusion. Three of these carriers American Airways, Eastern Air Transport and Transcontinental & Western Air changed their names respectively to American Airlines, Eastern Airlines, and Transcontinental & Western Air Inc. to avoid this restriction and continue in the airmail business. The administration of contracts would be divided between the Post Office, Interstate Commerce Commission, and the Department of Commerce. Beginning in 1938, rates would be set by the newly created Civil Aviation Bureau (Kane, 1998).

By the beginning of the Second World War, the domestic aviation environment of the Americas and Europe was in place, although the strain of the Great Depression was putting pressure on that system. Government ownership was the preferred method of domestic support and development in most of the world's nations. The U.S. government intervened in equally significant, though indirect ways to create a large, stable aviation system. A question occasionally arises from aviation interested individuals from outside the U.S. as to what factors account for the different i.e. indirect path taken toward the development of domestic aviation by the U.S. government. There are probably a number of concrete economic and geographical explanations, but the more intuitive and less obvious answer may lie in the basic, shared attitude of many of the individuals that originally colonized and later immigrated to the U.S., namely a general distrust of organized government. This distrust grows in direct proportion to the distance that government is from the individual or individuals in question. It has been said in a number of slightly varying ways that the citizens in the United States tend to believe that their government was invented by geniuses to be run by idiots (Friedman, 2000). These sentiments are clearly and forcefully expressed by such economists as Hayak, Milton Friedman, and other individuals associated with the so-called Chicago School. Simply put, government intervention distorts the functioning of free market forces preventing the efficient allocation of resources and the establishment of natural prices (Friedman, 1980, 1982; Hayak, 1960, 1980, 1994; Yergin and Stanislaw, 2002). Clearly such an attitude does not predispose the average U.S. citizen to favoring greater government involvement in their daily life. The federalization of airport screening in the wake of 9/11 probably reflects the confusion, shock, fear, and uncertainty created by those events far more than it represents a true belief that the government can perform this function better than private enterprise. It is likely that within a few years there will be increasing pressure to 'privatize' that that was once 'federalized' for just these reasons.

Lessons of War

During the first half of the twentieth century, the world would experience two great wars. The airplane would play a role in both of these conflicts. Although the airplane first went to war in 1911 with the Italian forces in North Africa, its role was to provide reconnaissance. In World War I, it would assume an offensive role first as a bomber and later in aerial combat with mounted machine guns. While World War I evokes images of flying aces such as Manfred von Richthofen, commonly called the Red Baron, twisting and turning in an aerial ballet with his opponents, the war also saw the first large scale bombing of such cities as London. On June 13, 1917 alone, the Germans dropped 118 high-explosive bombs on the city of London. The airplane had clearly arrived as a weapon of war.

If World War I saw the airplane become more than an observer of the action, then World War II saw it become an integral, vital part of the grand strategy of nations and allies. The war itself began with the Blitzkrieg of Poland and later much of Europe. The aircraft made these lightening strikes possible and devastating. The desperate Battle of Britain demonstrated the important role of aircraft for both offensive and defensive purposes. The aircraft in fact took several major leaps forwarding design and performance during the war years. One of the most significant developments was the turbojet aircraft. Germany followed this innovation with the Messerschmitt (Me-262), which was capable of carrying 550-pound bombs installed on the aircraft's wing racks as well as 12 R4M rockets fitted under the wings. The Me-163 Komet was fitted with a rocket motor that could propel it at almost 600 miles per hour and climb vertically at 11,810 feet per minute. Other advances during the war included the use of rocket boosters for short takeoffs, pressurized cabins, four-engine aircraft, forward-swept wings mounted over swept-back wings to establish stability at low speeds, and drag-resistant body designs (Badsey, 1990; Cooksley and Robertson, 1998).

Aircraft were not the only beneficiaries of the wartime push to innovation. The British development of radar was critical to the defense of Britain and the Allies' ability to avoid detection during bombing raids over Germany. This innovation led to early efforts at reducing aircraft detectability, stealth technology, through the use of deflected radar beams and radar-absorbing materials. Work was also begun on the use of thinner, flatter, heat-resistant materials for aircraft construction. Finally, unmanned, armed aircraft and guided missiles would make their appearance toward the end of the war (Cooksley and Robertson, 1998).

In short, the aircraft came out of these two conflicts a more powerful and deadlier device. As has always been the case with aviation, however, the innovations developed for military application also can have important impacts on the civilian sector. By 1946, aircraft such as the Douglas DC-6 would be carrying 102 passengers at 20,000 feet in a pressurized cabin (Badrocke and Sunston, 1999). Commercial aviation was coming of age and prepared to launch the world on the path to globalization.

Coming Out with Different Agendas

As World War II was coming to an end, the Allied powers would turn at least some of their attention back to the issue of creating an international aviation system. This interest would result in the Chicago Conference (Chapter 3), but the countries attending that conference had been changed by the years of war in ways that would echo through the halls in Chicago. It has been said that the United States was the only country to emerge from World War II richer. In fact, the U.S. gold reserves at the end of the war totaled $20 billion, two-thirds of the world's total (Matloff, 1959). The U.S. would be responsible for more than half of the total manufacturing production of the world and account for one third of the production of all types of goods (Ashworth, 1975). In the aviation area, the United States production of aircraft had risen by 1945 to 49,761 per year, up from 5,856 in 1939. It would account for more aircraft per year than the combined manufacturing of Britain and the USSR (Overy, 1980).

For its part, the USSR had not only lost 20-25 million citizens between 1941 and 1945, it had lost a substantial portion of its infrastructure (Hosking, 1985). It is estimated that in the transportation sector alone the USSR 'was hit by the destruction of 65,000 kilometers of railway track, loss of or damage to 15,800 locomotives, 428,000 goods wagons, 4,280 river boats, and half of all the railway bridges in the occupied territory' (Nove, 1969; 285). The losses to infrastructure were devastating in the nations of other Allied and Great Powers as well. In 1946, German national income and output was one-third of its 1938 level (Landes, 1969). Japanese real income had fallen to only 57 percent of its 1934-1936 levels and exports were only 8 percent of the 1934-1936 figures (Allen, 1981). Italy's gross national product had declined by 40 percent to its 1911 level (Ricossa, 1972). The Allied Powers, with the exception of the U.S., had not fared any better. By 1944, years of war and occupation had left France with a situation where 'most of the waterways and harbors were blocked, most of the bridges destroyed, much of the railway system temporarily unusable' (Wright, 1968; 264). The French national income in 1945 was half of its 1938 level. In Great Britain, years of bombing had severely weakened the industrial base and damaged the overall civilian infrastructure. Exports had fallen to 31 percent of their 1938 figures with a resulting surge in the British trade deficit (Kennedy, 1981).

It is with this backdrop that the Allied and Neutral powers would meet in Chicago to decide the shape of the post-war international aviation system. The fact that the meeting would take place even before the conclusion of the war was an indication of the importance this young industry had gained in the eyes of world governments and their citizens. While the industry itself was young, the arguments heard in Chicago were old. The aviation community had heard them before Chicago and would hear them again over the subsequent years. The successes and failures of Chicago would live on in the international aviation system of today.

References

Allen, G.S. (1981), *A Short Economic History of Japan*, London.
Ashworth, W.A. (1975), *A Short History of the International Economy Since 1850*, London.
Badrocke, M. and Sunston, B. (1999), *The Illustrated History of McDonnell Douglas Aircraft from Cloudster to Boeing*, Osprey, Oxford.
Badsey, S. (1990), *Modern Air Power: Fighters*, Gallery Books, New York.
Bedwell, D. and Wegg, J. (2000), *Silverbird: The American Airlines Story*, Plymouth Press, Boston.
Cooksley, M.K. and Robertson, B. (1998), *Air Warfare: The Encyclopedia of Twentieth Century Conflict*, Frank Cass, London.
Davies, R.E.G. (1984), *Continental Airlines: The First Fifty Years*, Pioneer Publications, The Woodlands, TX.
Davies, R.E.G. (1998), *Airlines of the United States Since 1914*, Smithsonian Institution Press, Washington, D.C.
Friedman, M. (1980), *Free to Choose*, Harcourt Brace Jovanovich, New York.
Friedman, M. (1982), *Capitalism and Freedom*, University of Chicago Press, Chicago.
Friedman, T.L. (2000), *The Lexus and the Olive Tree*, 2nd ed., Farrar, Straus & Giroux, New York.
Glines, C.V. (1968), *The Saga of the Airmail*, D. Van Nostrand, Princeton, N.J.
Groenewedge, A.D. (1996), *Compendium of International Civil Aviation*, International Aviation Development Corporation, Quebec.
Hayek, F.A. (1960), *The Constitution of Liberty*, University of Chicago Press, Chicago.
Hayek, F.A. (1980), *Individualism and Economic Order*, University of Chicago Press, Chicago.
Hayak, F.A. (1994), *Hayek on Hayek: An Autobiographical Dialogue*, University of Chicago Press, Chicago.
Hosking, G.A. (1985), *A History of the Soviet Union*, London.
Jones, G. and Jones, G.P. (1999), *U.S. Airways*, Ian Allan, Shepperton, England.
Kane, R.M. (1998), *Air Transportation*, 13th ed., Kendall/Hunt Publishing, Dubuque, IA.
Kennedy, P.M. (1981), *The Realities Behind Diplomacy*, London.
Landes, D. (1969), *The Unbound Prometheus: Technological Change and Industrial Development in Western Europe from 1970 to the Present*, Cambridge.
Marriott, L. (1998), *British Airways Book*, 2nd ed., Plymouth Publishing, Plymouth, MI.
Matloff, M. (1959), *Strategic Planning for Coalition Warfare, 1943-1944*, Washington, D.C.
Nove, A. (1969), *An Economic History of the USSR*, Harmondsworth.
Overy, R.J. (1980), *The Air War, 1939-1945*, New York.
Pimlott, J. (1998), *The Illustrated History of the German Air Force in World War II*, Motorbooks International, Osceola, WI.
Ricossa, A. (1972), 'Italy 1920-1970' in C. Cipolla (ed.), *The Fortuna Economic History of Europe*, London.
Roseberry, C.R. (1991), *Glenn Curtiss: Pioneer of Flight*, Syracuse University Press, Syracuse, NY.
Sochor, E. (1990), *The Politics of International Aviation*, University of Iowa Press, Iowa City.
Tischauser, L.V. (2002), 'Wright Brothers', in Tracy Irons-Georges (ed.), *Encyclopedia of Flight*, pp. 785-786, Salem Press, Pasadena, CA.
Wirth, D. and Young, J. (1980), *Ballooning: The Compete Guide to Riding the Winds*, Random House, New York.
Wright, G. (1968), *The Ordeal of Total War, 1939-1945*, New York.

Yergin, D. and Stanislaw, J. (2002), *The Commanding Heights: The Battle for the World Economy*, Simon & Schuster, New York.

Chapter 3

Chicago, the Windy City

Crosswinds

The wind can be a friend or a foe to the air traveler. A strong headwind can add time to your journey. A strong tailwind can help speed you along your way. Crosswinds, however, are unpredictable, often dangerous. At the very least they can make it very difficult to maintain your planned course and reach your planned destination. Chicago has long been called the Windy City and anyone who has ever looked out over the lakefront on a fall day can understand the nickname. It is perhaps fitting that Chicago was the chosen site for the most famous aviation conference in history. The events that happened and didn't happen at Chicago still echo in the events of today. To understand the forces that created the international aviation landscape of today, you must understand Chicago.

Even as U.S. President Franklin D. Roosevelt and British Prime Minister Winston Churchill were meeting in Quebec to plan the cross-channel invasion of Normandy and turn the tide of war in Europe, the topic of a general meeting to discuss the future of air transportation came up as an issue. U.S. politicians had already begun to explore the nature of a post-war aviation system. Henry Wallace, the U.S. Vice-president, proposed a global network of air routes and international airports under the envisioned United Nations while Clare Boothe Luce denounced this notion as 'globaloney' in her maiden address to the U.S. Congress. Edward Warner, the vice-chairman of the U.S. Civil Aviation Bureau, envisioned air navigation agreements that would prevent the 'return to the evil days when air transportation was regarded with caution and suspicion' (Sochor, 1990: 4). The British had also been considering the issue of aviation. At the 1943 Dominion and Empire Conference and a May 1944 meeting of the Dominion ministers there were discussions about creating some system of reciprocal rights. In a White Paper shortly after the 1944 meeting, the British proposed an international regulatory body with the power to decide on routes, frequencies, and fares. Clearly, the crosswinds would be blowing in Chicago.

Setting the Table

When the delegates arrived in Chicago on November 1, 1944, they found four proposals awaiting them on shaping the international environment. The opening message of President Roosevelt called on the delegates 'not to dally with the thought of creating great blocs of closed air, thereby tracing in the sky the conditions of future war' (Sochor, 1990:8). His call was for an open sky that could be exploited for the good of all mankind. Not surprisingly, the U.S. proposal called for system of complete market access without restrictions on routes, frequency, and fares. The British who rightly feared that the large, undamaged aviation infrastructure, commercial fleet, and manufacturing capacity of the U.S. would dominate the war ravaged systems of Europe saw the U.S. proposal as self-interest masquerading as philosophical principle. The British plan reiterated their earlier White Paper calling for a tightly regulated system governed by an independent international regulatory body. The Canadian proposal attempted to offer a compromise between the U.S. and British positions by creating a multilateral regulatory body that would allow for limited competition within the system. The last proposal, jointly sponsored by the Australians and New Zealanders, called for the international ownership and management of all international air service. Committee I of the Chicago Conference would clearly have its work cut out for it.

Meanwhile, the other three committees worked on the technical issues of the conference eventually completing work on the Interim Agreement on International Aviation, the Chicago Convention on International Civil Aviation, and the International Air Transport Agreement. The first treaty or convention established a temporary organization called the Provisional International Civil Aviation Organization to operate until the permanent organization created in the second document came into effect, the International Civil Aviation Organization (ICAO). The third convention is also known as the Five Freedoms Agreement (Table 3.1 lists the freedoms of the air including the subsequently added sixth, seventh, and eighth freedoms). The first two freedoms are known as technical freedoms. The remaining freedoms deal with the commercial rights of aviation to pick up and discharge passengers and cargo to, from and through foreign nations.

While the technical committees were concluding their work, Committee I was deadlocked. Despite several exchanges between Roosevelt and Churchill on the issues facing the Committee and a series of private meetings between the key players, there would be no compromise on the basic positions of either the U.S. or Great Britain. The U.S. might have the planes to fly, but without landing rights they had only half the resources needed for a viable international system of carriers. They needed landing rights and Great Britain had potential landing sites galore. In fact, as the conference was opening the British publicized a 'plan' for creating an all-Commonwealth airline called the All-Red Line after the cartographic practice of showing Commonwealth nations in red. This All-Red line would be given exclusive rights to land on Commonwealth territory. In a world in which the sun never set on the British flag, the All-Red Line was a reminder that the British did not come to the table empty-handed nor would they allow a system of international aviation to be put in place that created serious disadvantages for Britain and other small aviation nations.

Table 3.1: The Freedoms of the Air

Freedom	Description
First	The right to fly over the territory of a contracting State without landing
Second	The right to land on the territory of a contracting State for non-commercial purposes
Third	The right to transport passengers, cargo and mail from the State of registration of the aircraft to another State and set them down there
Fourth	The right to take on board passengers, cargo and mail in another contracting State and to transport them to the State of registration of the aircraft
Fifth	The right to transport passengers, cargo and mail between two other States as a continuation of, or as a preliminary to, the operation of the third or fourth freedoms
Sixth	The right to take on board passengers, cargo and mail in one State and to transport them to a third State after a stopover in the aircraft's State of registration and vice versa
Seventh	The right to transport passengers, cargo and mail between two other States on a service which does not touch the aircraft's country of registration
Eighth	The right to transport passengers, cargo and mail within the territory of a State which is not the aircraft's State of registration (full cabotage)
Ninth	The right to interrupt a service

Just as it began to seem that nothing would be achieved in Committee I, the Netherlands broke the deadlock by suggesting that the British might join in an agreement on the first two freedoms of overflight and technical landing or stopover. The Netherlands then moved immediately to guarantee these rights as part of a multilateral agreement. The British agreed to this proposal which became the fourth treaty or convention to come out of the Chicago Conference. The

International Air Services Transit Agreement would eventually be signed by all of the participants and go into effect on June 30, 1945. It is now recognized by over 100 nations. The International Air Transport Agreement which contained the remaining commercial frèedoms would be signed by 19 of the participants, but 9, including the U.S., would subsequently denounce it. The remaining nations would not endorse it, primarily for its fifth freedom condition. One final document would come out of the Convention. This form, the Bilateral Agreement for the Exchange of Routes and Services, would be adopted as part of the Final Act and serve to move the international aviation community forward in the absence of a broader, multilateral agreement on commercial aviation rights. The gavel fell on December 7, 1944 ending the Chicago Conference and the governmental delegates went home with their treaties and the bilateral form to decide on the next steps in the process of creating an international aviation system.

Not all of the individuals present in Chicago, however, went home immediately. Airline executives who had attended the conference as delegates or advisors to their national governments had quickly realized the implications of a failure by the conference to reach a broad multilateral agreement on commercial rights and fares. Showing admirable restraint, they waited until December 6th to begin discussions on the formation of a trade association for international carriers. This new association would be their voice in the international system and, they hoped, fill the void left in the commercial aviation system by the events in Chicago. The newly formed International Air Transport Association (IATA) called its first meeting in Havana in April 1945.

A Bilateral World

Without a multilateral agreement, it was left to the national governments of the world to begin the process of negotiating bilateral air service agreements. In fact, the United States had opened bilateral talks with the Dominions, Chinese, and Russians even before the conference began and quickly returned to this process after the conference signing a bilateral agreement with Spain on December 2, 1944, Denmark and Sweden on December 16, 1944, Iceland on January 27, 1945, Canada on February 7, 1945, and Switzerland and Norway on July 13, 1945 (Kane, 1998). However, it was not until 1946 that the United States and Great Britain were ready to sit down again and discuss the aviation issues that had not been resolved at Chicago. The agreement that emerged from these talks would be called the Bermuda Agreement and would, by agreement of both governments, become the model for all of the future agreements either side would negotiate. This form would henceforth replace the Chicago form as the world's standard Air Service Agreement.

The United States agreed to accept the British position on fares and rates which allowed the airlines to mutually set these matters subject to prior approval by both governments. The United Kingdom agreed to allow airlines to unilaterally set their own capacity i.e. aircraft size and service frequency subject to subsequent review for unfair practices. Other key features of the agreement included designated (or named) routes and multiple carrier designation. In total, 'the Agreement clearly favored the United States which then accounted for about 60 percent of the world's passenger airline traffic and which had the largest and most efficient international airlines' (Toh, 1998: 61). This may reflect the fact that the British were also in negotiations with the U.S. over a US$3.75 billion loan to rebuild its economy and thus had to negotiate from a position of some weakness (Sochor, 1990). As a concession to the British, the United States did agree to allow the International Air Transport Association (IATA) to set international fares and cargo rates. They also decided to limit their pursuit of fifth freedom rights which are seen in aviation circles as placing a foreign carrier in too close a competition for domestic traffic with a state's national carriers (Toh, 1998). By 1947, over 100 bilaterals had been signed around the world and the fare-setting power of IATA accepted in subsequent aviation accords (Sochor, 1990).

The most recently amended bilateral between the US and UK illustrates the key points of bilaterals as well and the specific and restrictive nature of such air service agreements (Air Transport Association of America, 2001). Under the portion of the air service agreement entitled United Kingdom Routes: Atlantic combination air service is the following list:

Table 3.2: U.S.-U.K. Bilateral Agreement - U.K. Routes

(A) UK Gateway Points	(B) Intermediate Points	(C) Points in US Territory
London, Manchester, Prestwick/Glasgow, Belfast. Any UK Point, excluding London.	Points in Luxembourg, The Netherlands and The Republic of Ireland. Points in Belgium, France and Germany.	Atlanta, Boston, Charlotte, Chicago, Dallas/Ft Worth, Denver, Detroit, Houston, Las Vegas, Los Angeles, Miami, New Orleans, New York, Orlando, Phoenix, Philadelphia, San Diego, San Francisco, Seattle, Tampa, Washington/ Baltimore. Up to two points to be selected and notified to the United States.

In addition to the Atlantic combination air service, lists are provided of named routes for Atlantic regional combination air service, Atlantic combination air service via Canada, Atlantic combination air service beyond to Mexico City, Atlantic combination air service beyond to South America, Atlantic combination service beyond to Japan, Atlantic combination service beyond to the Pacific, Atlantic combination service beyond to Australia, Pacific combination service, Pacific combination service via Tarawa, Bermuda combination service, Caribbean combination service, Caribbean combination air service, Atlantic all-cargo service, Atlantic all-cargo service beyond to South America, Atlantic all cargo service beyond to Mexico, Pacific all-cargo services, Pacific all-cargo service via Tarawa, Bermuda all-cargo service, Caribbean all-cargo service, and Caribbean all-cargo air service.

Conversely, the principle of reciprocity demands that similar lists of named routes be included for U.S. passenger and all-cargo service. The following is the list of United States Routes: Atlantic combination service.

Table 3.3: U.S.-U.K. Bilateral Agreement - U.S. Routes

(A) US Gateway Points	(B) Intermediate Points	(C) Points in UK Territory	(D) Points Beyond
Anchorage, Atlanta, Boston, Charlotte, Chicago, Cincinnati, Dallas/Ft Worth, Detroit, Houston, Los Angeles, Miami, Minneapolis/St.Paul, Newark, New York, Philadelphia, Pittsburgh, Raleigh-Durham, San Francisco, Seattle, St. Louis, Washington/ Baltimore. Up to 3 points to be selected and notified to the United Kingdom.	Shannon	London, Prestwick/ Glasgow. Any UK point exc. London.	Berlin, Frankfurt, Hamburg, Munich, Oslo, one point in Western Europe to be selected.

These excerpts demonstrate the reciprocal exchange of named routes as well as the application of fifth freedom (beyond) rights between the U.S. and the U.K. By the old bilateral standards, the US-UK agreement was considered liberal in that it did not include capacity (aircraft size and route frequency) restrictions.

As an example of further restrictions, the U.S.-Japanese bilateral distinguishes between incumbent carriers which were provided for by the 1952 agreement (Northwest and United Airlines for the U.S. and Japan Airlines and All Nippon

Airways for the Japanese) and non-incumbent carriers (Delta Air Lines, American Airlines, and Continental Airlines) in naming routes. It also includes sections on restricted frequency routes. In this case, non-incumbent airlines are permitted to operate up to forty-two additional aggregate weekly round-trip frequencies on the following city-pair markets: Tokyo-New York, Tokyo-Chicago, Tokyo-San Francisco, Tokyo-Los Angeles, Tokyo-Honolulu, Tokyo-Guam/Saipan, Osaka-Los Angeles, Osaka-Honolulu, Nagoya-Honolulu, and Fukuoka-Honolulu (Air Transport Association of America, 2001).

Looking Back

Looking back on the Chicago Conference, it is clear that no compromise could have bridged the gap between the basic U.S. and British positions. In the tug-of-war between free markets and political reality, political reality was the victor. Ironically, the lever that had allowed the British to hold off the U.S. push for open skies would not long survive the end of World War II. The British Empire would be replaced by a much looser Commonwealth of independent nations with the right to determine the disposition of their own landing rights. Unfortunately, the system created by the major aeronautical players to meet their needs would not give these newly emerging nations a great deal of clout in the international system even if it did recognize their sovereign rights to control their own airspace.

The United States for all of its philosophical preaching on open skies was not willing to grant more open access to the U.S. market as it proved later when it renounced the International Air Transport Agreement rather than grant foreign carriers greater fifth freedom rights through the U.S. (Sochor, 1990). This was seen as an admission by the U.S. that there could be no stable commercial aviation system without reciprocity between countries (de la Rochere, 1971). While the United States was able to use its power and prestige following the war to sign a number of bilateral agreements advantageous to the U.S. carriers, it did so by giving up the right to allow the markets to determine price. The U.S. would again be accused of abandoning philosophical principle in favor of commercial and political reality when it began to take up the cause of open skies again after airline deregulation (Chapter 5). Frederik Sorensen of the European Commission Air Transport Policy Unit has said that '[o]pen skies is an American term which, as we see it, is synonymous with a free for all system depending on the good behavior of air carriers and only partial opening of the market' (1998: 125).

Looking Ahead

Out of the ashes of the post-World War II world, the phoenix of international aviation took off. If it did not fly as high as some would have liked or take the paths its creators envisioned, it did at least fly. The winds blowing out of Chicago did not make its flight either smooth or steady, but it has remained aloft. The next decades would see less dramatic but no less significant progress in the world of international aviation. The two international organizations born in Chicago, ICAO and IATA, would build on the framework laid out there (Chapter 4) only to have many of the structures set in place challenged by deregulation of the U.S. airline industry (Chapter 5) and liberalization in European (Chapter 6) and Asian (Chapter 7) markets. The events of the past would come back to challenge the future and demand that the world community grapple with them again.

The preamble to the Convention on International Civil Aviation laid out the goals of the Chicago Convention as follows:

> WHEREAS the future development of international civil aviation can greatly help to create and preserve friendship and understanding among nations and peoples of the world, yet its abuse can become a threat to the general security; and
>
> WHEREAS it is desirable to avoid friction and to promote that cooperation between nations and peoples upon which peace of the world depends;
>
> THEREFORE, the undersigned governments having agreed on certain principles and arrangements in order that international civil aviation may be developed in a safe and orderly manner and that international air transport services may be established on the basis of equality of opportunity and operated soundly and economically; (Reprinted in Sochor, 1990).

This vision of international aviation as a global force for peace was perhaps utopian, but air travel has certainly brought the world closer together in time and space. Unfortunately, the events of 9/11 have temporarily replaced this unifying vision with a grimmer reality. This reality too is overstated. An airplane was merely the tool used to perpetrate the destruction of 9/11. Like any tool, it serves the wishes of its user; the terrorists used their tool to drive the world apart. Others continue to use it to bring the world together. While the vision of ICAO has proven elusive, the goals have also presented their own challenges. As we will see in the next chapter ICAO would work hard to create a safe, orderly, and economical air transportation system and, by-and-large, they will achieve this goal.

The difficulty lies in the basis for this system – equality of opportunity. Free markets guarantee all the right to participate. They do not guarantee that the opportunities are equal or that the outcomes are equitable. In fact, free markets are about access not success and neither of these commodities is equally distributed. In a free market the opportunities of large, wealthy nations are greater than small, poor nations. The chances of success are also greater for the large and wealthy. Equity is about fairness, impartiality, and justice. Free markets are about competition and winner-take-all. Governments intervene in the market to provide opportunity and equity. All governments intervene to some extent. The level of intervention or regulation has been a subject for debate in economic and policy circles since Adam Smith. The push for liberalization in the airline industry would raise these issues once again for policy makers and the people they represent.

References

Air Transport Association of America (2001), 'Air Service Rights in U.S. International Air Transport Agreements: A Compilation of Scheduled and Charter Service Rights Contained in U.S. Bilateral Aviation Agreements', Washington, D.C.

De la Rochere, J.D. (1971), *La Politique des Etats-Unis en matiere d'aviation civile*, Libraire de Droit et de Jurisprudence, Paris, pp. 30-36.

Kane, R.M. (1999), *Air Transportation*, 13th edition., Kendall/Hunt Publishing, Dubuque, Iowa.

Sochor, E. (1990), *The Politics of International Aviation*, University of Iowa Press, Iowa City.

Sorensen, F. (1998), 'Open Skies in Europe', in U.S. Department of Transportation (ed.), *FAA Commercial Aviation Forecast Conference Proceedings: Overcoming Barriers to World Competition and Growth*, pp. 125-132, Office of Aviation Policy and Plans, Washington, D.C.

Toh, R.S. (1998), 'Toward an International Open Skies Regime: Advances, Impediments, and Impacts', *Journal of Air Transportation World Wide*, vol. 3, pp. 61-70.

Chapter 4

Shaping the World

First Chicago Then the World

The interim Agreement on International Civil Aviation established the framework for a provisional International Civil Aviation Organization (PICAO), which functioned until 1947 when the required number of countries ratified the agreement to create a permanent organization. Over the coming years the International Civil Aviation Organization (ICAO) would work to develop the standards and practices followed by much of the world's aviation community. They would do so amidst the push and pull of the Cold War, the rapid development of aviation technology, and the limited funding often available to organizations associated with the United Nations. Like the United Nations, their actions could not be enforced on the world community, but could only be considered advisory. ICAO would thus struggle like the U.N. to achieve a consensus that would allow it to foster and develop the aviation system while balancing the needs of a diverse and fractious constituency.

The other organization born in Chicago, the International Air Transport Association, would receive recognition of its role at the 1946 bilateral talks between the U.S. and U.K. It would not suffer from the kind of tension that divided ICAO. Its members, international airlines, would set about the task of setting the fares, dividing the world's international routes, establishing the standards for interlining (transfer between carriers), and devising the methods of revenue sharing that would govern the international aviation system until these powers were slowly eroded by domestic air transport deregulation and international liberalization (Chapter 5). ICAO and IATA would work together on many issues related to safe air transport operation, standardization of documentation and procedures, and the development of legal agenda such as the Warsaw Convention on airline liability. Together these two organizations would shape the post-World War II international aviation system.

Setting the Standards

The International Civil Aviation Organization (ICAO) is composed of appointed representatives of all nations interested in international civil aviation (now totaling 188 contracting states). ICAO is governed by a sovereign body, the Assembly, which meets at least once every three year. Each nation represented has one vote on key matters and majority rules. The governing body of ICAO is the Council. The Council is elected from the Assembly for a three-year term and is composed of

33 members elected from three categories of ICAO general members. The first category is states of chief importance to air transport. The second is states that make the largest contribution to the provision of air navigation facilities. The final category is composed of states designated to insure that all of the regions of the globe are represented. Table 4.1 provides a list of the nation's currently serving on the Council.

Table 4.1: ICAO Council Membership

Algeria	Japan
Argentina	Lebanon
Australia	Mauritius
Brazil	Mexico
Cameroon	Nigeria
Canada	Pakistan
China	Paraguay
Costa Rica	Republic of Korea
Cuba	Russian Federation
Czech Republic	Saudi Arabia
Egypt	Senegal
Ethiopia	Spain
France	Sweden
Germany	United Kingdom
India	United States
Ireland	Venezuela
Italy	

These nations maintain a permanent presence at ICAO's headquarters in Montreal, Canada where they are responsible for the day-to-day operations of the organization. The Council adopts the Standards and Recommended Practices (SARPs) and approves the Procedures of Air Navigation Services (PANS) that are the heart of the work of ICAO. Assisting the Council are the Air Navigation Commission which is responsible for technical matters, the Air Transport Committee responsible for economic matters, the Committee on Joint Support of Air Navigation Services, and the Finance Committee. Proposals to amend or add new SARPs come from ICAO-sponsored international meetings, deliberative bodies within the organization itself, the Secretariat, the United Nations or other interested international organizations. ICAO works closely with such organizations as the World Meteorological Organization, the International Telecommunications Union, the Universal Postal Union, the World Health Organization, the International Maritime Organization (all U.N. affiliated), the International Air Transport Association, the Airports Council International, the

International Federation of Air Line Pilots, and the International Council of Aircraft Owner and Pilots Association (all non-governmental organizations).

Once an issue is brought to ICAO for consideration, it is referred to the Air Navigation Commission, which is composed of fifteen persons who have 'suitable qualifications and experience in the science and practice of aeronautics.' These individuals are nominated by Contracting States and appointed by the Council. The Commission is assisted by the Air Navigation Bureau and panels and working groups nominated by Contracting States and appointed by the Commission. These individuals serve based on their personal expertise and not as representatives of any Contracting State. Once the Commission submits a SARP to the Council, a two-thirds vote of its members is required for adoption. If a majority of the Contracting States do not disapprove it, the SARP becomes effective on the established date. SARPs are considered binding, although States that cannot comply can file a 'difference' that is published by ICAO in Supplements to Annexes. This process takes roughly 5-7 years to reach completion which means that the work of ICAO progresses slowly. PANS are developed in a similar way, however, they are not binding and no difference needs to be filed. Table 4.2 lists the annexes and areas, which are covered by ICAO.

Table 4.2: Annexes to the ICAO Convention

Annex	Subject
1	Personnel licensing
2	Rules of the Air
3	Meteorological Service
4	Aeronautical Charts
5	Units of Measurement to be used in operations
6	Operation of Aircraft
7	Aircraft Nationality and registration
8	Airworthiness of Aircraft
9	Facilitation
10	Aeronautical Telecommunications
11	Air Traffic Service
12	Search and Rescue
13	Aircraft Accident Investigation
14	Aerodromes
15	Aeronautical Information Service
16	Environmental Protection
17	Security
18	Safe Transport of Dangerous Goods

Other activities of ICAO include joint financing of navigation service on the high seas or in areas where no nation can be charged with the responsibility.

Iceland and Greenland are examples of the latter. Considering that their own aircraft represent less than 3 percent of the trans-Atlantic traffic, the burden for navigational services is shared by other nations. The Legal Affairs Committee prepares drafts for key international conferences related to aviation such as the Geneva (1948) and Rome (1952) Conventions. ICAO's Technical Co-operation Programme works with the United Nations Development Programme (UNDP) on projects aimed at developing the aviation system of developing nations. The Trainair programme provides assistance to national and regional civil aviation training institutes. Finally, ICAO provides expert services such as site selection and design of airstrips and design of air traffic control systems. The magnitude of work of ICAO seem overwhelming, particularly in light of their limited funding. Much of their efforts depend on the support, both technical and monetary, that comes from the Contracting States (ICAO, 2002).

The key to understanding ICAO is in realizing that like the United Nations in general it has *no* independent enforcement power; it can not make its members implement any of its standards. Its main bodies may act to support or condemn certain actions by members that relate to aviation, but this is an exercise in public relations and free expression. When or if a vote is taken on the issue of SARPs or PANS, it is the perfunctory end to months or years of consensus building at ICAO. If consensus is not initially achieved on certain issues, then all parties revise, rework, or reframe the issue until consensus is obtained. It is a painstaking process, but it has and is producing some very positive results. After years of debate, ICAO established in January 1999, the Universal Safety Oversight Program which 'consists of regular, mandatory, systematic, and harmonized safety audits carried out by ICAO in all 187 countries…it has proven effective in identifying and correcting safety deficiencies in areas of personnel licensing and airworthiness and operations of aircraft' (ICAO, 2002: 1). The program has been expanded to include air traffic service and airports. ICAO has been requested to help in the resolution of deficiencies through educational activities, funding and technical coordination, and the creation of a Quality Assistance Function. Given the politically sensitive nature of safety for governments and airlines, the Safety Oversight Program was a great victory for ICAO in their efforts to further advance the cause of international aviation. Most recently, ICAO has been directed by its Assembly to establish a Universal Security Oversight Audit Programme that would assess the implementation of ICAO security-related SARPs (ICAO, 2002).

Setting the Fares

Under the 1945 Articles of Association, the aims of the International Air Transport Association are:

> To Promote safe, regular, and economical air transportation for the
> benefit of the peoples of the world, to foster air commerce, and to
> study the problems connected therewith;

To provide means for collaboration among the air transport enterprise engaged directly or indirectly in international air transport service;

To cooperate with the newly created International Civil Aviation Organization and other international organizations (IATA, 2002).

In the early years, IATA worked on such issues as the Multilateral Interline Traffic Agreements, Passenger and Cargo Services Conference Resolutions, and Passenger and Cargo Agency Agreements & Sales Agency Rules. The Interline Agreements involved insuring acceptance of other carrier's tickets and waybills. The Conference Resolutions prescribed standard formats and specifications for tickets and waybills. The Agency Agreements governed the relationships between IATA airlines and their accredited agents. A Clearing House was also established in 1947 to handle debt settlements between carriers largely arising from interlining.

It was the role of IATA's Traffic Conferences that would eventually come under intense scrutiny by a liberalizing world air transportation system. Under the Bermuda Agreement of 1946, IATA was delegated the role of establishing fares and rates subject to government approval. According to IATA, the goal of the system was to establish 'coherent fares and rates patterns'. Such a system would avoid 'inconsistencies between tariffs affecting neighboring countries – and thereby avoiding traffic diversion' (IATA, 1996). In effect, there was a set fare for any given international route that any IATA member was expected to charge. If there continued to be an imbalance in the revenues earned by the designated carriers on such a route, then a revenue-sharing or pooling agreement could be worked out to equalize the revenues of both sides (Taneja, 1988). There were intermittent efforts in ICAO to question the tariff (fare) setting role of IATA, but during the last such effort ICAO concluded that 'at present, there is no justification for ICAO to undertake specific studies and other economic work on the subject of airline tariffs' (Sochor, 1990: 17).

Following the events discussed in Chapter 5, IATA was forced to reconsider its role in fare setting. It did so first by establishing a 'two-tier' system. Under this system, the IATA Trade Association became responsible for technical, legal, financial, and traffic services. The Tariff Coordination became responsible for fares and rates. An airline could participate in the Trade Association without participating in the Tariff Coordination activities. Over time, IATA has placed increasing emphasis on the trade association activities and come to derive much of its funding from the educational and product marketing activities of the Association. For all intents and purposes, the new IATA does not engage in fare or rate setting but allows these activities to be the domain of the airlines themselves.

A New Day Dawning

As the decade of the 1970s was coming to a close, there were few in the international aviation system that realized that the 'end of an era' was coming, but the passage in the United States of the Airline Deregulation Act of 1978 would be such a watershed. For the cozy system of routes and fares set up by IATA, it would mean radical change. For ICAO, this new era would mean more issues of safety and security would be added to their already full plate of issues.

References

International Air Transport Association (1996), 'Early Days', electronic edition, www.iata.org.

International Air Transport Association (2002), electronic edition, www.iata.org.

International Civil Aviation Organization (2002), electronic edition, www.icao.int.

International Civil Aviation Organization (2002), 'Meeting Caps Most Productive Triennium in Recent ICAO History', News Release, October 9, pp. 1-4.

Sochor, E. (1990), *The Politics of International Aviation*, University of Iowa Press, Iowa City.

Taneja, N.K. (1988), *The International Airline Industry*, Lexington Books, Lexington.

Toh, R.S. (1998), 'Towards an International Open Skies Regime: Advances, Impediments, and Impacts', *Journal of Air Transportation World Wide*, vol. 3, pp. 61-70.

Chapter 5

A Brave New World

New Deal

In 1976, the British gave notice to the U.S. government that it was terminating Bermuda I. According to the British, Bermuda I gave American carriers a disproportionate share of the traffic in large measure due to the liberal fifth freedom rights granted to U.S. carriers. It had been thirty years since the events at Chicago and the signing of Bermuda I. The world was now a very different place. The Asian miracle saw, first Japan, then other Asian nations achieve double digit levels of economic growth. Between 1950 and 1973, the Japanese gross domestic product grew at a rate of 10.5 percent a year. By the 1970s, the Japanese were producing over half the world's tonnage of shipping and as much steel as their U.S. counterparts (Kennedy, 1987). In Europe, most of the nations were back to their pre-war levels of output by 1950. Between the period 1950-1970, European gross domestic product grew on average 5.5 percent a year while industrial product rose 7.1 percent (Landes, 1969). By contrast, the U.S. economy had lost the relative advantages it possessed coming out of World War II. At the Bretton Woods conference in 1944, the world monetary system had been established pegging all major currencies to the U.S. dollar. Unfortunately, U.S. policies to finance both the war in Vietnam and domestic, social spending without increasing taxes had led the government to print more money, i.e. increase the money supply. This in turn led to inflation and put pressure on the international monetary system. This system was abandoned in 1973 (Solomon, 1982). Rising inflation, declining shares of exports, and new foreign competition at home were taking their toll on the U.S. economy.

For the British, the time appeared right to make a change. For their part, the U.S. government fearing a complete breakdown of the commercial air traffic with Great Britain agreed to sign what became known as Bermuda II in 1977. This bilateral agreement virtually eliminated multiple carrier designations, established capacity limitations, and redressed the imbalance in fifth freedom rights. Bermuda II was seen as a major policy setback by the U.S. government and a direct challenge to competitive markets.

Not Taking it Laying Down

To demonstrate its commitment to air transport liberalization, the U.S. initiated three actions in 1978. The first action was to issue a statement entitled 'Policy for the Conduct of International Air Transportation'. This statement declared the U.S. intention to 'trade competitive opportunities, rather than restrictions' in order to expand competition and reduce prices (95th Congress, 1978). This policy was a denunciation of Bermuda II and a clear challenge to the rest of the aviation community. Shortly afterwards, the U.S. Civil Aeronautics Board (CAB) issued an order to IATA to 'show cause' why they should not be considered an illegal cartel as prohibited by U.S. anti-trust law. Since IATA membership was restricted to international carriers whose major tasks included setting fares and capacity, there was little argument of violation. This was also a warning to U.S. carriers that their participation in the tariff and capacity setting activities of IATA would not be acceptable. Finally, in late 1978, the U.S. became the first nation in the world to deregulate its air transport industry with the passage of the Airline Deregulation Act (Toh, 1998).

The purpose of the Airline Deregulation Act was 'to encourage, develop, and attain an air transportation system which relies on competitive market forces to determine the quality, variety, and price of air services, and of other purposes'. The Act phased out the CAB with its market control of entry/exit, pricing, and service levels. The proponents of deregulation argued that regulation forced competition based solely on service quality and thus created fares that in many cases were 50 percent higher than comparable intrastate (unregulated) fares. Studies had concluded that regulation also forced carriers to accept low, uneconomical load factors, raised labor costs, protected inefficient carriers, and prevented them from establishing economies of scale that would allow them to lower unit prices (Caves, 1962; Douglas and Miller, 1974; Jordon, 1970; Kahn, 1971). It should be noted that several studies found that the average cost per passenger did not fall as firm size increased which tended to indicate that airlines were not natural monopolies that should be subject to regulation (Eads, Nerlove, and Raduchel, 1969; Straszheim, 1969; White, 1969). On the other hand, larger aircraft and increasing density (increased frequency of flights, additional seats in existing flights) did appear to lower unit costs (Caves, Christensen, and Thetheway, 1984; Graham and Kaplan, 1982). Overall, deregulation was expected to improve service to the public, lower fares, allow carriers to achieve higher profits, and create a more competitive airline industry through the entry of new carriers as well as the freer regulatory environment afforded to existing competitors (Kane, 1998). These proponents have noted that there are more carriers flying today than in 1978 and that prices have fallen. Morrison and Winston (1997) have estimated that airfares fell 33 percent in real terms between 1976 and 1993. They attribute at least 20 percent of this decline to deregulation itself which increased competition and reduced costs at large and medium airports. A recent study of international carriers found that the major U.S. carriers as a whole are most cost competitive than all but some of the lower wage Asian carriers (Oum and Yu, 1998).

While the impact of deregulation is still under debate, it is clear that following deregulation many U.S. carriers were forced to undergo a painful process of restructuring that not all of them completed successfully. The financial crisis in the early 1980s hit all of the U.S. carriers hard and led to industry consolidation and the creation of the hub-and-spoke system. In addition to the disappearance of such pre-deregulation carriers as Eastern Air Lines and Pan Am, more than two hundred new-entrant carriers have started and failed. By the early 1990s, another financial crisis had led the industry to develop complex holding structures, expand non-airline and/or discrete services, and race to create global seamless service through a network of strategic alliances (Rosen, 1995). Studies show that although there are more carriers flying, the top six carriers account for an increasingly large proportion of the total traffic. In 1985, the top six accounted for 62 percent of the domestic U.S. traffic. By the early 1990s, these same six controlled 86 percent (Kim and Singal, 1993). Several studies have even suggested that real prices fell faster under regulation than they did in the post-deregulation period (Dempsey and Goetz, 1992; Dempsey and Gesell, 1997). In addition, it has been suggested that deregulation did not benefit all consumers in terms of the level of service or price. Small, outlying communities have in fact lost some portion of the service they enjoyed prior to deregulation and the fact that they may be linked to a single dominant hub may also increase their fares (Goetz and Dempsey, 1989; Jones, 1998). While there are no studies examining the pre- and post-deregulation levels of service quality among U.S. carriers, there is a general consensus that it has declined significantly following deregulation and U.S. carriers are conspicuously absent from surveys ranking the service quality of international carriers (Kahn, 1990; Dempsey and Goetz, 1992; Towers and Perrin, 1991; Zagat, 1992).

The benefits and costs of domestic regulation can and have been the subject of an entire book (or series of books) and are mentioned here only because freeing domestic markets added philosophical and economic pressure to the liberalization of international markets. The arguments briefly presented here are also intended to suggest some of the effects that might occur in a truly deregulated international market. Deregulation in the U.S. market did appear to result in overall declines in fare prices and the appearance, at least temporarily, of new entrant carriers. These pressures forced the industry to restructure to lower costs as noted above by Oum and Yu (1998). Whatever the successes or failures of deregulation in the long run, the U.S. was now ready to push forward on the international scene with new initiatives designed to open international markets to greater competition and more market-based controls.

Encircling the World

In 1979, the U.S. passed the International Air Transportation Competition Act which set out three goals for future U.S. aviation policy. First, the U.S. would push for multiple carrier designations, permissive route authority, and no operational restrictions on capacity and frequency. Second, air fares would be freed to respond to consumer demand. Finally, the U.S. would work to eliminate discriminatory practices preventing U.S. carriers from effectively competing in international markets. Some of the practices targeted for change included foreign computer reservation systems that favored other national carriers, government user fees at international airports that were excessive compared to domestic only airports (the contention being that national governments were using these fees to subsidize smaller, local airports), and policies that required exclusive contracts for ground handling and other services (Toh, 1998).

The U.S. would now pursue its new open skies policy through the application of two levers. The first lever was laid out by the Director of the Bureau of Pricing and Domestic Aviation and the CAB. The so-called Encirclement Strategy called for the U.S. to bring pressure on smaller market countries to sign open skies agreements as a means of diverting traffic from larger aviation markets. The strategy was based on the assumption that open skies would lower fares between those countries involved in the bilateral agreement and cause passengers to change their traveling patterns in pursuit of lower fares. Two nations were primarily targeted for encirclement - Japan and Great Britain - because they represented the key entry ports for U.S. travelers to Asia and Europe respectively (Levine, 1979). The U.S. first targeted smaller market countries that generated very little third and fourth freedom traffic (to and from the U.S.) since these countries stood to gain by simply getting greater access to U.S. destinations. There could also be no question of exchanging domestic opportunities (cabotage) with these nations since they had little or no domestic markets to exchange for the sizable U.S. domestic market.

The second lever to open skies came through the application of the U.S. Department of Transportation's (DOT) policy on approving airline alliances. This policy based approval on either the coverage of the rights under existing bilateral or proven benefits to the U.S. (Gellman Research Associates, 1994). In addition, the U.S. DOT has granted immunity from anti-trust enforcement to alliances between carriers from open skies countries (see Chapter 10 for a further discussion), the arguments being that there were proven benefits to the U.S. deriving from these agreements. Anti-trust immunity allows competitors to coordinate on issues of pricing, capacity, and scheduling. Thus, they are able to achieve greater levels of operational integration, cut costing, and improved quality through coordination (Oum and Park, 1997).

Opening Up

Table 5.1 lists the open skies agreements signed by the U.S. to date and the dates of their signing. As the Encirclement Strategy dictated, countries approached first were small market nations. To understand the difference open skies has made in the bilateral process, it is interesting to note that the length of the bilateral agreements discussed in Chapter 3 between the U.S.-Great Britain and U.S.-Japan were sixteen pages in length. The U.S.-Netherlands agreement is one page. Under routes, there appears the following:

Netherlands

A.   The Netherlands via intermediate points to a point or points in the United States and beyond.

B.   The Netherlands Antilles via the intermediate points Santo Domingo, Port au Prince, Kingston, Montego Bay, Camaguey, and Havana, to Miami.

C.   The Netherlands Antilles to New York.

D.   The Netherlands Antilles to San Juan.

United States

A.   The United States via intermediate points to a point or points in the Netherlands and beyond.

B.   The United States via intermediate points to Aruba, Curacao, and St. Maarten and beyond (Air Transport Association of America).

There is no mention of pricing, capacity or frequency restrictions in these agreements. Clearly, Open Skies agreements have been helpful in saving the world's trees. One might ask whether they have achieved the goals set forth by U.S. policy and whether the consumers of the world have benefited from these new bilateral.

Conspicuously absent from the Open Skies list in Table 5.1 are two countries - Japan and Great Britain. Understanding the reasons for their absence illustrates several key issues in international aviation. To those outside the industry it may be surprising to discover that not all the disagreement during the course of the bilateral negotiations between these countries took place between national governments; airlines on both sides of the debate disagreed among themselves and thus did not present a unified voice to their respective governments. The 1952 agreement between the U.S.-Japan had given broad rights to three carriers - United, Northwest, and Japan Airlines. The remaining U.S. carriers and All Nippon Airlines (ANA) received limited access in the 1980s due to a series of Memoranda of Understanding between Washington and Tokyo. Although Northwest, an incumbent carrier, supported Open Skies, United Airlines did not favor such as agreement, which would have allowed more U.S. competition into the Japanese market. From a policy perspective, the non-incumbent U.S. carriers would have received more access under a 'not-quite-open-skies' agreement and felt that the U.S. should not push for Open Skies if that push jeopardized an overall agreement (Goldman, 1997). Similar issues surfaced in the Open Skies negotiations between the U.S.-U.K. As part of their Oneworld alliance American Airlines and British Airways had asked the U.S. government for anti-trust immunity which would only be granted in the presence of an Open Skies agreement. As Richard Branson, Chairman of Virgin Atlantic Airways has noted 'they thought they had the British Department of Transport in their pocket, which unfortunately at the time was

Table 5.1: Open Skies Agreements

Year	Month	Country	Year	Month	Country
2001	10	France	1997	7	Aruba
	9	Oman		2	Brunei
	5	Poland		10	Chile
	11	Sri Lanka		4	Costa Rica
				4	El Salvador
2000	11	Benin		4	Guatemala
	2	Burkina Faso		4	Honduras
	5	Gambia		6	Malaysia
	3	Ghana		12	Nether. Antilles
	10	Malta		5	New Zealand
	10	Morocco		5	Nicaragua
	2	Namibia		3	Panama
	8	Nigeria		12	Romania
	10	Rwanda		1	Singapore
	12	Senegal		3	Taiwan
	1	Slovak Republic			
	3	Turkey	1996	11	Jordan
				2	Germany
1999	8	Argentina			
	5	Bahrain	1995	5	Austria
	12	Dom Republic		5	Belgium
	4	Pakistan		12	Czech Republic
	12	Portugal		5	Denmark
	10	Qatar		5	Finland
	11	Tanzania		5	Iceland
	4	UAE		5	Luxembourg
				5	Norway
1998	11	Italy		5	Sweden
	4	S. Korea		5	Switzerland
	5	Peru			
	2	Uzbekistan	1992	10	Netherlands

probably true. They also thought that the U.S. Department of Transportation would be so eager to get rid of the Bermuda II disagreement, that it would be blind to the dire consequences such an alliance would hold for competition on the North Atlantic' (100).

As this quote indicates, the competitors in both countries were generally more interested in simply gaining more access to US-UK markets than pursuing a broad Open Skies agreement. Carriers such as British Airways and American saw Open Skies initially as the only way to gain even more from the system. However, even these two carriers began to have doubts when they realized the price that the European Union intended to extract for its approval. Access to Heathrow Airport in London, the number one destination airport for North Atlantic passengers, is tightly constrained. In order to free up landing slots for new entrant carriers, European officials have sought ways to encourage incumbent carriers to give up slots. It should be noted that unlike in the U.S. slots cannot be sold as an asset. In Europe, a carrier either uses a slot or loses it. The price of European approval was the surrender of 300 landing slots by British Airways and American (Phillips, 1999). British Airways 'apparently decided the price for opening up Heathrow to new competition might not be offset by revenues gained from a full alliance with American' (Morrocco, 1998: 45).

If opening up Japan and the United Kingdom were goals of open skies, then the policy has not yet been a complete success, however, the example of US-Japan and US-UK internal divisions illustrates the interplay that occurs in free market systems where competitors look to individual profit and advantage over mutual, assured benefits. According to Adam Smith, the Father of market economics, individuals each acting in their own self-interest was supposed to result in a more perfect distribution of good and determination of price. In the case of airline, market operation is never separated from government intervention. In a broader sense, Open Skies has helped to spread a more liberal environment for international pricing and capacity. In 1984, the U.S. signed a multilateral agreement with the European Civil Aviation Conference that created zones of reasonableness for each fare class allowing individual carriers latitude in setting prices. The U.S. also pushed for the inclusion of language within bilateral agreements that disallowed fares only with the mutual disapproval of the two parties to the agreement. This new pricing freedom placed tremendous pressure on IATA members to find ways around the IATA set fares. Many IATA members resorted to illegal discounting of fares through extra commissions to travel agents (Toh, 1998). These 'bucket shops' sold blocks of tickets at prices more competitive with U.S. carriers, but without sales receipt documentation that would be evidence of violation. Over time the zones of reasonableness became so broad that for all intents and purposes the market ruled in matters of pricing and IATA abandoned its role in fare setting.

Several studies by the U.S. Department of Transportation have concluded that Open Skies bilateral have been effective in lowering fares. In the 1999 report *International Aviation Developments: Global Deregulation Takes Off*, the DOT reported that fares in Open Skies markets dropped 17.5 percent between 1996 and 1998 compared to only a 3.5 percent drop in no-Open Skies markets. Fares increased slightly in non-Open Skies gateway-to-gateway markets, but dropped 11.1 percent in Open Skies markets. In the 2000 report *International Aviation Developments: Transatlantic Deregulation – The Alliance Network Effect*, the DOT concluded that average fares to open skies countries declined by 20 percent overall compared to 1996, and approached 25 percent in connecting markets beyond European gateways. Significantly, double-digit fare reductions have occurred even in gate-to-gate markets in open skies countries (3). This report goes on to suggest that the link between Open Skies and strategic alliances have created an 'alliance network effect' that has further lowered prices. In fact, it concludes that 'alliance-based networks are the principle driving force behind transatlantic price reductions and traffic gains' (5).

The Next Step

The U.S. deregulation of air transportation and the concomitant push for open skies would slowly erode the old system of international aviation set up in the post-World War II era. The liberalization and economic integration of Europe (Chapter 6) would further press the cause of liberalization. However, the fact remains that the system remains far from open. Branson (1998) has observed that the Virgin retail division in the U.S. 'has a rapidly growing chain of Megastores in this country (U.S.) selling CD's, books, computer games, etc. We employ several thousand U.S. staff and the increased competition our stores have brought clearly benefits the consumer. No one stands in our way when we want to invest...What a difference from aviation, where if Virgin wanted to establish a U.S. airline we would be restricted to a mere 25% of the voting shares, and thus prevented from exercising any form of control' (101).

The events of 9/11 have propelled the already slumping international airline industry to the brink of one of its greatest disasters, but in every crisis there is also the possibility of creating new futures. Some of these possible new futures will be the subject of Chapters 14-16, but first it is important to understand the way today's airlines have attempted to create global seamless networks that extend their reach throughout the world and promise to get you anywhere you want to go in the ever shrinking globe.

References

Air Transport Association of America (2001), *Air Service Rights in U.S. International Air Transport Agreements: A Compilation of Scheduled and Charter Service Rights Contained in U.S. Bilateral Aviation Agreements*, Air Transport Association of America, Washington, D.C.

Branson, R. (1998), 'Luncheon Address', *FAA Commercial Aviation Forecast Conference Proceedings: Overcoming Barriers to World Competition and Growth*, March 12-13, pp. 99-102.

Caves, R. (1962), *Air Transport and Its Regulators: An Industry Study*, Harvard University Press, Cambridge, MA.

Caves, R.E., Christensen, L.R. and Tretheway, M.W. (1984), 'Economies of Density versus Economies of Scale: Why Trunk and Local Service Airline Costs Differ', *Rand Journal of Economics*, vol. 15, pp. 471-489.

Dempsey, P.S. and Gesell, L. (1997), 'Airline Management: Strategies for the 21st Century', Coast-Aire Publications, New York.

Dempsey, P.S. and Goetz, A. (1992), 'Airline Deregulation and Laissez Faire Mythology', Quorum Books, Westport, CT.

Douglas, G.W. and Miller, J.C. (1974), *Economic regulation of Domestic Air Transport: Theory and Policy*, The Brookings Institution, Washington, D.C.

Eads, G., Nerlov, M. and Raduchel, W. (1969), 'A Long-Run Cost Function for the Local Service Airline Industry: An Experiment in Non-Linear Estimation', *Review of Economics and Statistics*, vol. 51, pp. 258-270.

Gellman Research Associates (1994), 'A Study of International Airline Codesharing', report submitted to Office of Aviation and International Economics, Office of the Secretary of Transportation, U.S. Department of Transportation, Washington, D.C.

Goetz, A.R. and Dempsey, P.S. (1989), 'Airline Deregulation Ten Years After: Something Foul in the Air', *Journal of Air Law and Commerce*, vol. 54, pp. 927-963.

Goldman, M. (1997), 'Negotiating not-quite-open-skies', *The Journal of Commerce*, November 1, p. 4.

Graham, D.R. and Kaplan, D.P. (1982), 'Airlines Deregulation is Working', *Regulation*, vol. 6, pp. 26-32.

Jones, J.R. (1998), 'Twenty Years of Airline Deregulation: The Impact on Outlying and Small Communities', *Journal of Transportation Management*, vol. 10, pp. 33-43.

Jordan, W.A. (1970), *Airline Regulation in America: Effects and Imperfections*, Johns Hopkins University Press, Baltimore, MD.

Kahn, A.E. (1971), *The Economics of Regulation*, Wiley, New York.

Kahn, A.E. (1990), 'Deregulation: Looking Backward and Looking Forward', *Yale Journal of Regulation*, vol. 7, pp. 325-354.

Kane, R.M. (1998), *Air Transportation*, 13th edition, Kendall/Hunt Publishing Company, Dubuque, IA.

Kennedy, P. (1987), *The Rise and Fall of the Great Powers*, Random House, New York.

Kim, E.H. and Singal, V. (1993), 'Mergers and Market Power: Evidence from the Airline Industry, *American Economic Review*, vol. 83, pp. 549-569.

Landes, D. (1969), *The Unbound Prometheus: Technological Change and Industrial Development in Western Europe from 1970 to the present*, Cambridge.

Levine, M.E. (1979), 'Civil Aeronautics Memo by Michael E. Levine', *Aviation Daily*, March 8, pp. 1-7.

Morrison, S.A. and Winston, C. (1997), 'The Fare Skies: Air Transportation and Middle America', *The Brookings Review*, vol. 15, pp. 42-45.

Morrocco, J.D. (1998), 'Open Skies Impasse Shifts Alliance Plans', *Aviation Week and Space Technology*, November 9, pp. 45-46.

Oum, T.H. and Park, J. (1997), 'Airline Alliances: Current Status, Policy Issues, and Future Directions', *Journal of Air Transport Management*, vol. 3, pp. 133-144.

Oum, T.H. and Yu, C. (1998), *Winning Airlines: Productivity and Cost Competitiveness of the World's Major Airlines*, Kluwer Academic Press, Boston, MA.

Phillips, E.H. (1999), 'Oneworld Late, But Powerful', *Aviation Week and Space Technology*, August 23, pp. 63-64.

Rosen, S.D. (1995), 'Corporate Restructuring: A labor perspective' in P. Cappelli (ed.), *Airline Labor Relations in the Global Era: The New Frontier*, pp. 31-40, ILR Press, Ithaca.

Solomon, R. (1982), *The International Monetary System*, Harper & Row, New York.

Straszheim, M.R. (1969), *The International Airline Industry*, The Brookings Institution, Washington, D.C.

Toh, R.S. (1998), 'Towards an International Open Skies Regime: Advances, Impediments, and Impacts', *Journal of Air Transportation World Wide*, vol. 3, pp. 61-70.

Towers and Perrin (1991), *Competing in a New Market: Is Airline Management Prepared?*, Towers and Perrin, San Francisco, CA.

U.S. Congress (1978), *Hearings before the Subcommittee on Aviation of the Committee on Commerce, Science and Transportation*, United States Senate, 95th Congress Second Session on S.3363, pp. 19-20.

U.S. Department of Transportation (1999), *International Aviation Developments: Global Deregulation Takes Off*, Department of Transportation, Office of the Secretary, Washington, D.C.

U.S. Department of Transportation (2000), *International Aviation Developments: Transatlantic Deregulation - The Alliance Network Effect*, Department of Transportation, Office of the Secretary, Washington, D.C.

White, L.J. (1979), 'Economies of Scale and the Question of "Natural Monopoly" in the Airline Industry', *Journal of Air Law and Commerce*, vol. 46, pp. 545-573.

Zagat, W. (1992), *Zagat United States Travel Survey*, Zagat, New York.

Chapter 6

The View From Europe

Different Markets, Different Views

From a historical and geographic standpoint, Europe can be said to include all the nations west of the Russian Ural mountains, however, this chapter will focus primarily on the 15 nations of the European Union (Table 6.1) with a brief look at the 13 nations, primarily eastern European, that have asked to be considered for membership in the European Union (Table 6.2). These nations represent a very diverse set of languages, cultures, histories, and geographies. As Table 6.1 shows, the landmass of the EU countries ranges from 2,586 square kilometers for Luxembourg to 547,030 square kilometers for France. Likewise, the population of EU countries ranges from 448,569 for Luxembourg to 59,778,002 for the United Kingdom. This diversity in size and population is reflected in the level of aviation infrastructure within these countries as well as the importance of aviation to domestic travel and commerce. The geographic location of nations also influences the ability of potential hub city airports to attract traffic. The countries requesting consideration for admission to the EU under enlargement plans also shows considerable diversity in size and population ranging from Malta with an area of 316 square kilometers and 397,499 people to Turkey with an area of 780,580 square kilometers and 67,308,928 people.

There are a number of key differences between the air transport market in Europe and the U.S. that have influenced the development of and approach to domestic deregulation and international liberalization. The Chicago Convention of 1944 led to the adoption of a one airline policy in most of the nations of Europe. This airline, the de jure flag carrier, was seen as more of an instrument of state policy than a moneymaking enterprise (Graham, 1995). The typical European carrier was completely or partially owned by the state which would provide direct financial assistance to carriers '(1) to compensate airlines for the imposition of a public service obligation; (2) to develop and operate domestic service; (3) to provide service to economically underdeveloped regions; (4) to encourage the acquisition and operation of specific airplanes; or (5) simply to cover an airline's operating losses' (Taneja, 1988: 59). This flag carrier would develop its national hub, usually at the nation's capital, and dominate that hub accounting for over 50 percent of the departures (Borenstein, 1992). The network of airline routes would reflect national requirements and former colonial ties. As a whole, the old European air transport market would be characterized by low productivity, high unit costs, and high fares. In contrast, the U.S. domestic market was substantially larger than that of any single EU nation and benefited from a number of privately owned carriers throughout its history, although it too received government assistance in its early development from air mail rates (Graham, 1995; Sinha, 2001).

Table 6.1: Information on European Union Nations

Country	Area*	Population**	Airports (paved)
Austria	83,858	8,169,929	55 (24)
Belgium	30,510	10,274,545	42 (24)
Denmark	43,094	5,368,854	116 (28)
Finland	337,030	5,183,545	160 (73)
France	547,030	59,765,983	477 (270)
Germany	357,021	83,251,851	625 (325)
Greece	131,940	10,645,343	79 (65)
Ireland	70,280	3,883,159	41 (17)
Italy	301,230	57,715,625	135 (97)
Luxembourg	2,586	448,569	2 (1)
Netherlands	41,526	16,067,754	28 (20)
Portugal	92,391	10,084,245	67 (40)
Spain	504,782	40,077,100	133 (85)
Sweden	449,964	8,876,744	255 (147)
U.K.	244,820	59,778,002	470 (332)

Source: CIA Factbook.
* Square Km. **Estimated July 2002 figures. Data on airports from 2001.

Table 6.2: Information on Selected EU Enlargement Nations

Country	Area*	Population**	Airports (paved)
Bulgaria	110,910	7,621,337	215 (129)
Cyprus	9,250	767,314	15 (12)
Czech Rep.	78,866	10,256,760	121 (44)
Estonia	45,226	1,415,681	32 (8)
Hungary	93,030	10,075,034	43 (16)
Latvia	64,589	2,366,515	25 (13)
Lithuania	65,200	3,601,138	72 (9)
Malta	316	397,499	1 (1)
Poland	312,685	38,625,478	122 (83)
Romania	237,500	22,317,730	61 (24)
Slovakia	48,845	5,422,366	34 (17)
Slovenia	20,273	1,932,917	14 (6)
Turkey	780,580	67,308,928	120 (86)

Source: CIA Factbook.
* Square Km. **Estimated July 2002 figures. Data on airports from 2001.

Another feature that distinguishes the European market from the U.S. is the higher level of inter-modal competition from automobiles and high-speed trains. The average length of a haul in Europe is 750 kilometers, half the U.S. average length of a haul. This increases the competition from other modes of transportation and has limited the ability of airlines to develop hub-and-spoke systems like their U.S. counterparts. This in turn has limited consumer ability to achieve reduced fares by accepting indirect routing over direct flights to destination. With the exception of the northeastern corridor of the U.S., train service does not offer a viable substitute to air travel for U.S. consumers (Graham, 1995; Sinha, 2001). European carriers also face competition from a well-developed air charter market. In the early 1990s, charter service in the U.S. accounted for less than 2 percent of all passenger miles, but more than 25 percent of the passenger miles in Europe.

These European charter passengers were predominantly leisure travelers, leaving scheduled carriers to serve business travel needs (Sinha, 2001). Finally, there is a significant difference in the product mix between U.S. and European carriers. For U.S. carriers, only 15.4 percent of the departures in 1990 were international while international departures represent 52.9 percent of the departures of European carriers (Sinha, 2001). In short, it was neither feasible nor probably possible to institute U.S. style deregulation in Europe.

The European Way

When the European Economic Community, a predecessor of the current European Union, was formed in 1957, it established a Common Transport Policy, but failed to include aviation in the original draft (Button, 1997). This oversight was corrected in a 1986 ruling by the European Court of Justice which declared that air transport would henceforth be subject to the competition rules of the Treaty of Rome. The following year, the Council of Ministers adopted the so-called First Package which allowed multiple designation of carriers on country-to-country routes and high volume city-to-city routes, fifth freedom rights on city-to-city routes up to 30 percent of capacity, automatic approval of discount fares up to 55 percent, and double approval of full fares. The Second Package, adopted in 1990, included a double-disapproval provision for full fares and an extension of 5th freedom rights to city-to-city routes up to 50 percent of capacity. Protection was also granted for routes designated as public service obligations. The Third, and final, Package was implemented in 1993 and ended on April 1, 1997. This package granted full access to all routes including cabotage which went into effect on April 1. It removed all restrictions on fares subject to the right of the European Commission to intervene in matters of predatory pricing and seat (capacity) dumping. All distinctions were removed between charter and scheduled carriers and freedom was granted to start an airline provided it was 1) EU owned, 2) financially sound, and 3) in compliance with all safety requirements (Graham, 1997, 1995; Sinha, 2001).

Results to Date

There have been few studies to date on the effects of the three packages. The early packages, combined with the more liberal bilaterals signed during the 1980s, did appear to have increased the frequency on some routes and reduced leisure (but not business class) fares, particularly where multiple carrier designation allowed new market entry (Button and Swann, 1989; Graham, 1995). Morrell (1998) has found that the number of cross border routes served increased by 11 percent between 1989 and 1992. This number rose to 25 percent between 1992 and 1995. The number of flights operated also increased during these periods by 14 and 18 percent respectively. The average frequency on all intra-EU routes increased from 13.9 departures per week in 1989 to 15.5 in 1992. Seat capacity did not increase between 1989-1992, but did go up after 1992 on routes that were served by three or more carriers. A 1995 study by the Civil Aviation Authority of Great Britain also found that consumers only gained from lower fares, better service, and better connecting flights when there were at least three competitors on a given route. In effect, actual, rather than threatened, entry was essential to realizing benefits from liberalization (Abbot and Thompson, 1989; Humphreys, 1996). A study by the European Commission (1996) concluded that competition had little effect on routes run as a monopoly or duopoly. Unfortunately, approximately 94 percent of the intra-EU routes fall into this category.

The effect of liberalization on established EU carriers has until recently been relatively limited. Carriers such as British Airways and KLM appear to have worked to improve their long haul market and hub system more than their intra-EU system (CAA, 1995). While one of the key features of the first two packages was the extension of fifth freedom rights, evidence indicates that few carriers actually exploited these rights (Graham, 1995). Some of the peripheral EU countries did initially attempt to exploit the intra-EU opportunities of cabotage, but many of these services were discontinued due to limited profitability (Morrell, 1998). Thus, there was generally no third carrier entry in many markets, certainly not by the traditional flag carriers.

Another goal of deregulation and liberalization is the creation of new entrants. Between 1992-1995, there was a net gain of six carriers (Morrell, 1998). The most successful of these carriers are Ireland's Ryanair and the UK's EasyJet and Virgin Express. In 2001, these carriers posted significant profits compared to their traditional counterparts in the EU. In fact, it appears that 2001 will be a turning point for the low-cost European entrants. Industry experts expect them to increase their share of intra-European passenger traffic from the current 7 percent to over 14 percent in the next five years (Binggeli and Pompeo, 2002). Analysts, however, are somewhat divided over the extent to which low-cost carriers can continue to post gains in the EU market given some of the EU's more unique problems (Binggelli and Pompeo, 2002; R2A, 2002).

With liberalization, particularly the implementation of the Third package, charter operators in the EU were presented with a number of options. They could now (1) enter scheduled service in a head-to-head competition with EU flag carriers; (2) enter scheduled service on leisure routes; or (3) stay in the core charter market and develop their long haul operations. Evidence to date shows that option 1 was not very successful for these operators (Air Europe, Dan Air, Trans European). Some carriers did have limited success on certain routes (Maersk Air, Transwede, Transavia), but generally charter operators have not provided a serious challenge to the established carriers (Morrell, 1998).

UK Experience

Among the EU countries, the UK has attempted to apply a policy of liberalization in its domestic markets for the longest period of time. It remains dominated by a single carrier, British Airways and continues to show signs that 'inequalities of opportunity' exist among the UK carriers. Richard Branson of Virgin Airlines has consistently complained that British Airways has the British Department of Transport in their pocket (Branson, 1998). According to Graham (1995), the New Right which dominated UK politics during the 1980s when British Airways was privatized insisted that privatization could not damage the airline's international competitive strength and so 'the consequent protection of BA's position, and the reconstruction of its finances prior to privatization in 1987, not only exacerbated the long-term problems created by the airline's dominance of the UK air transport industry but, simply, were factors incompatible with the stimulation of competition' (148). He suggests that three other factors prevented the Civil Aviation Authority from achieving its goals of greater liberalization. The first factor was business failure and consolidation. The same phenomena also occurred in the U.S. market and limited the level of competition in many areas. The second factor was the 'goal' of developing a UK carrier to serve the secondary London airport, Gatwick, to relieve congestion at Heathrow. The final factor is BA itself who dominates at the UK airport of Heathrow which continues to be the primary airport of London. Despite these problems, the UK has managed to maintain a higher level of viable internal competition than other EU countries. Barrett (1999) has reported that the productivity on routes between Ireland and the UK has resulted in higher levels of traffic and faster falling fares than that of the 14 other airlines of the Association of European Airlines. Liberalization has also allowed UK carriers to achieve lower unit costs and higher productivity than their EU counterparts (Alamdari, 1998).

The Netherlands

With a total area of only 41,526 square kilometers and a population of 16,067,754 (Table 6.1), the Netherlands does not have a significant domestic market. Not surprisingly, the focus of KLM, the Netherlands flag carrier, has been on international markets. As the airline of the first country to sign an open skies agreement (Table 5.1), KLM has focused its attention on long haul operations across the North Atlantic, forming a strategic alliance with the U.S. carrier Northwest. While the details of this alliance are discussed more fully in chapters 8-11, it is important to note that KLM and Northwest were the first to receive anti-trust immunity from the U.S. government based on the existence of an open skies agreement. This has allowed them to coordinate closely on issues of schedules, pricing, and capacity which in turn has resulted in a financially strong network with a high level of network density (frequency) and a market presence greater than its geographic scope would suggest (Merrill Lynch, 1999).

Remaining Obstacles

The EU has faced a number of hurdles in its efforts to liberalize. First, there is the continuing issue of airline subsidies. In 1993 alone, six EU carriers - Air France, Olympic, Iberia, TAP-Air Portugal, Alitalia, and Aer Lingus - required government subsidies to remain in business (Graham, 1995). Most recently, the Belgium government has stepped in to salvage something of its flag carrier, Sabena. These subsidies, while approved by the European Commission, have been vigorously opposed by other members of the EU. This apparent preference of governments for national carriers flies in the face of the objective to remove such barriers to free trade in the EU as a whole. It also keeps excess capacity in the European market in a way similar to the liberal bankruptcy laws of the U.S. In both cases, artificial barriers prevent the market from adjusting quickly in market demand downturns and spread the problem to other carriers.

The EU has also not seen the level of new entrants into liberalized markets that the United States witnessed after deregulation. In part this is a function of the slot allocation problem in Europe. Under the IATA-agreed rules accepted by the EC, slots must be allocated on a non-discriminatory basis, but historic rights may be considered. Given the pattern of European air transport development, the traditional flag carrier will have superior access to slots at the major airports which tend to be those that face capacity restrictions. Since slots cannot be sold as in the United States, it is in the best interest of airlines to maintain historic rights to these slots by exercising at least the minimum number of departures. Thus, it is very difficult for new entrants to gain the landing slots required to offer competition at these hubs. The European Commission has attempted to open up slots as a prerequisite for approving exemptions from competitive rules for airline alliances, but this has not been enough at many airports.

Low cost new entrants face other problems as well. First, the low-cost segment in Europe is smaller than in the U.S. and there is overlap between the charter carriers who may sell up to a third of their seats without the hotel package that normally accompanies it and the traditional flag carriers who offer discounted weekend travel. Second, if the U.S. pattern holds, then the first entrant into the markets (route) will be able to stimulate new growth and capture the market share. Later entrants with similar costs structures will find it more difficult to generate traffic. At the moment, there are still a number of routes not served by low-cost carriers so there is room for growth. From the EU consumer perspective, however, this pattern has meant that low-cost carriers have tended to avoid the direct competition that could further lower prices. They have also tended to avoid head-to-head competition with the traditional carriers, but long term growth will eventually require them to challenge these very carriers and their business class yields (Binggeli and Pompeo, 2002). Like Southwest in the U.S., many of these entrants have adopted a no-frills, secondary airport strategy that does seem to be gaining some momentum. Once again, the problem appears to be a lack of routes with sufficient origin and destination traffic to support entry, even if airport capacity restraints and other factors did not hinder them (Morrell, 1998).

Future EU Liberalization

It seems quite likely that the EU will eventually enlarge by admitting most, if not all, of the countries in Table 6.2. Like the original 15 EU nations, these nations share many of the same structural and historic problems that have inhibited greater liberalization of their air transport markets. In an effort to prepare for entry into the EU, the air transport industry of these nations has begun to reorganize by 1) placing new organizational and management structure into place including privatization, strategic alliances, and joint ventures with Western firms, 2) attempting to reorient their networks westward to attract the tourism markets, 3) acquiring more western aircraft, and 4) upgrading their infrastructure (Graham, 1995).

While it does not appear to be productive to argue over whether the approach to deregulation and liberalization taken by the EU was better than the U.S., the evidence to date suggests that consumers in the EU have not yet benefited to the same extent as consumers in U.S. markets (Sinha, 2001). This may simply be a function of time, however, a number of authors have suggested that there is reason to believe that the EU will never achieve the level of fares or the connectivity of U.S. markets. Taneja (1988) has argued that two factors are likely to keep fares higher in Europe than the U.S. The first is the policy of EU governments of maintaining inefficient EU carriers with subsidies and other benefits. This not only keeps excess capacity in the marketplace, but allows inefficient carriers to continue to operate using more expensive equipment, less efficient route structures, and less productive labor. The second reason is the overall higher cost structure of EU airlines that is partly a function of higher input costs such as labor, but is also the result of shorter average lengths of flights. Graham (1995) has gone on to argue that the hubbing patterns in the EU create a 'considerable degree of inertia' (154). In connection with hubs, he has cited two factors that inhibit the connectivity of EU markets. First, these hubs continue to be national in nature and dominated by the flag carrier. Second, regional carriers can only operate in connection with these national carriers. This means that 'peripheral regions are likely to be linked by direct flights to national air hubs, but not more widely to the EU itself' (167). As noted in the previous chapter, smaller, outlying areas often experience declines in service levels and higher fares caused by routing to a major hub dominated by a single carrier (Goetz and Dempsey, 1989; Jones, 1998). The very unevenness of the population within the EU means that the traffic demands on some routes will not support significant frequency. This is likely to continue to hinder connectivity patterns and necessitate transfers across hubs (Graham, 1995).

Looking Backward and Forward

Looking back on the European experience, the diversity of the European market and the political nature of the integration process itself would have precluded a U.S. style deregulation nor would such a process have been likely to produce any 'better' results for the air transport markets. Given the constraints, liberalization and deregulation have achieved a good deal in terms of opening markets and providing consumers with a greater range of choices. The EU still faces many challenges including 1) integration of the enlargement countries, 2) questions on airline subsidies, 3) questions on cross-border mergers and acquisitions, 4) questions on the level of consolidation and competition necessary to achieve consumer benefits, 5) questions on the means of protecting and encouraging new entrant carriers, and 6) questions on providing public service obligations (or essential services as it is called in the U.S.) to communities that may be disadvantaged by liberalization and deregulation. As we will see in Chapter 16, the Europeans are also asking questions of others as well. In this case, they are asking to extend their single market across the Atlantic to North America. Answering this question will prove as difficult for North American governments, airlines, and consumers as liberalization and integration has been for the EU.

References

Abbott, K. and Thompson, D. (1989), *Deregulating European Aviation: The Impact of Bilateral Liberalization*, Center for Business Strategy Working Paper Series no. 73, London.

Alamdari, F. (1998), 'Trends in Airline Labor Productivity and Costs in Europe', *Journal of Air Transportation World Wide*, vol. 3, pp. 71-88.

Barrett, S.D. (1999), 'Peripheral Market Entry, Product Differentiation, Supplier Rents, and Sustainability in the Deregulated European Airline Market – a Case Study', *Journal of Air Transport Management*, vol. 5, pp. 21-30.

Binggeli, U. and Pompeo, L. (2002), 'Hyped Hopes for Europe's Low-cost Airlines', *McKinsey Quarterly*, no. 4.

Borestein, S. (1992), 'Prospects for Competitive Air Travel in Europe' in W.J. Adams (ed.), *Singular Europe: Economy and Policy of the European Community After 1992*, University of Michigan Press, Ann Arbor.

Branson, R. (1998), 'Luncheon Address', *FAA Commercial Aviation Forecast Conference Proceedings: Overcoming Barriers to World Competition and Growth*, U.S. Department of Transportation, Washington, D.C.

Button, K.J. (1997), 'Developments in the European Union: Lessons for the Pacific Asia Region' in C. Findley, C.I. Sien and K. Singh (eds.), *Asia Pacific Air Transport: Challenges and Policy Reform*, Institute of Southeast Asian Studies, Singapore.

Button, K.J. and Swann, D. (1989), 'European Community Airlines-Deregulation and its Problems', *Journal of Common Market Studies*, vol. 37, 259-282.

CIA Factbook (2002), www.odci.gov/cia/publications/factbook.

Civil Aviation Authority (1995), *CAP 654 The Single Aviation Market: Progress So Far*, Civil Aviation Authority, London.

European Commission (1996), *Impact of the Third Package of Air Transport Liberalization Measures COM 96*, European Commission, Brussels.

Goetz, A.R. and Dempsey, P.S. (1989), 'Airline Deregulation Ten Years After: Something Foul in the Air', *Journal of Air Law and Commerce*, vol. 54, pp. 927-963.

Graham, B. (1995), *Geography and Air Transport*, John Wiley and Sons, New York.

Graham, B. (1997), 'Air Transport Liberalization in the European Union: An Assessment', *Regional Studies*, vol. 31, pp. 87-104.

Jones, J.R. (1998), 'Twenty Years of Airline Deregulation: The Impact on Outlying and Small Communities', *Journal of Transportation Management*, vol. 10, pp. 33-43.

Humphries, B. (1996), 'The UK Civil Aviation Authority and European Air Services Liberalization', *Journal of Transport Economics and Policy*, vol. 3, pp. 213-220.

Merrill Lynch (1999), *Global Airline Alliances: Global Alliance Brands Create Value*, Merrill Lynch, Pierce, Fenner & Smith, Inc.

Morrell, P. (1998), 'Air Transport Liberalization in Europe: The Progress so Far', *Journal of Air Transportation World Wide*, vol. 3, pp. 42-60.

R2A (2002), Unisys R2A Scorecard: Airline Industry Cost Measurement, Unisys Corporation.

Sinha, D. (2001), *Deregulation and Liberalization of the Airline Industry: Asia, Europe, North America, and Oceania*, Ashgate, Aldershot.

Taneja, N.K. (1988), *The International Airline Industry: Trends, Issues and Challenges*, Lexington Books, Lexington, MA.

Chapter 7

The View From Asia

Covering a Lot of Ground

According to the ICAO regional classification, the Asia-Pacific is composed of 34 nations covering 16,000 kilometers. It extends from Afghanistan in the west to Tahiti in the east and from Mongolia in the north to New Zealand in the south. The Asia-Pacific accounts for roughly 50 percent of the total world population and was responsible for 25% of the world's scheduled passenger traffic in 2001 (ICAO, 2002). This figure is actually down somewhat from previous years when the Asian miracle saw double-digit economic growth for this region which was reflected in the aviation forecasts for both passenger and freight traffic. ICAO has projected that the region could increase its share of traffic to 42 percent by 2020 (Sinha, 2001).

According to Taneja (1988), the growth in Asian-Pacific aviation can be attributed to a number of factors including high-growth export-oriented economies, productive, lower cost airlines, and coordination and cooperation between airlines and their respective governments. He also cited the pro-competitive policies of the governments of the U.S. and Asia for some of this growth. The Asian financial crisis has slowed the growth rates in both economic and aviation terms, but growth is predicted to return in 2003-2004 (ICAO, 2002). While there is a great deal of variation in the general approaches of the countries in the Asia-Pacific region, they too have been on a path toward greater deregulation and liberalization even if the pace has been somewhat slower and more uneven than the North American and European markets.

Variations on a Theme

Graham (1995) divides the Asia-Pacific into five categories: (1) China, (2) the wealthy states of the West-Pacific Rim-Japan, Brunei, South Korea, Singapore, Taiwan, and Hong Kong as well as Thailand, Malaysia, Indonesia, and the Philippines, (3) the East Asian low-income nations of Vietnam, Cambodia, Laos, and Myanmar, (4) Australia, New Zealand, and the Southwest Pacific islands, and (5) the South Asian nations of India and Pakistan. These divisions will be used to explore the aviation environment in Asia.

China

With a population of almost 1.3 billion and an area of 9,596,960 square kilometers (Table 7.1), China could not be left out of any discussion of aviation even if it had not experienced some of the highest economic growth rates of the past decade, however, until 1988 China had only one state airline, CAAC which was a division of the Civil Aviation Administration of China. This same division also ran the air traffic control system and administered airports in China. CAAC has now been divided into six regional airlines - Air China, China Eastern, China Southern, China Northern, China Northwest, and China Southwest - which were expected to run as more or less independent carriers by 1995. In addition to Cathay Pacific and its subsidiary Dragonair, Hong Kong based carriers that have now reverted to Chinese authority, there were 26 other airlines operating in China as of 1999. This includes 11 carriers directly governed by the CAAC and 15 regional carriers. The three largest airlines, China Southern, China Eastern, and Air China control 41 percent of the domestic market. In April 2001, the CAAC announced plans to merge nine airlines under its control into three larger groupings - China Southern Airlines Group, China Eastern Airlines Group, and Air China Group (Centre for Asian Business Cases, 2002). In response to this consolidation, five of China's regional carriers have announced plans to form an alliance. The China Sky Aviation Enterprise Group will include Shandong Airlines, Shanghai Airlines, Shenzen Airlines, Sichuan Airlines, and Wuhan Airlines. Together this alliance would control roughly 12 percent of China's domestic market (Aviation Daily, 2001). In other efforts to restructure Chinese aviation, the CAAC has announced plans to overhaul the domestic air route network, permit ticket discounting, encourage airport alliances, and raise air transport service fees (Centre for Asian Business Cases, 2002; Aerospace Daily, 2001). Although passenger traffic is predicted to grow at a rate of approximately 11 percent a year through 2010, it still represents a small percentage of the domestic Chinese market (Graham, 1995). In order to meet the expected demands, China and the CAAC must focus on improving the infrastructure within China.

Several factors have hindered the growth of civil aviation in China. First, the country remains a relatively low-income nation which limits the internal demand for air travel, even if there were no restriction on travel imposed by the Chinese government. Second, while inbound traffic has increased with economic growth, there has not been a significant growth in outbound traffic (again, largely reflecting the policies of the Chinese government). Third, there have been a number of recent crashes by Chinese carriers leading to questions of overall system safety. Fourth, there is a shortage of experienced airline pilots. Finally, the air traffic control system and the airport infrastructure need major upgrading requiring a good deal of investment from government or private sources (Graham, 1995). Despite its potential, China has yet to embrace a more liberal domestic or international policy in regard to aviation and is not likely to achieve anything like its true potential until it does, but even without such a policy the number of Chinese passengers is likely to experience significant growth over the next two decades fueled mainly by rising standards of living.

The West Pacific Rim

This area not only includes the Asian Tiger economies of South Korea, Singapore, Taiwan, and Hong Kong, but the all-important North American gateway of Japan. It is also home to some of the strongest and largest carriers in the Asian region, notably Singapore Airlines, Thai Airways, Korean Airlines, and Japan Air Lines (JAL). Differing views on privatization are reflected in the fact that carriers in this area range from wholly-owned government operations such as Garuda to partially-owned carriers such as Singapore and Malaysian to private carriers such as JAL. Whether privately or governmentally owned, Asian carriers continue to be treated as flag carriers by and large, receiving preferential government treatment in matters of international aviation. While there has not been extensive effort to deregulate domestic markets, international routes tend to be highly competitive both within the region and to Europe and North America. Five of the countries in this area have open skies agreements with the United States - Singapore, Taiwan, Malaysia, Brunei, and South Korea. Of these countries, Singapore, Taiwan, and Brunei have little or no domestic markets. The focus of growth has been almost exclusively long-haul international travel making open skies a good option.

Singapore Airlines, partially privatized sixteen years ago, has consistently been rated one of the best international carriers in the world. It flies one of the most modern fleets in the industry to over 40 countries (BBC News, 1999). Until 2001, it was also a consistently profitable carrier as well. In fact, the airline not only weathered the Asian financial crisis well but used its assets to good advantage purchasing stakes in other financially troubled Asian carriers such as Air New Zealand (BBC News, 2001a). In 1999, Singapore Airlines purchased 49 percent of the British carrier, Virgin Atlantic (BBC News, 1999). The economic slowdown that began prior to 9/11 combined with the aviation slump following the terrorist attacks led the carrier to post profits for the period April to November 2001 that were 90 percent below the prior year. Despite these problems, they continue to remain one of the strongest competitors in Asia (BBC News, 2001a).

Thai Airways who along with Singapore Airlines is a member of the Star Alliance was even harder hit by the aviation crisis that followed 9/11. In September 2001, the board of Thai was forced to resign amid labor disputes and bomb threats that capped off a year of carrier losses. Thai debt has been estimated at roughly 18 times its equity and the airline is considered to be overstaffed with a total workforce of 25,000 compared to Singapore Airlines' 14,000. The carrier which is 93 percent owned by the Thai government was planning to begin the process of privatization but is currently facing a major restructuring and cost-cutting effort in an attempt to regain profitability (BBC News, 2001b). Of the Asian carriers included in the Oum and Yu (1998) study of cost competitiveness, Thai had the lowest input costs in the region but was twice as inefficient as the next worst carrier in the region.

South Korea has three carriers - Korean Airlines, Korean National Airlines, and Asiana. Korean Airlines and Asiana are privately owned while Korean National is the government carrier. Beginning in 1992, the government ceased to set fares, although the Korean domestic air travel has not seen significant drops in fares. The entry of Asiana in 1988 did begin to increase passenger enplanements but again had little or no effect on fares. In effect, the Korean government has allowed a collusive duopoly to form following changes made in 1994.by permitting Korean Airlines and Korean National to agree on the allocation of new traffic on

Table 7.1: Information on Selected Asia-Pacific Nations

Country	Area*	Population**	Airports (paved)
Australia	7,686,850	19,546,792	421 (282)
China	9,596,960	1,284,303,705	489 (324)
Cook Islands	240	20,811	7 (1)
Fiji	18,270	854,346	27 (3)
India	3,287,690	1,045,845,226	335 (234)
Indonesia	1,919,440	231,328,092	490 (156)
Japan	377,835	126,974,628	173 (142)
Malaysia	329,750	22,662,365	116 (34)
New Zealand	268,680	3,908,037	106 (44)
Pakistan	803,940	147,663,429	120 (85)
Philippines	300,000	84,525,639	275 (77)
Singapore	693	4,452,732	9 (9)
Taiwan	35,980	22,548,009	39 (36)
Thailand	514,000	62,354,402	110 (59)
Vietnam	329,560	81,098,416	34 (17)

Source: CIA Factbook.
*Square Km. **Estimated July 2002 figures. Data for airports from 2001.

different routes, allowed Asiana greater route freedom, and agreed to allow more than one carrier to serve a city-pair only when the number of passengers exceeded a set limit (Sinha, 2001).

Korean Airlines and Asiana were also hard hit by the Asian crisis, however, these problems were overshadowed in many ways by the decision of the U.S. Federal Aviation Administration to downgrade them from a Category 1 to a Category 2, meaning that they failed to meet the minimum international safety standards set by ICAO. As a result of this action, Asiana, the second largest carrier in South Korea lost its code-sharing pact with American Airlines costing it an estimated US$16 million. Korean Airlines had earlier lost its international alliance with the U.S. carrier Delta Air Lines after a series of accidents in 1999. Following joint efforts by the Korean government and the FAA, Category 1 status was renewed. Korean Airlines has also made a series of changes that have allowed it to rejoin the SkyTeam alliance with Delta and Air France.

Malaysia was another country hit very hard by the Asian crisis. During that crisis, Garuda, one of the two Indonesian international and government-owned carriers, nearly collapsed. Since 2000, Garuda has returned to profitability by rationalizing its fleet and cutting unprofitable routes. It is scheduled to begin the process of privatization in 2003. The other international carrier, Merpati Nusantara Airlines was once a subsidiary of Garuda, but was delinked in 1997 and has since captured almost 38 percent of the domestic market.

As you will remember from Chapter 5, the United States policy of encirclement was aimed at opening up the Japanese market as the key Asian market from North America. The policy has been less than successful to date. Japanese policy has been marked by a strict regulation of the aviation system since the so-called 'aviation constitution' was adopted in 1972 dividing the market among the three Japanese carriers - Japan Air Lines (JAL), All Nippon Airways (ANA), and Japan Air Systems (JAS). JAL was to serve the main domestic truck routes and the international market. ANA was assigned short-haul international charter flights and other domestic trunk routes. JAS was to serve primarily on local routes. Little or no competition was allowed between these carriers. In 1986, the Council for Transport Policy, recommended the privatization of JAL, the introduction of greater domestic competition, including new entrant carriers, and the end of JAL's international monopoly (Yamaichi and Ito, 1996). In 1996, a zone fare system was introduced allowing carriers to offer a discount up to a 50 percent of the minimum fare, however, fares for all carriers operating on the same routes are the same. Although new entrants are now allowed in the market, restrict regulation and limited airport capacity has hindered the development of more carriers (Graham, 1995). The most successful new entrant has been Skymark which has recently applied for several new routes following the decision of ANA to abandon them as part of a re-thinking of its domestic route structure. This re-thinking was triggered by the decision of the Japanese government to allow JAL and JAS to merge under a new holding company, Japan Airlines Systems Corporation (Reuters, 2002). Overall, Japanese consumers do not appear to have benefited from the more liberal policies of the government, although there is some evidence that airlines have been able to lower their own costs (Sinha, 2001). Internationally, JAL and ANA suffer from high input costs and lower efficiency than most of their U.S. and European competitors and all but Thai Airways in Asia. According to Oum and Yu (1998), these carriers were 52.7 and 63.5 percent less cost competitive in 1993 than the benchmark U.S. carrier American Airlines.

East Asian Nations

Three characteristics define this group of nations. First, they all are among the poorest nations in the world. Second, they have all experienced war and civil unrest that have left their economies and their transportation systems in ruins. Finally, they will each require substantial foreign investment to rebuild their economies and their airlines (Sinha, 2001). These nations have sadly been left out of the Asian miracle. With the exception of Vietnam which is showing some sign of recovery, there does not appear to be much room for hope in the near future.

Australia and New Zealand

The first act regulating aviation in Australia was the Navigation Act of 1920, but confusion over the role of state and Commonwealth governments in air transport regulation led to an amended Air Navigation Act in 1936. According to this act, the Commonwealth was authorized to control air transportation with other countries and within the two territories of Australia. It was left to the states to control intra-state air transportation, although this did not keep the Commonwealth government from attempting to regulate intra-state aviation.

One of the most significant aviation policies of the Australian government occurred in the 1950s when then Prime Minister Robert Menzies decided that it was essential to prevent a monopoly from developing in Australian domestic airline service. The Two Airline Policy became official in 1952 with the passage of the Civil Aviation Agreement Act. Henceforth, there would be two carriers in Australia. Trans-Australian Airlines (later Australian Airlines), the state-owned carrier, would operate alongside the privately owned Australian National Airways (later Ansett). The government guaranteed the loans of Australian National up to a specified limit and later loosened the requirement that all government employees fly Trans-Australian. International service would be the province of Qantas. In 1957, the government further declared that two and only two truck carriers would exist in Australia and established a Rationalization Committee composed of a member of each airline and a coordinator nominated by the Transport Minister. The Airlines Equipment Act of 1958 authorized the government to restrict the size of each carrier's fleet. In 1961, two additional acts authorized the Rationalization Committee to establish timetables, frequencies, aircraft types, capacity, fares, freight levels, and overall load factors on groups of routes.

By 1981, criticism of the Two Airline Policy led to the Holcroft Inquiry which recommended a pricing policy based on cost that would be nationally consistent and allow discounted fares to be determined by the airlines. This same year Trans-Australia Airlines was made a public company, although the government continued to maintain effective ownership. Other actions in 1981 created an Independent Air Fares Committee to review fares, approve discounts, and change fare formulas to consider cost and efficiency and strengthened the government's ability to control the capacity of regional and cargo carriers through licensing of aircraft imports (Sinha, 2001).

Overall, limited information suggests that while the Two Airline Policy did create a stable aviation system of high yield, profitable carriers with an excellent safety record, it was characterized by higher costs and lower productivity (Kirby, 1979; Sinha, 2001). The perception of Australian consumers was that it also resulted in higher fares than the deregulated market of the U.S. Under pressure, the Australian government decided in 1990 to deregulate its domestic market. In the first year of deregulation, the Australian market experienced a growth of 66 percent and average air fares dropped 41.3 percent, however, both of these numbers have fluctuated in the years since then in part due to the entry and failure of new carriers. Forsyth (1991) has argued that entry into the Australian market was destined to be difficult because of the advantages incumbent carriers possessed, particularly in terms of airport and terminal access. In a further effort to foster competition, the Australian government proposed a single trans-Tasman aviation market with New Zealand, granted Air New Zealand greater fifth freedom rights, and opened up the international market to other carriers (after allowing Qantas to purchase Australian). Recently, two new carriers have entered the Australian domestic market, Impulse Airlines and Virgin Blue (owned by Richard Branson of Virgin Airlines). The entry of these new carriers has led to price wars on the main routes of competition which have temporarily lowered fares to Australian consumers, however, a 2001 decision by the Australian Competition and Consumer Commission has approved the acquisition of Impulse Airlines by Qantas who has also signaled its intent to improve fleet allocation and costs to more effectively compete against the lower cost Virgin Blue (Cahners Publishing Company, 2000; M2 Communications Ltd., 2001a; M2 Communications Ltd., 2001b).

Airline deregulation in New Zealand actually predates that of Australia having begun in 1983 with the abolishment of domestic fare and entry controls. The flag carrier, Air New Zealand, was privatized in 1989 and Australian-based Ansett was invited to set up a subsidiary to serve the New Zealand domestic market, however, internationally the market continued to be restricted, particularly between New Zealand and its near neighbor Australia. Beginning in 1992, there was some movement to provide greater flexibility in pricing, fares, and capacity in international service between the two countries. Like the Australian market, New Zealand has found it difficult to retain new entrant carriers. Kiwi Airlines started service in 1995 between Australia and New Zealand, but halted operations in 1996. After Ansett New Zealand and its parent company began to experience financial difficulty, Qantas considered making a financial investment in the New Zealand carrier. When this deal fell through Qantas New Zealand was allowed to begin domestic service (Sinha, 2001). In an interesting twist on Australian-New Zealand aviation relations, Air New Zealand went on to purchase Ansett Australia in 2000 only to cut it loose on September 12 when it was placed in voluntary administration (bankruptcy). Following allegations that they had stripped Ansett of assets before its collapse, Air New Zealand agreed to pay the administrators of Ansett NZD180 million (M2 Communications, 2001, 2002). Singapore Airlines had purchased 25 percent of Air New Zealand, but this share was reduced to 4.3 percent after the New Zealand government renationalized the carrier in October 2001 (BBC News, 2001). In the most recent twist to the Australian-New Zealand aviation relationship, a major alliance was announced between Quantas and Air New Zealand that would see Qantas invest $550 million in Air New Zealand, assuming a 15 percent stake in the company (Air New Zealand, 2002).

South Asia

The South Asian region includes India, Pakistan, Bangladesh, Sri Lanka, and the small Himalayan states of Nepal and Bhutan. India is second only to China in population and since the 1991 crisis triggered by the collapse of the Soviet Union, a major trading partner of India, has been on a path toward economic liberalization. Until the early 1990s, the Indian government maintained a virtual monopoly on the airline industry with the market divided between Indian Airlines who served the domestic market and Air India who provided international service and limited connecting flights. Under the Air Corporation Act of 1953, these two government-owned carriers were the only ones permitted to offer air service in India. The open skies policy introduced in 1990 allowed air taxi operations, charters, and new entrants to begin serving the domestic market. In 1993, Indian Airlines was allowed to begin international operations to the Gulf countries where many expatriate Indians worked. Indian Airlines continues to have the bulk of the domestic markets, however, their share has declined to only about 46 percent as of 2000 due to two new private carriers, Jet Airways and Sahara Airlines. Other new entrants have not fared as well. The list of failed carriers includes Modiluft, a joint venture between the Modi group of India and Lufthanse, Air Asiatic, Continental Air Link, UB Air, Damania, East West, and NPEC. These failures can be attributed to several factors including overexpansion, high debt, and continued government control over routes served, aircraft imported, and feeder service requirements. In addition to these burdens, carriers are prohibited from exiting loss making routes and required to purchase state controlled aviation fuel at almost twice the world price. The Indian market also suffers from a lack of infrastructure, particularly in the areas of air traffic control and airport facilities (Sinha, 2001). Despite suggestions by Sinha and Sinha (1997) that the Indian market could surpass the potential of China in areas of aviation, there has not been a major increase in domestic passenger traffic. According to Gallagher and Jenkins (1996), the Indian market is more price and income elastic than the developed nations of the West. Therefore, traffic growth responds more favorably to changes in fares rather than changes in income.

The Pakistani government has deregulated the domestic market, but has not seen significant results from this effort. The flag carrier, Pakistan International, remains partially government owned and continues to retain the majority of the domestic traffic. Like Indian Airlines, its most lucrative international routes are to the Middle East. While it is the only carrier in Pakistan authorized to offer international service, it does face competition from foreign carriers exercising fifth freedom rights (Graham, 1995).

Resuming Growth

According to the most recent ICAO forecast, passenger traffic for all of Asia was flat for 2001 unlike world figures overall which posted a negative growth rate of 2.9 percent. Estimates for 2002 through 2004 show a positive growth rate of 3.5, 7.9, and 7.0 respectively. The principle generator of traffic in Asia has normally been trade which is closely tied to economic growth and Asian policies of export-oriented led development, however, tourism has increasingly been used as a means to development both nationally and regionally (Hodder, 1992; Hitchcock, King, Parnwell, 1993). The World Trade Organization (1994) has suggested that Australia's efforts to deregulate and liberalize their air transport are a model for developing the tourism sector of an economy. The extent to which the rest of Asia continues on a path toward further liberalization will determine which Asian carriers emerge and/or remain world competitive (Graham, 1995).

References

Aerospace Daily (2001), 'CAAC Readies for Airport, Carrier Alliance', October 30, Aviation Week Group.

Aviation Daily (2001), 'Six China Carriers Join Forces, Will be Fourth Largest Group', June 21, Aviation Week Group.

BBC News (1999), 'Branson sells 49% of Virgin Atlantic', BBC News wireservice, December 20.

BBC News (2001), 'South Korea to probe airline industry', BBC News wireservice, August 20.

BBC News (2001), 'Air New Zealand renationalized', BBC News wireservice, October 4.

BBC News (2001), 'Singapore Airlines sees profits slide', BBC News wireservice, November 26.

BBC News (2001), 'Thai Airways may collapse', BBC News wireservice, November 16.

Cahners Publishing Company (2000), 'Virgin Blue Launches Service; Second Route to Debut Sept. 7', Gale Group wireservice, September 4, www.findarticles.com.

Centre for Asian Business Cases (2002), *Preparing for China's Entry to the WTO: China's Airline Industry*, The University of Hong Kong School of Business, Hong Kong.

CIA Factbook (2002), www.odci.gov/cia/publications/factbook.

Forsyth, P. (1991), 'The Regulation and Deregulation of Australia's Domestic Airline Industry' in K.J. Button (ed.), *Airline Deregulation: International Experiences*, David Fulton, London, pp. 48-84.

Gallagher, T. and Jenkins, D. (1996), 'Going when the Price is Right', *Airfinance Journal*, February, pp. 38-40.

Graham, B. (1995), *Geography and Air Transport*, John Wiley and Sons, New York.

Hitchcock, M., King, V.T. and Parnwell, M.J.G. (1993), 'Introduction' in M. Hitchcock, V.T. King and M.J.G. Parnwell (eds.), *Tourism in South East Asia*, Routledge, London, pp. 1-31.

Hodder, R. (1992), *The West Pacific Rim: An Introduction*, Belhaven Press, London.

ICAO (2002), 'One Year After 11 September Events ICAO Forecasts World Air Passenger Traffic will Exceed 2000 Levels in 2003', Press Release of International Civil Aviation Authority, September 10, Montreal.

Kirby (1979), 'An Economic Assessment of Australia's Two Airline Policy', *Australian Journal of Management*, vol. 5, pp. 105-118.

M2 Communications Ltd. (2001), 'Air New Zealand Denies Stripping Ansett Assets', Gale Group wireservice, November 13, www.findarticles.com.

M2 Communications Ltd. (2001), 'Virgin Blue may be able to Open Review into Qantas' Takeover of Impulse Airline', Gale Group wireservice, September 7, www.findarticles.com.

M2 Communications Ltd. (2002), 'Air New Zealand Increases Flights in Asia after Ansett Collapse', Gale Group wireservice, www.findarticles.com.

Oum, T.H. and Yu, C. (1998), *Winning Airlines: Productivity and Cost Competitiveness of the World's Major Airlines*, Kluwer Academic Publishers, Boston.

Reuters (2002), 'Skymark Plans to Double Domestic Routes', Reuters Newswire, October 25.

Sinha, D. (2001), *Deregulation and Liberalization of the Airline Industry*, Ashgate, Burlington.

Sinha, T. and Sinha, D. (1997), 'A Comparison of Development Prospects in India and China', *Asian Economics*, vol. 27, pp. 123-126.

Taneja, N.K. (1988), *The International Airline Industry: Trends, Issues, and Challenges*, D.C. Heath and Co., Lexington.

Part II
Present Realities

Chapter 8

The Defining Deal of the Next Century?

A New Model?

While the United States circled and the Europeans attempted to integrate the economies of 15 different countries, the airlines looked for ways to provide global service in a bilateral world. Part of the push for global networks is based on studies that indicate that consumers choose an airline based on schedule first rather than price and prefer to fly with an airline serving a large number of cities (Tretheway and Oum, 1992). Consumers also prefer nonstop or single carrier connecting service to non-interline connecting service. Interlining refers to the situation whereby a consumer changes from one carrier to another, but carriers with interlining agreement can provide for the seamless service of joint ticketing and baggage transfers while non-interline connecting service requires the consumer to make all of these arrangements (Dempsey, 2001). If bilateral agreements prevented carriers from achieving nonstop or single carrier connecting service, then carriers needed to find ways to imitate this service to attract consumers. The strategic alliance seemed to offer an answer.

Less than a decade ago, conventional wisdom suggested that the primary business decision corporations had to deal with was to 'make or buy'. In other words, do we engage in arm's-length contractual relationships to obtain important resources or do we internally develop and/or purchase the resources to carry out our strategic plan. The arm's-length contractual choice created so-called transaction costs, costs of buying and selling. These costs include the time and financial resources involved in selecting partners, negotiating the deal, and monitoring the relationship to insure contract compliance. These costs could be substantial depending on the number of suppliers to be considered, the reputation of suppliers, and the information available on actual supplier costs. These costs multiplied exponentially for corporations with many suppliers. Not surprisingly, firms also felt at the mercy of suppliers when it came to guaranteeing deliveries and quality. These costs and the lack of control led many to adopt the 'GM model'. The 'GM model' was a vertically integrated company that sought to do it all, making its own spark plugs, radiators, lights, ballbearings, etc. Ownership eliminated transaction cost uncertainty and provided greater control of the operational aspects of the relationship. This obsession with 'owning' in the United States led to the merger mania of the 1980s and the takeover mania of the 1990s. During the three busiest years of the 1990s (1998-2000), merger deals totaled almost 44 trillion which was more than the preceding 30 years combined (Henry, 2002). Greater economic integration in Europe has also led to an increase in owning, often fueled by economic crises that create deals out of stressed companies in many industries. However, evidence indicates that this obsession is waning in many industries and regions. A recent *Business Week* study indicates one reason why the trend is declining. According to their study, 61 percent of the 'buyers' actually destroyed shareholder wealth by picking bad acquisitions and paying too much for them (Henry, 2002).

According to a recent article in *Business Week*, 'the defining deal for the next decade and beyond may well be the alliance, the joint venture, the partnership' (Sparks, 1999: 106). This article argues that alliances provide more flexibility, speed, informality, and economy than traditional business arrangements. These qualities can make them ideal in rapidly changing business environments. Industries cited as embracing the alliance movement include media, entertainment, airlines, financial services, pharmaceuticals, biotech, and high tech. In Part II of the book, we will examine the present reality of international aviation; the present reality is alliances. The next four chapters will examine the strategic alliance in an airline context and attempt to answer the following questions: What is it, how does it form, what are the benefits and challenges it presents, who benefits from alliances, and what is the future of alliances in the airline industry?

Defining the Terms

A strategic alliance can be defined a 'relatively enduring interfirm cooperative arrangement, involving flows and linkages that utilize resources and/or governance structures from autonomous organizations, for the joint accomplishment of individual goals' (Parke, 1991: 581). In other words, a strategic alliance is an agreement between two independent firms to share resources in a jointly governed project that helps each individual firm achieve specific, not necessarily shared, goals. Unfortunately, strategic alliances can also be defined as arrangements 'characterized by inherent instability arising from uncertainly regarding a partner's future behavior and the absence of a higher authority to ensure compliance' (Parke, 1993: 794). Doorley (1993) found that 60 percent of the alliances he examined had a survival rate of only four years. Less than 20 percent survived for ten years. An Anderson Consulting survey found that 61 percent of corporate partnerships were either outright failures or performing below expectations (Sparks, 1999). Michael Porter of Harvard University believes that we should not be surprised by these numbers since he sees alliances as transitional rather than stable arrangements that rarely result in sustainable competitive advantage (Porter, 1990). Hamel (1991) has even suggested that many alliances are simply a race to learn in which the winner will eventually establish dominance in the partnership or dissolve it before its partner can catch up.

While the old business model equated control with ownership, control in alliance arrangements is gained through one of three means. The first means of control is through active participation in the management of the enterprise or operation. The second means of exercising control is through withholding or threatening to withhold some resource or capability vital to the success of the overall operation and/or desired by the other partner. The final means of control is through legal or de facto prohibitions on the actions of alliance partners. Areas where firms might seek control include daily operations, quality of products or services, physical assets, brand name, tacit knowledge of procedures and processes, and codified knowledge such as computer reservation systems (Contractor and Kundu, 1998). Whichever means of control partners select, the fact remains that most interfirm alliances involve attempts by competitors to cooperate in some aspect of their operation. It has been suggested that such firms have an 'inalienable de facto right to pursue their own interests' (Buckley and Casson, 1988:34). This perception, however, may make it inevitable that problems will arise as partners seek to control the alliance to their benefit. Another reason for instability in alliance arrangements may be the failure of partners to clearly define objectives and establish means of measuring performance. A surprising 49 percent of alliances in a recent survey did not have formal performance guidelines (Sparks, 1999). Chapter 9 will address the literature on instability and the relationship to alliance activities in the airline industry.

Table 8.1: Alliance Summary, 1994-2000

	1994	1995	1996	1997	1998	1999	2000
Number of alliances	280	324	389	363	502	513	579
With equity stakes	58	58	62	54	56	53	-
Without equity	222	266	327	309	446	460	-
New alliances	21	34	26	56	84	79	72
Number of airlines	136	153	159	177	196	204	220

Source: Airline Business June 1994-June 2000. Reporting of equity change in 2000.

Alliances in the Airline Industry

According to Oum and Yu (1998), the first international alliance of the modern era was between Air Florida and British Island in 1986. It was not until the mid-1990s, however, that alliances in the airline industry began to soar. Table 8.1 summarizes the alliance activity documented by *Airline Business* over the seven years of its alliance survey. There are several striking trends in these numbers. First, the total number of alliances has risen almost 45 percent from 1994 to 1999 (see Figure 8.1). Second, the majority of alliances do not involve equity stakes and those that do are declining. Third, between one-quarter and one-sixth of the reported total yearly alliances are newly created. Finally, the number of airlines participating in some form of alliance is increasing.

Figure 8.1: Number of Alliances, 1994-1999

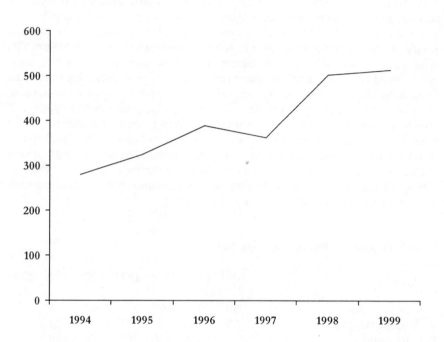

The term 'strategic alliance' covers a multitude of different forms or types of arrangements in the airline industry, possibly more than in any other industry. To understand the airline alliance, it is necessary to understand that alliance activities can range from a simple, single route codeshare or bundle of codeshares all the way to the newly created 'mega-alliances' created by international groups of competing airlines such as Star, Oneworld, Qualiflyer, and Wings. Table 8.2 lists the most common types of alliance activities and a basic definition of each.

Not only is there a wide range of alliance activities or types in existence, there is also a large number of type combinations that can be created between any two or more carriers. However, not all types are equally likely to occur. Several studies have reported that the most common types of alliances involve codesharing, blockspace/franchising/feeding agreements, joint marketing, and joint service agreements (Table 8.3). Least common are alliances involving the sharing and/or adoption of information technology systems, including computer reservation systems. This is probably not surprising given the proprietary nature of such information in the airline industry (Rhoades and Waguespack, 2000; Zwart, 1999).

An airline's choice of alliance partner and alliance type is a function of its objectives which are believed to center around four strategic drivers. The first and traditionally most popular driver has been the need to gain entry into international markets restricted by bilateral agreements. Alliances allow foreign carriers to 'serve' international destinations without obtaining the right through country-negotiated bilateral agreements, a political process that many carriers have found difficult to influence. The second driver is the desire to build a global, seamless network that allows consumers to reduce travel costs, take advantage of expanded frequent flyer programs, and obtain better services. The third driver of alliance formation is cost reduction. Cost reduction can be achieved in several ways. Alliances can be used to enter and develop a new market without an actual 'presence' in that market. In this case, the entering carrier may rely on its alliance partner to provide the aircraft, ground handling, maintenance, customer service personnel, and other services in the new market. Carriers may also seek to reduce costs through arrangements creating joint activities such as marketing, maintenance, insurance, parts pooling, etc. These joint activities not only reduce redundancy but may create cost savings through economy of scale effects. A fourth driver can be the desire to maintain market presence in an area whose traffic pattern and growth make it unprofitable to serve alone (Merrill, Lynch, Pierce, Fenner and Smith, Inc., 1998; Oum and Yu, 1998). For many airlines, their alliance activity is driven by more than one objective and clearly carriers may have a different set of objectives for each market or region that they serve. This diversity of objectives can make the scope and depth of interaction within an alliance important issues in negotiating and governing the alliance.

Doing the Deal

Judging by the quickening pace of international alliance formation, the negotiating table has become the latest playground for global firms. What remains to be answered is 'Who's on whose team today? What game are we playing? What are the rules and objectives of the game?'.

The international joint venture (IJV) used to be the preferred mode of conducting international business, but a joint venture is a legally separate entity with a mission and administration separate from that of its parents. The alliance, on the other hand, can be formed and dissolved quickly and 'entail little if any paperwork - maybe only a handshake' (Sparks, 1999: 134). According to Jurgen Weber, CEO of Lufthansa Airlines, the Star alliance started with a 2½ page contract and its members 'will cooperate forever as long as we like it' (Feldman, 1998: 27). This sounds very similar to a comment made by Leo Mullin, CEO of Delta Airline. Mullin declared that Delta was 'extraordinarily committed to the Atlantic Excellence Alliance' (Flint, 1999: 33). So committed in fact that less than a year later, Delta announced the termination of its involvement and its new partnership with Air France (Hill, 1999).

Table 8.2: Definition of Alliance Activities

Alliance Type	Definition
CODESHARE	One carrier offers service under another carriers' flight designator
BLOCKSPACE	One carrier allocates to another seat to sell on its flight
REVENUE SHARING	Two or more carriers share revenues generated by joint activity
WET LEASE	One carrier rents the aircraft/personnel of another
FRANCHISING	One carrier 'rents' the brand name of another for the purpose of offering flight service but supplies its own aircraft/staff
COMPUTER RESERVATION SYSTEM	One carrier shares and/or adopts the reservation system of another
INSURANCE/PARTS POOLING	Two or more carriers agree to joint purchase
JOINT SERVICE	Two carriers offer combined flight service
MANAGEMENT CONTRACT	One carrier contracts with another carrier to manage some aspect of its operation
BAGGAGE HANDLING/ MAINTENANCE	One carrier contracts with another to provide services/personnel/facilities at specified sites
JOINT MARKETING	Two or more carriers combine efforts to market joint services/activities
EQUITY SWAP/ GOVERNANCE	Two or more carriers swap stock and/or create joint governance structures

According to the Webster's dictionary, to negotiate is 'to confer with another so as to arrive at the settlement of some matter: to arrange for or bring about through conference, discussion, and compromise'. By this definition, humanity and the businesses they form have been about the business of negotiating for a long time. Governance (the act of governing or establishing a structure to carry out the actions of an organization) has an equally long pedigree. What is new is the application of negotiation and governance to strategic alliances.

Table 8.3: Alliances by Type

Alliance Type	Description	Percentage of Total
Type I	Codeshare	29%
Type II	Block-Space	15%
Type III	CRS/Accting/IT	2%
Type IV	Pooling	6%
Type V	Joint Service	13%
Type VI	Commercial Agreements	3%
Type VII	Facilities/Ground Handling	9%
Type VIII	Marketing	16%
Type IX	Equity	7%

Source: Zwart, M.L. (1999), 'Duration and Stability of Strategic Alliances in the Airline Industry'.

Coming to the Table

Negotiation occurs when two or more parties with interdependent goals or objectives decide to resolve an issue or dispute through peaceful means when there is no clear or established method or procedure for reaching agreement (Lewicki, Litterer, Saunders, and Minton, 1993). Given the recent development of the alliance movement, alliances are likely to involve a great deal of negotiation in their formation as well as after initial establishment since there is no rulebook for alliance formation, no accepted practices. However, there is in fact very little research on alliance negotiation. Alliance research has examined motives for alliance formation (Alter and Hage, 1983), governance and control (Yan and Gray, 1994), alliance performance (Yan and Gray, 1994), alliance structure (Parkhe, 1993), and partner selection (Geringer, 1991). It has not focused on the negotiating process that 'created' the alliances themselves. In the airline industry, there are no studies of this aspect of alliances. Therefore, our first step will be to review the existing studies on alliance negotiation for hints to the processes that might come into play in the airline industry. Then we will examine a study currently underway in the airline industry.

The negotiation process has often been viewed as a win-lose, my position-your position event (Fisher and Ury, 1991). According to this view, the goal of a negotiation is to maximize one's own benefits through whatever means necessary. Negotiation is seen as a competitive sport with its own strategies and tactics.

There are lists of negotiating games (Acuff and Villere, 1993) and influencing tactics (Kipnis, 1976; Zimbardo, 1993). There are techniques for creative negotiation (Shea, 1993) and achieving a win-win outcome (Fisher and Ury, 1991). There are experts suggesting when to bargain hard, to soft-sell or to be rational. In fact, negotiation theory suggests that the greater the bargaining power of a participant the higher their level of control in the outcome of the process (Yan and Gray, 1994, Blodgett, 1991) and that negotiators who believe that they have a power advantage will tend to use hard negotiating tactics (Bacharach and Lawler, 1981). Recent research has found that absolute power is not associated with U.S. bargaining tactics. The issue was relative power. Relative power increases when the other party in the negotiation is believed to have alternatives to the current negotiation or current partner, however, many negotiators appear to be unaware of the other options for themselves or their negotiating partners. In fact, many 'negotiators believe that they have few or no alternative partners or strategic options to an alliance' (Rao and Schmidt, 1998; 681). These findings are consistent with antedotal accounts of alliance negotiation that found that many alliances do not have clear goals, objectives, or measures of performance (Sparks, 1999).

Other factors that might be expected to influence negotiations and negotiating tactics include partner trust (Gulati, 1995), time horizons of negotiators (Axelrod, 1981, 1984), and cultural distance between negotiating parties (Boyacigiller, 1990). Much of the theory behind negotiation interaction is based on game theory. Game theory examines the conditions that lead to cooperation or defection. One such condition is future expected interaction; partners are more likely to cooperate if they know that the relationship will continue in the future. Over time, cooperative behavior can lead to trust. Rao and Schmidt (1998) found that negotiators who believed that they would cooperate in the future used more rational tactics in negotiation and focused on the exchange of information and benefits. However, they also reported that once trust is established, negotiators tended to use more hard negotiating tactics. They suggested that using soft tactics early in a relationship might be designed to engender trust in potential partners.

Given the international nature of many alliances, the cultural distance between partners has begun to receive more attention. Several recent studies suggest that cultural differences do affect negotiating style and tactics (Tinsley and Pillutla, 1998; Morris, Williams, Leung, Larrick, Mendoza, Bhatnager, Li, Kondo, Luo, and Hu, 1998). These differences include the tendency to use competitive negotiating styles, self-enhancement, joint problem solving, and self-interested or maximizing individual gain strategies or tactics. Negotiation becomes even more complex in multilateral settings (Cole, 1998; Goldsmith, 1998). In addition to cultural issues, multilateral negotiations have been characterized by the formation of coalitions, the assumption of wider roles by negotiating parties (scapegoat, blocker, etc), and the tendency to oversimplify problems and issues (Devine, 1990).

How the Airlines Do It?

As noted earlier, there are currently no published studies of negotiating practices within the global airline industry. Preliminary results of one study indicate that there is a good deal of variation in airline approaches to alliances. Two thirds of the airlines responding indicate that they have an established procedure for alliance negotiation, however, there was wide variation in the level and detail of this procedure. Airlines most likely to have such a procedure were involved in ten or more alliances involving a wide range of activities. The most active airlines also had established procedures for evaluating the following aspects of potential partner performance: service quality, operating procedures, maintenance practices, safety quality, route structure, and financial performance. They were also more likely to continue to audit these aspects after alliance formation. When asked how often they initiated alliance talks with potential partners, most respondents indicated that they did so less than half of the time. Not surprisingly, the smaller the carrier and the less active they were in alliances, the more likely they were to have no standard procedures and to examine only the route structure of prospective partners. One question where we found considerable variation was alliance labor relations. Carriers were evenly divided as to whether labor issues were routinely considered in the negotiating process. They were also divided over the question of whether a carrier representative from industrial relations was included in the alliance negotiations and in the alliance evaluation process (Rhoades, Waguespack and Marett, 2000).

Setting Up House

Once the deal is done, alliance partners need to establish some mechanism for implementing the relationship. While these issues should ideally be considered in the initial negotiating phase, antidotal evidence suggests that this is often not the case. As noted earlier, one of the appeals of the strategic alliance model is that it does not involve the highly structured environment of a traditional joint venture. On the other hand, research in the aerospace industry has found that the performance of semi-structured strategic alliances was higher than their unstructured counterparts. An unstructured alliance was defined as one in which all tasks within the scope of the alliance were distributed out to alliance partners and performed separately. A semi-structured alliance distributed product development and manufacturing tasks out separately but carried out sales and marketing activities jointly. It should also be noted that the study reported that 'the organizational structure set up to manage an alliance was chosen several years after the project is launched' (Dussauge and Garrette, 1995: 525). In the case of the aerospace industry, many alliances involved research and development. Dussauge and Garrette (1995) have suggested that the structure in these relationships was instituted only after the partners become convinced of the viability of the alliance. Thus, establishing a structure, even a semi-structured relationship, may be a sign of greater commitment to the alliance.

The question of whether certain structural types of arrangements (such as joint marketing, separate R&D versus separate marketing, joint R&D) were better than others was not specifically addressed in this study nor in the alliance literature in general. However, we might speculate on several industry-related differences. In research intensive industries such as aerospace, competitive advantage rests in the ability to develop proprietary technology. Therefore, separate product development (R&D) projects provide alliance firms greater protection of these vital assets. Marketing and sales are usually not viewed as being a key source of advantage. Likewise, the production of many aerospace products such as airplanes may well lend itself to some co-production activities. On the other hand, airlines consider marketing related activities such as computer reservation and yield management systems to be a major source of competitive advantage. An alliance that is structured to 'jointly' provide these types of activities is likely to be seen as much riskier in the airline industry. In fact, there is some evidence that joint ventures between firms in highly concentrated industries involving marketing and after-sales service tend to be unstable (Kogut, 1988). There seems to be even more problems when the alliance involves one partner marketing another partner's products in its own domestic market (Doz, 1988; Doz, Hamel, and Prahalad, 1990).

Structuring Your Airline Alliance

One issue that appears repeatedly in the popular accounts of airline alliances is the level of time and coordination required by many alliance arrangements. There are several issues involved. First, alliances often involve information sharing and/or the 'outsourcing' of some activities to alliance partners. This requires trust. As Jurgen Weber, CEO of Lufthansa, has noted a key issue in many alliances is trust and the willingness to sell the other's seats just as forcefully as your own (Feldman, 1998). According to past research, trust is a function of three factors: Ability, benevolence, and integrity. Trust develops when the trustor believes that the trustee has the ability to do what they promise, the desire to do good for the trustor, and the value set that is consistent with that of the trustor (Cook and Wall, 1980; McFall, 1987; Sitkin and Roth, 1993). Mayer, Davis, and Schoorman (1995) have suggested that the perceived integrity of a partner is more important early in the relationship when other information is not available. Benevolence develops in a relationship over time. In fact, the outcome of prior trusting behavior will influence a partner's perception of the ability, benevolence, and integrity of other parties in a relationship. A second key factor is differences in corporate culture and philosophy. Atlantic Excellence members found that different philosophies on service quality, pricing, and other important operational issues created problems. Strong personalities and size differences between members also contributed to the perception and resolution of problems (Feldman, 1998). A third factor affecting coordination is the number of partners involved. As noted above, the more parties involved in a negotiating situation the more potential there is for disagreement and gamesmanship. A fourth factor is the compatibility of partner systems. The final factor relates to the very real limitations placed on international airlines by laws restricting foreign ownership and limiting the scope of allowed activities. Initial results from the earlier mentioned survey of international airlines confirm these problems in alliance governance. The most frequently cited problem with alliance partners was incompatible systems, policies or procedures. The second most frequently cited problem related to differences in national and/or corporate culture and the affect of these differences on communications (Rhoades, Waguespack and Marett, 2000).

The result of these limitations is that airline alliances are coordinated or managed by committee; agreement is achieved by arriving at the lowest common denominator or minimally acceptable standard to all members (Feldman, 1998). The Star alliance has struggled with governance arrangements. They have reduced the number of coordinating committees from 25 to 15 and established a policy group to oversee the activities of these committees. At the highest level, the management board consists of the CEOs of each partner airline (Feldman, 1998; Nelms, 1999). Oneworld is establishing a similar executive structure (Nelms, 1999). Wings, the oldest of the mega-alliances, has opted for a somewhat different model which entails a much higher level of carrier integration of advertising, sales forces, etc. The Wings model reduces some of the problems of coordination by committee but it also demands that alliance partners relinquish some of their independence.

Strange Bedfellows

Whiles airlines appear committed to the idea of an alliance world, there are many problems facing alliances as they try to provide the seamless service that their founders hope to achieve. If the negotiating and governance process looks complex, then imagine the complexity of day-to-day activity. Micheal E. Levine, the Executive VP-Marketing for Northwest Airlines has said that 'the hardest thing in working on an alliance is to coordinate the activities of people who have different instincts and a different language, and maybe worship slightly different travel gods, to get them to work together in a culture that allows them to respect each other's habits and conviction, and yet work productively together in an environment in which you can't specify everything in advance' (1993: 69). Resolving these human issues as well as the legal issues surrounding alliances is one of the chief challenges of the alliance movement and one of the causes of instability in alliance arrangements. Chapter 9 will examine the issues surrounding alliance instability while Chapters 10 and 11 will explore the stumbling blocks to alliance performance.

References

Acuff, F.L. and Villere, M. (1993), 'Games Negotiators Play', in *Negotiation: Readings, Exercises, and Cases* in R.J. Lewicki, J.A. Litterer, D.M. Saunders, J.W. Minton (eds.), Irwin, Boston.

Alter, F.L. and Hage, J. (1993), *Organizations Working Together*, Sage, Newbury Park.

Anderson, E. (1990), 'Two Firms, One Frontier: On Assessing Joint Venture Performance', *Sloan Management Review*, vol. 31, pp. 19-30.

Axelrod, R. (1981), 'The Evolution of Cooperation among Egoists', *American Political Science Review*, vol. 75, pp. 306-318.

Axelrod, R. (1984), *The Evolution of Cooperation*, Basic Books, New York.

Bacharach, S.B. and Lawler, E.J. (1981), *Bargaining: Power, Tactics, and Outcomes*, Jossey Bass, San Francisco.

Blodgett, L.L. (1991), 'Partner Contributions as Predictors of Equity Share in International Joint Ventures', *Journal of International Business Studies*, vol. 22, pp. 63-78.

Boyacigiller, N. (1990), 'The role of expatriates in the management of interdependence, complexity, and risk in multinational corporations', *Journal of International Business Studies*, vol. 21, pp. 357-383.

Buckley, P. and Casson, M. (1988), 'A Theory of Cooperation in International Business' in F.J. Contractor and Peter Lorange (eds.), *Cooperative Strategies in International Business*, D.C. Heath & Company, Lexington.

Cole, J. (1998), 'Space Stations Cost Could Hit $24 Million', *Wall Street Journal*, March 23, A2.

Contractor, F. and P. Lorange (eds.), *Cooperative Strategies in International Business*, Lexington Books, Lexington, pp. 31-54.

Contractor, F.J. and Kundu, S.K. (1998), 'Modal Choice in a World of Alliances: Analyzing Organizational Forms in the International Hotel Sector', *Journal of International Business Studies*, vol. 29, pp. 325-358.

Cook, J. and Wall, T. (1980), 'New Work Attitude Measures Trust, Organizational Commitment and Personal Need Fulfillment', *Journal of Occupational Psychology*, vol. 53, pp. 39-52.

Dempsey, P.S. (2001), 'Carving the World into Fiefdoms: The Anticompetitive future of International Aviation', Working Paper.

Devine, T. (1990), 'A Preemptive Approach in Multilateral Negotiation: Charles Evans Hughes and the Washington Naval Conference', *Negotiation Journal*, vol. 6, pp. 369-381.

Doorley III, T.L. (1993), 'Teaming Up for Success', *Business Quarterly*, vol.57, pp. 99-103.

Doz, Y.L. (1988), 'Technology Partnerships between Larger and Smaller Firms: Some Critical Issues' in F. Contractor and P. Lorange (eds.), *Cooperative Strategies in International Business*, Lexington, pp. 317-338.

Doz, Y.L., Prahalad, C.K. and Hamel, G. (1990), 'Control, Change, and Flexibility: The Dilemma of Transnational Collaboration' in C.K. Bartlett, Y. Doz and G. Hedlund (eds.), *Managing the Global Firm*, Routledge, London, pp. 117-143.

Dussauge, P. and Garrette, E. (1995), 'Determinants of Success in International Strategic Alliances: Evidence from the Global Aerospace Industry', *Journal of International Business Studies*, vol. 26, pp. 505-530.

Feldman, J (1998), 'Making Alliances Work', *Air Transport World*, June, pp. 27-35.

Fisher, R. and Ury, W. (1991), *Getting to Yes: Negotiating Agreement Without Giving In*, Penguin Books, New York.

Flint, P. (1999), 'Alliance Paradox', *Air Transport World*, April, pp. 33-36.

Gallacher, J. (1994), 'Airline Alliance Survey', *Airline Business*, June, pp. 25-53.

Gallacher, J. (1995), 'Airline Alliance Survey', *Airline Business*, June, pp. 26-53.

Gallacher, J. (1996), 'A Clearer Direction', *Airline Business*, June, pp. 23-51.

Gallacher, J. (1997), 'Partners for Now', *Airline Business*, June, pp. 26-67.

Gallacher, J. (1998), 'Hold your Horses', *Airline Business*, June, pp. 42-81.

Goldsmith, C. (1998), 'After Trailing for Year, Airbus Aims for 50% of the Market', *Wall Street Journal*, March 16, A1.

Gulati, R. (1995), 'Does Familiarity Breed Trust? The Implications of Repeated Ties for Contractual Choice in Alliances', *Academy of Management Journal*, vol. 38, pp. 85-112.

Hamel, G. (1991), 'Competition for Competence and Inter-partner Learning within International Strategic Alliances', *Strategic Management Journal*, vol. 12, pp. 83-104.

Henry, D. (2002), 'Mergers: Why Most Big Deals Don't Pay Off', *Business Week*, October 14, pp. 60-70.

Hill, L. (1999), 'Global Challenger', *Air Transport World*, December, pp. 52-54.

Kipnis, D. (1976), *Powerholders*, University of Chicago Press, Chicago.

Kogut, B. (1988), 'Joint Ventures: Theoretical and Empirical Perspectives', *Strategic Management Journal*, vol. 9, pp. 319-332.

Levine, M.E. (1993), 'Interview', *Air Transport World*, January, pp. 69-70.

Lewicki, R.J., Litterer, J.A., Saunders, D.M. and Minton, J.W. (1993), 'Introduction', *Negotiation: Readings, Exercises, and Cases*, Irwin, Boston.

Mayer, R.C., Davis, J.H. and Schoorman, F.D. (1995), 'An Integrative Model of Organizational Trust', *Academy of Management Review*, vol. 20, pp. 709-734.

McFall, L. (1987), 'Integrity', *Ethics*, vol. 98, pp. 5-20.

Merrill Lynch, Pierce, Fenner & Smith Inc. (1998), *Global Airline Alliances: Why Alliances Really Matter from an Investment Perspective*, Merrill Lynch, Pierce, Fenner & Smith Inc., New York.

Morris, M.W., Williams, K.Y., Leung, K., Larrick, R., Mendoza, M.T., Bhatnagar, D., Li, L. Konda, M., Luo, J.L. and Hu, J.C. (1998), 'Conflict Management Style: Accounting for Cross National Differences', *Journal of International Business Studies*, vol. 29, pp. 729-748.

Nadler, D.A. and Tushman, M.L. (1997), *Competing by Design: The Power of Organizational Architecture*, Oxford University Press, Oxford.

Nelms, D.W. (1999), 'Getting Their Acts Together', *Air Transport World*, April, pp. 27-36.

O'Toole, K. (1999), 'The major Airline Alliance Groupings', *Airline Business*, July, pp. 36-65.

Oum, T.H. and Yu, C. (1998), *Winning Airlines: Productivity and Cost Competitiveness of the World's Major Airlines*, Kluwer Academic Publishers, Boston.

Parkhe, A. (1991), 'Interfirm Diversity, Organizational Learning, and Longevity in Global Strategic Alliances', *Journal of International Business Studies*, vol. 22, pp. 579-601.

Parkhe, A. (1993), 'Strategic Alliance Structuring: A Game Theoretic and Transaction Cost Examination of Interfirm Cooperation', *The Academy of Management Journal*, vol. 36, pp. 794-829.

Pekar, P. and Allio, R. (1994), 'Making Alliances Work - Guidelines for Success', *Long Range Planning*, vol. 27, pp. 54-65.

Porter, M.E. (1990), *The Competitive Advantage of Nations*, Free Press, New York.

Rao, A. and Schmidt, S.M. (1998), 'A Behavioral Perspective on Negotiating International Alliances', *Journal of International Business Studies*, vol. 29, pp. 665-694.

Rhoades, D.L., Waguespack, B. and Marett, P. (2000), 'The Mating Habits of International Airlines: Alliance Formation and Governance', working paper, Embry-Riddle Aeronautical University.

Rhoades, D.L. and Waguespack, B., Jr. (2000), 'Divorce Airline Style', working paper, Embry-Riddle Aeronautical University.

Shea, G. (1993), 'Creative Negotiating' in *Negotiation: Readings, Exercises, and Cases*, in R.J. Lewicki, J.A. Litterer, D.M. Saunders, J.W. Minton (eds.), Irwin, Boston.

Sitkin, S.B. and Roth, N.L. (1993), 'Explaining the Limited Effectiveness of Legalistic "Remedies" for Trust/Distrust', *Organizational Science*, vol. 4, pp. 367-392.

Sparks, D. (1999), 'Partners', *Business Week*, October 25, pp. 106-112.

Tinsley, C.H. and Pillutla, M.M. (1998), 'Negotiating in the United States and Hong Kong', *Journal of International Business Studies*, vol. 29, pp. 711-728.

Tretheway, M.W. and Oum, T.H. (1992), *Airline Economics: Foundation for Strategy and Policy*, The Centre for Transportation Studies, University of British Columbia.

Yan, A. and Gray, B. (1994), 'Bargaining Power, Management Control, and Performance in United States-China Joint Ventures: A Comparative Study', *Academy of Management Journal*, vol. 37, pp. 1478-1517.

Zimbardo, P.G. (1993), 'The Tactics and Ethics of Persuasion' in *Negotiation: Readings, Exercises, and Cases* in R.J. Lewicki, J.A. Litterer, D.M. Saunders, J.W. Minton (eds.), Irwin, Boston.

Zwart, M.L. (1999), 'Duration and Stability of Strategic Alliances in the Airline Industry', Dissertation at Maastricht University.

Chapter 9

Unstable Creations

The Love of Your Life

Whenever the topic of strategic alliances comes up, someone will invariably compare them to a 'marriage'. Like marriages, alliances often require partners of different background, preferences, and objectives to develop a common vision of the future that may demand sacrifices from both partners in order to achieve objectives that neither partner could accomplish alone. Like marriages, alliances are subject to disagreement, selfish consideration, cheating, re-negotiation, divorce, and possibly even widowhood. Some alliances may be love matches. Others may be marriages of convenience. In fact, in view of the broad application of the term strategic alliance in the airline industry (see Chapter 8), it is possible that code sharing, for example, is not a marriage at all, simply holding hands. In any event, it is reasonable to ask a number of questions about alliances. How long will this alliance last? What should I look for in a good partner? How do I avoid conflicts? How can I make the best of this alliance?

The *Airline Business* annual alliance survey has done a commendable job of documenting the growth and development in airline alliances. It has not, however, highlighted the other side of the coin - failures. Based on a careful analysis of the *Airline Business* survey, Rhoades and Waguespack (2000) have found that the number of alliance failures over the past three years has been roughly equivalent to the number of new alliances (approximately 24 percent of the yearly total). A number of the 'dead' alliances lasted less than a year. This has led a number of industry experts to agree with Leo Mullin, CEO of Delta Airlines, when he calls alliances 'an inevitable but not hazard-free' step in the evolution of the airline industry (Flint, 1999: 33). In addition to these failures, there have been numerous press accounts of family squabbles including the KLM-Northwest fight over KLM's equity investment and voting rights, the KLM/Northwest debate with Alitalia over the Malpensa Airport, the United-Lufthansa disagreements over joint purchasing, the Northwest-Continental equity investment debate, and Thai Airways' dissatisfaction with the addition of Singapore Airlines to the Star alliance.

The purpose of this chapter is to lay the foundation for a conceptual understanding of the issues of duration and stability in strategic alliances. Since there has been very little research to date specifically addressing the issue in an aviation context, we will explore theory and research from other industries and suggest ways that it may be applied to airline alliances. Finally, we will address one typology of airline alliances that seeks to answer the questions we have just posed and discuss the results of a recent test of that typology.

What Does It All Mean?

The first step in understanding the issues is achieving a consensus on the meaning of our terms. From an alliance point-of-view, failure occurs when one or all parties fail to achieve their objectives. Obviously, it is possible for one member to achieve their goals when other parties do not. This type of failure can occur either because of a problem in the objective-setting process or because of deliberate action on the part of one member. As noted in Chapter 1, a surprising number of firms enter into alliances without clearly defined objectives or established means of measuring performance. A more ominous reason for failure is the possibility that one or more partners enter an alliance seeking to gain competitive advantage (Buckley and Casson, 1988; Hamel, 1991). Given this definition, a terminating alliance is only unsuccessful if it is 'unplanned and premature from the perspective of either or both partners' (Inkpen and Beamish, 1997: 182). Duration simply refers to the length of time between the initiation of an alliance and its termination.

Researchers have defined instability in terms of changes in equity and/or governance control, termination, and duration (Franko, 1971; Killing, 1983; Kogut, 1989). From a theoretical perspective, instability should be separated from duration and termination. If a stable relationship is defined as one in which there have been no major changes in the relationship design to either increase or decrease the linkages between firms, then an alliance could terminate without experiencing instability. Actions which would indicate instability include changes in strategic direction, renegotiation of contracts or agreements, and reconfiguration of ownership and/or management structure (Yan, 1998). It would not include alliance termination. A stable alliance may terminate when the strategic goals of partners have been met or when the strategic needs of partners change. By the same token, an unstable alliance will not necessarily end in termination. Instability may arise because partners are adjusting their expectations or objectives. It may indicate that partners have decided to commit themselves to even higher levels of interaction or to a longer term strategy to disengage from or de-emphasize the relationship.

Lasting Relationships

Given the high failure rates already cited, it is reasonable to ask what factors contribute to longevity. Bleeke and Ernst (1995) have categorized alliances based on three factors - market strength of partners, motivation of alliance partners, and alliance outcome - to create six classes or types of alliances. These six types are 1) collisions between competitors, 2) alliances of the weak, 3) disguised sales, 4) bootstrap alliances, 5) evolutions to a sale, and 6) complementary equals. According to their typology, an alliance between a weak firm and a strong firm can be either a disguised sale, that is, it will result in the weaker firm failing to gain strength and being acquired (and, hence, the alliance terminated) by the stronger firm or a bootstrap alliance in which the weaker firm increases its strength and dissolves the alliance. In their typology, only one type of alliance will survive longer than the median age of seven, complementary equals. This alliance involves two firms with truly complementary skills, assets and/or resources. Unfortunately, many alliances are entered in the belief that partner complementarity exists. It is usually only in the process of implementing the alliance that partners discover incompatibility. The other weakness of the Bleeke and Ernst (1995) typology is that it is post hoc; it classifies alliances after the outcome of the alliance is known. It does not predict which alliances will succeed nor does it lay out conditions for success.

Park and Cho (1997) examined the market strength of code sharing partners and its effect on market share performance, presumably a goal of such alliances. They found that the most successful alliances occurred between partners of equal size. They also reported that the performance effects were greater in growing markets with few competitors and flexible market share changes. Here, at least, we have two factors that might be useful in selecting partners and/or predicting alliance outcome.

Khanna, Gulati and Noria (1998) offer us another way. They focus not on the strengths of alliance partners but on the nature of the benefits arising from alliance activity. They suggest that alliances create two types of benefits - common and private. Common benefits 'accrue to each partner in an alliance from the collective application of the learning both firms go through as a consequence of being part of the alliance' (195). By contrast, private benefits can accrue to a firm that can pick up partner skills and apply them to areas unrelated to alliance activity. In the case of an alliance with purely common benefits, 'all firms must finish learning in order for any of them to derive the common benefits' (197). Thus, such alliance may be expected to last longer and result, even if terminated, in a successful alliance from the viewpoint of all parties. The alliance with purely private benefits is indeed a race to see which partner can finish learning first. That partner will then have no further incentive to incur alliance costs and will terminate the relationship. In reality, most alliances are a combination of both types of benefits. It is the ratio of private to common benefits that will affect a firm's decision to stay in or quit an alliance. All things being equal, the greater the scope of the alliance relative to the total market scope of the partners, the greater the common benefits and the lower the private benefits. In this regard, the mega alliances with their increased alliance scope relative to firm scope should create more common benefits and last longer than their narrow alliance scope competitors. In connection with learning in alliance arrangements, Simonin (1999) has suggested that the more ambiguous and tacit the information to be transferred the longer the process will take. In other words, it should be more difficult for a Singapore Airlines to transfer the rich, experience-laden knowledge that has made it an industry leader in service quality than to train alliance partners in line maintenance procedures.

A number of studies have examined the role of resource commitment to alliance duration. Resource commitment involves dedicating assets to a particular use in such a way that their redeployment to other uses would result in some level of cost to the firm. By limiting strategic flexibility and acting as a barrier to exit, the willingness to commit resources lessens the perception of opportunistic behavior on the part of other alliance members (Parkhe, 1993). The more nonrecoverable, alliance-specific the investment the greater the potential effect on alliance duration.

Changing Times

Resource commitment can also have a positive effect on alliance stability and performance (Freeman, 1987; Heide and Johns, 1988; Smith and Aldrich, 1991). Resource commitment effects stability for much the same reason as it increases duration, namely that it creates incentives to stay in the relationship rather than quit. Its effect on performance is due to the link between resource commitment, firm control, and involvement in operations. The higher the level of commitment by the firm the more likely it is to exercise control in the alliance and seek involvement in decision making (Anderson and Gatignon, 1986; Root 1987). On the other hand, high levels of commitment are often associated with more alliance complexity. The more complex the relationship the greater the 'fundamental problem of cooperation' (Ouchi, 1980: 130). Alliances that involve greater coordination and integration of resources require a level of trust and interaction that is generally foreign to competitive firms. The more highly concentrated the industry, the more unstable the relationship may be, particularly when the scope of the venture involved marketing and after-sales service (Kogut, 1989). The need for higher levels of coordination and integration is also likely to increase problems relating to incompatible systems, procedures, training, and organizational/national cultures.

According to Yan (1998), four forces act to destabilize alliance arrangements: unexpected changes in the environment, undesirable alliance performance, obsolescing bargain effects, and interpartner competitive learning. Clearly, changing environmental conditions and poor performance can cause partners to reevaluate/restructure their relationship. The obsolescing bargain occurs when the foreign partners' relative bargaining power erodes over time as it invests increasing, unrecoverable resources in a local economy. Finally, the race to learn can lead to various strategic maneuvering in an alliance. Yan (1998) also cites four factors that can increase alliance stability: the political and legal environment at founding, the initial resource mix, the initial balance of bargaining power, and the interpartner, pre-venture relationship. As we have discussed earlier in this book, the airline industry is currently facing a series of challenges to the existing political and legal structure that has governed the industry since the end of World War II. When this challenge is added to alliance-specific differences in resource mix, balance of power, and pre-venture relationships, the results can be volatile.

Scott (1992) has noted that the forms organizations establish at founding are likely to persist over their lifespan. This is called structural inertia. The initial form may reflect the task environment (Stinchcombe, 1965), the characteristics of executives (Mintzberg and Waters, 1980) or top management team (Eisenhardt and Schoonhoven, 1990) or institutional factors such as laws, organizational or national culture (Meyer and Scott, 1983). The initial resources and bargaining power partners bring into an alliance can also create stability as can a pre-alliance relationship of trust and respect. The stability of the alliance depends on the delicate balance between these eight forces.

A Balancing Act

In a 1997 article in the *Journal of Air Transportation Management*, Rhoades and Lush proposed an alliance typology that involved another delicate balancing act. Their typology was based on the premise that airline alliances could be classified according to two dimensions: commitment of resources and complexity of arrangement. In general, the typology predicted that the level of resource commitment should increase both the duration and stability of alliances while the complexity of the alliance arrangement should decrease both duration and stability. These predictions are consistent with theory and research in other industries. The difficulty lies in assessing the interaction effects of these two dimensions on duration and stability. For example, what is likely to happen to an alliance that involves a low level of resource commitment to a complex task requiring partners to integrate different systems, cultures, or tasks. Rhoades and Lush (1997) attempted to address this difficulty by assigning each of the activities defined in Chapter 8 to an 'alliance type' based on the level of resource commitment and complexity. Figure 9.1 outlines a refined version of the typology used in a recent test of the model. Type I alliances involve low levels of resource commitment and complexity. The relatively simple nature of the activity should make them more stable and lasting. However, these types of code sharing arrangements are normally driven by the desire for market access and/ or market presence in a restricted or undeveloped market. The lasting nature of Type I alliance could change if liberalization continues and carriers can enter markets freely in their own right. On the other hand, financial crisis in the wake of 9/11 has seen cost-cutting carriers withdraw from increasingly marginal routes in favor of alliance partners.

Diagonally across from Type I alliances is Type IX. These alliances involve multiple activities, complex integration efforts, extensive resource commitment, shared decision making, and, often, equity investment. High resource commitment makes the exit cost of these alliance types high. On the other hand, the complex nature of the tasks to be coordinated and integrated will make these alliances unstable as well. On balance, resource commitment should provide Type IX partners with greater incentives to work through complexity. Type III alliances involve low complexity and high resource commitment should make these alliance some of the most durable. On the diagonal from Type III are Type VIII alliances that tend to involve low levels of resource commitment and high complexity. These types of arrangements should experience some of the highest failure rates. An increasing focus on quality may make the potentially undesirable outcomes of some of these complex and important activities too great to bear. Of course, it is possible that the cost savings benefits of these arrangements and/or airport specific restrictions on facilities or eligible grand handling firms will override the destabilizing effects of complexity.

Figure 9.1: Alliance Activity by Type

	-	COMPLEXITY	+	
	Type III (IT) Accounting services CRS links Data processing Freight IT IT Development	**Type VI (Management)** Commercial agreements Commercial support mgmt Management contract MOU Spares mgmt cooperation Strategic partnership	**Type IX (Equity)** Equity	+
R E S O U R C E S	**Type II (Block-Space)** Block seat agreements Block space agreements Feeding agreement Franchise agreement Revenue sharing Wet lease	**Type V (Joint-Service)** Cargo cooperation Freight handling Joint cargo terminal Joint flight Joint freighter flight Joint route development Joint venture Schedule coordination Shared routes	**Type VIII (Marketing)** Coop on sales Gen sales agency Joint mkt Joint FFP Joint advertising Mkting agreement Mkting alliance Reservations	D U R A T I O N
	Type I (Code-Share) Cargo code-share Code sharing	**Type IV (Pooling)** Fuel purchasing Financial access arrangements Joint insurance purchase Freight return pool Joint purchase Pool agreement Revenue pooling Space swap	**Type VII (Ground Facilities)** Slot-sharing Maintenance Catering JV Joint check-in Ground handling Shared terminal Shared lounge Through check-in	-
	+	DURATION	-	

A recent study tested the typology predictions on duration using data from the *Airline Business* surveys. Gudmundsson and Rhoades (2000) found that alliances in general were at greater risk of termination in year 2. The rate of termination decreased from years 3 to 6. Four types of alliance arrangements demonstrated a lower risk of termination, Type IV-pooling, Type VIII-marketing, Type II-block space, and Type I-codesharing. Type V (joint service) and Type VII (ground/facilities) showed a significant relationship with higher risk of early termination. Type IX (equity) alliances were also associated with high risk of termination. The remaining two types of alliances, Type III (CRS/IT) and Type VI (commercial agreements) contained too few cases to test. While this study did not provide unqualified support for the typology, it does demonstrate that different alliance activities are at greater risk for termination.

The Gudmundsson and Rhoades (2000) study also found that the more extensive the alliance i.e. the more types of activities involved the lower the risk of termination. Since each additional alliance activity adds incrementally to the level of resource commitment, this finding is supportive of the general proposition that resource commitment increases duration. Table 9.1 lists the membership of the so-called mega-alliances which have been created as broad alliances involving increasingly complex webs of activities. At present, there are four, however, the possibility exists that approval of a Northwest-Continental-Delta alliance by the U.S. Department of Transportation could result in consolidation into three global alliances (Ott, 2002). The attempt by mega-alliances to increase the breadth and scope of partner activity also supports the contention of Khanna, Gulati, and Noria (1998) that the higher the level of common benefits to private the more likely the alliance is to survive. In the case of the mega-alliances, resource commitment appears to outweigh complexity as a factor in alliance duration. In the case of Type IX equity alliances, the troubles of shared governance and organizational control have created instability in a number of alliances, notably KLM-Northwest and Northwest and Continental, although it has not necessarily resulted in termination of the overall alliance.

To date, there has been no test of the stability predictions of the typology. As Rhoades and Lush (1997) noted in their original article, 'instability in and of itself is not necessarily a "bad thing." It can be an indication that the parties in the alliance are committed to establishing a successful partnership' (113). On the other hand, too much instability should have a negative effect on an alliance's ability to function and produce profitable returns. Testing the stability predictions would require a careful year-by-year survey of changes (major and minor) within alliances. A related area of study would be to examine the possibility of sequencing as it relates to alliance stability and duration. For example, are alliances that begin their relationship with relatively simple, low resource activities and then move to more complex arrangements more successful than those who jump right into equity and/or other complex activities.

Creating a Stable World

In the new global environment even confirmed bachelors are considering the prospect of marriage, but alliance-seeking partners should not forget that the cost of divorce may be high. In the race to establish global networks capable of generating higher revenues and capturing the high yield business passenger, alliance shy airlines could well lose out or be relegated to niche, low cost segments. In view of the potential costs, there are two critical factors for improving alliance duration and stability.

Table 9.1: Members of the Mega-Alliances

Oneworld	SkyTeam	Star	Wings
Aer Lingus	Aeromexico	Air Canada	KLM
American Airlines	Air France	Air New Zealand	Northwest
British Airways	Alitalia	All Nippon Airways	
Cathay Pacific	Czech Airlines	Austrian Airlines	
Finnair	Delta Air Lines	bmi British Midlands	
Iberia Airlines	Korean Air	Lauda Air	
LanChile		Lufthansa Airlines	
Qantas Airways		Mexicana	
		SAS	
		Singapore	
		Thai Airways	
		United Airlines	
		Varig	

Source: Ott (2002), 'Alliances may be fewer, but savings will improve', *Aviation Week and Space Technology*, November 18, pp. 65-68.

First, carriers must invest time in partner selection and relationship development. The initial step in partner selection is determining the desired partner profile. To do this, airlines need to have a clear understanding of their goals and objectives for such a relationship as well as the part that alliance will play in their overall strategic plan. They must consider options, next best alternatives, costs (including the opportunity costs), and expected benefits (Berardino and Frankel, 1998a). An airline that is unable to do this should take this as a sign that their strategy and the objectives stemming from it are not clearly defined. If stability and duration are important measures of success for alliance-seeking partners, then airlines should not only look at compatibility on key factors (service, safety, route structure, etc) but previous alliance behavior. Research has found that the more experience an alliance partner has in alliance arrangements the more likely they are to enter alliances in the future (Gulati, 1999) and the better they may be at generating value from such arrangements (Anand and Khanna, 1997). On the other hand, a pattern of broken alliances may indicate a lack of alliance commitment or unfocused alliance objectives.

Successful marriages or alliances do not simply happen; they are the result of commitment, hard work, and sacrifice. Alliance partners need to invest time in building the relationship and creating the structure that it will operate under. Antedotal evidence suggests that one of the most underestimated aspects of alliances has been the time commitment required to coordinate alliance activities. While the time spent in these activities can clearly be beneficial to relationship building, it is also possible to suffer from diminishing returns and alliance burnout. Too much togetherness may be bad for the 'marriage' (Feldman, 1998).

The second key to success and stability lies in finding ways to measure, track, and allocate common benefits. Berardino and Frankel (1998a) have suggested that successful alliances must insure that no partner is made worse off for joining the alliance. In fact, it must be better off than if it had chosen its next best alternative. In essence, they suggest that alliances devise a way to keep score. The process of devising this scoring system can not only help partners to clarify goals and objectives, but build the relationships that are necessary for long term alliance success. In a second article, Berardino and Frankel (1998b) discuss ways to maximize mutual benefits. In their view, this requires carriers to act as a single unit. They outline eight organizing principles: 1) exclusivity, 2) long-term contracts, 3) costly exit penalties, 4) costly ejection penalties, 5) agreement on accounting principles, 6) participation in the same equity markets, 7) partnership profit sharing, and 8) commitment of resources.

In principle, their arguments are valid. Recent speculation about the possible exit of Thai Airways from the Star Alliance has centered on calculations of the benefits (or losses) that Thai might expect in an alliance that includes Singapore Airlines. There are several problems facing carriers attempting to develop a score keeping system. The first problem is legal; without anti-trust immunity this type of benefit analysis is not possible. The second problem concerns the scorekeeper and the system of score keeping itself. Initially, these issues may need to be handled by a third party facilitator or negotiator. Finally, carriers must be prepared to deal with the results of this score keeping. Oum and Park (1997) have reported an analysis of the BA-USAir alliance that concludes that BA gained additional profit of $27.2 million while USAir gained only $5.6 million during the first quarter of 1994. Although there is no estimate on USAir profits from its next best alternative, it is certainly possible that such lopsided benefits could over time create strain in any alliance. Creating a scoring system will likely require alliance partners to address issues of benefit imbalance and systems to allocate benefits among partners.

Love and Marriage

Alliance termination or instability in and of itself is not a bad thing. Unexpected changes in the environment or new strategic considerations may dictate alliance termination or change. Instability may also indicate a willingness on the part of alliance partners to work out problems, to redress benefit/cost issues, or to create a better, stronger relationship. This is surely not a bad thing given the newness of alliance partnering in the airline industry. Termination and instability become a problem when they result in alliance relationships that fail to meet their objectives or generate their anticipated benefits. There are no guarantees of success in life or alliances. There are also no risk-free ways to create global, seamless aviation service. Sometimes you have to take the good with the bad.

References

Anand, B.N. and Khanna, T. (1997), 'Do Firms Learn to Create Value?', working paper, Harvard Business School.

Anderson, E. and Gatignon, H. (1986), 'Modes of Entry: A Transaction Cost Analysis and Propositions', *Journal of International Business Studies*, vol. 17, pp. 1-26.

Barardino, F. and Frankel, C. (1998b), 'Alliances: the next step', *Airline Business*, October, pp. 68-71.

Berardino, F. and Frankel, C. (1998a). 'Keeping Score', *Airline Business*, September, pp. 82-87.

Bleeke, J. and Ernst, D. (1995), 'Is Your Strategic Alliance a Sale?', *Harvard Business Review*, vol. 73, pp. 97-105.

Buckley, P.J. and Casson, M. (1988), 'A theory of cooperation in international business' in Farok J. Contractor and Peter Lourange (eds), *Cooperative strategies in international business*, Lexington Books, Lexington.

Doorley III, T.L. (1993), 'Teaming up for Success', *Business Quarterly*, vol. 57, pp. 99-103.

Eisenhardt, K. and Schoonhoven, C.B. (1990), 'Organizational growth: Linking Founding Team Strategy, Environment, and Growth among Semiconductor Ventures, 1978-1988', *Administrative Science Quarterly*, vol. 35, pp. 504-529.

Feldman, J.M. (1998), 'Making alliances work', *Air Transport World*, vol. 35 (6), June.

Flint, P. (1999), 'Alliance Paradox', *Air Transport World*, April, pp. 33-36.

Franko, L. (1971), *Joint Venture Survival in Multinational Companies*, Praeger, New York.

Freeman, R.E. (1987), 'Review of the Economic Institutions of Capitalism, by O.W. Williamson', *Academy of Management Review*, vol. 12, pp. 385-387.

Gudmundsson, S.V. and Rhoades, D.L. (2000), 'Can this marriage be saved? Survival rates in airline alliances', Paper presented at the Air Transportation Research Group Conference, Amsterdam, July 2000.

Gulati, R. (1999), 'Network Location and Learning: The Influence of Network Resources and Firm Capabilities on Alliance Formation', vol. 20, pp. 397-420.

Hamel, G. (1991), 'Competition for Competence and Inter-partner Learning within International Strategic Alliance [Special Issue]', *Strategic Management Journal*, vol. 12, pp. 83-104.

Heide, J.B. and Johns, G. (1988), 'The role of dependence balancing in safeguarding transaction-specific assets in conventional channels', *Journal of Marketing*, vol. 52, pp. 20-35.

Inkpen, A.C. and Beamish, P.W. (1997), 'Knowledge, bargaining power, and the Instability of International Joint Ventures', *Academy of Management Review*, vol. 22, pp. 177-202.

Khanna, T., Gulati, R. and Nohria, N. (1998), 'The Dynamics of Learning Alliances: Competition, Cooperation, and Relative Scope', *Strategic Management Journal*, vol. 19, pp. 193-210.

Killing, J.P. (1983), *Strategies for Joint Venture Success*, Praeger, New York.

Kogut, B. (1989), 'The Stability of Joint Ventures: Reciprocity and Competitive Rivalry', *Journal of Industrial Economics*, vol. 38, pp. 183-198.

Meyer, J.W. and Scott, W.R. (1983), *Organizational Environments: Ritual and Rationality*, Sage, Beverly Hills.

Mintzberg, H. and Waters, J.A. (1982), 'Tracking Strategy in an Entrepreneurial Firm', *Academy of Management Journal*, vol. 25, pp. 465-499.

Ott, J. (2002), 'Alliances may be fewer, but savings will improve', *Aviation Week and Space Technology*, November 18, pp. 65-67.

Ouchi, W.G. (1980), 'Markets, bureaucracies, and Clans', *Administrative Science Quarterly*, vol. 25, pp. 129-142.

Oum, T.H. and Park, J. (1997), 'Airline alliances: current status, policy issues, and future directions', *Journal of Air Transport Management*, vol. 3, pp. 133-144.

Park, N.K. and Cho, D. (1997), 'The effect of strategic alliance on performance', *Journal of Air Transport Management*, vol. 3, pp. 155-164.

Parkhe, A. (1993), 'Strategic Alliance Structuring: A Game Theoretic and Transaction Cost Examination of Interfirm Cooperation', *Academy of Management Journal*, vol. 36, pp. 794-829.

Rhoades, D.L. and Lush, H. (1997), 'A Typology of Strategic Alliances in the Airline Industry: Propositions for Stability and Duration', *Journal of Air Transportation Management*, vol. 3, pp. 109-114.

Rhoades, D.L. and Waguespack, B., Jr. (2000), 'Divorce Airline Style', working paper at Embry-Riddle Aeronautical University.

Root, F.R. (1987), *Entry Strategies for International Markets*, Lexington Books, Lexington.

Scott, W.R. (1992), *Organizations: Rational, natural, and open systems 3rd ed.*, Prentice-Hall: Englewood Cliffs.

Simonin, B.L. (1999), 'Ambiguity and the Process of Knowledge Transfer in Strategic Alliances', *Strategic Management Journal*, vol. 20, pp. 595-624.

Smith, A. and Aldrich, H.E. (1991), 'The role of trust in the transaction cost economics framework', paper presented at the annual meeting of the Academy of Management, Miami.

Stinchcombe, A.L. (1965), 'Organizations and social structures', in James G. March (ed.), *Handbook of Organizations*, Rand McNally, Chicago.

Yan, A. (1998), 'Structural Stability and Reconfiguration of International Joint Ventures', *Journal of International Business Studies*, vol. 29, pp. 773-796.

Yan, A. and Zeng, M. (1999), 'International Joint Venture Instability: A Critique of Previous Research, A Reconceptualization, and Directions for Future Research', *Journal of International Business Studies*, vol. 30, pp. 397-414.

Chapter 10

Stumbling Blocks: The Slippery Legal Slope

A Bumpy Ride

Two of the key reasons for establishing strategic alliances in the airline industry are lowering costs and creating seamless global networks capable of simulating the non-interlining service preferred by customers on a global basis, however, the road to the land of seamless service and ever declining costs has not been a smooth one for alliance partners. Two key issues have bedeviled alliances in their alliance efforts. The first, anti-trust or competitiveness policy, is a legal issue that threatens to limit the ability of alliance partners to reduce costs through greater coordination of operations, fares, schedules, and aircraft. The second issue, airline and alliance quality, is an organizational issue that requires airlines with different cultures, markets, cost structures, and business priorities to agree on standards and implement them in such a way that they are consistent across airlines and achieve a level of quality that is satisfactory to the passengers of all the carriers involved. The purpose of this chapter is to examine the first of these issues and its effect on airlines and consumers. Chapter 11 will then look at quality issues bedeviling airlines and alliances.

Benefiting from Alliances?

On June 11, 1996, American Airlines and British Airways announced their proposed alliance setting off a firestorm of controversy on both sides of the Atlantic that has yet to be resolved. This partnership was to be the cornerstone of a broader alliance, Oneworld. ' It would compete directly with the Star alliance created by United, Lufthansa, SAS, Air Canada, and Varig. At the heart of this firestorm were competing airlines (and airline groups), consumer groups, and elected and appointed officials from the U.S., Great Britain, and other European nations. The ensuing debate on the merits of this alliance centered on the issues of competitiveness and consumer benefit. It raised questions about the motives of airline alliances, the regulatory philosophy of various world governments, and the long-term best interest of world air travelers. This debate reached a fever pitch with the announcement that United Airlines and US Airways have agreed to merge and that British Airways and KLM are discussing the possibility of merger. While it should be noted that both the BA-KLM and United-US Airways talks have officially ended, the issues of consolidation and competitiveness have continued to raise questions and concerns. The turmoil in the industry caused by the events of September 11th is likely to revive talk of consolidation in many regions and force governments to once again grapple with the questions consolidation raises. Key questions are who benefits from competition, how much competition is desirable, what form should it take, and what role do governments have in protecting competition.

Consumers benefit from markets that offer a wide choice of products and services at the lowest possible prices. These benefits are best achieved in a marketplace where there are many buyers and many sellers. Sellers compete by following one of two generic strategies: differentiation or cost leadership. In other words, they choose to develop for sale products or services that differ from rival firm products in qualities or characteristics for which consumers are willing to pay higher prices to obtain or by selling products or services similar to rival firms at a lower cost. There are a number of situations where competition is or becomes limited. To encourage innovation in firms, governments issue patent protection for a period of time, in effect, granting the developing firm a temporary monopoly. This allows the firm to recover the costs of development as well as reap additional financial rewards for taking the risk of development. In other cases, industry forces such as high capital or research and development costs have led to industry consolidation in order to achieve economies of scale. This consolidation tends to lower unit costs, but it also confers 'market power' on the remaining firms in the industry. A firm can be said to have market power when it can affect the market price of its product or service and/or limit rivals from competing in the market. Market power is closely related to the concept of 'market share' or the percentage of a given market controlled by a particular firm.

Antitrust law (competitive policy as it is commonly called in Europe and Asia) is that body of principles and statutes whereby governments seek to promote forms of competition that benefit society and consumers. In many cases, this means restraining the use of market power by firms within an industry or preventing mergers or acquisitions that would create excessive market power. While all countries have some statutes addressing the behavior of firms within their domestic markets, the background and philosophy of countries regarding business itself, the role of government, and the limits of free enterprise differ. In this chapter, we will examine the background and philosophy of antitrust law and its application to aviation in the United States, Europe, and Asia. We will attempt to chart the future direction of antitrust enforcement and discuss critical issues impacting airline alliances.

The Politics of Antitrust

In the years following the American Civil War (1861-1865), the United States witnessed a renewed westward expansion fueled by the growth of the U.S. railroad industry. As the economy became more integrated, there was an effort by a number of smaller companies to combine their businesses to increase market power. The most notorious effort involved Standard Oil, led by John D. Rockefeller. The Standard Oil 'trust' was a device to gain market power by requiring participants to transfer stock from their company to a trustee in exchange for trust certificates. This trustee was then empowered to fix prices, control output, and allocate markets to other trust members. A series of scandals fueled the public perception that 'trusts' were designed to drive smaller competitors out of business through the use of predatory tactics. Public outcry led the U.S. Congress to pass a series of acts designed to curb activities that sought to restrain trade or establish excessive market power. Anti-'trust' legislation was born.

United States

The first U.S. legislation dealing with anti-trust was the Sherman Act (1890) which was concerned with 'horizontal restraints' i.e. agreements between rival firms in the same market or industry that sought to fix prices, restrain output, divide markets, exclude other competitors or erect barriers that impeded free markets. In 1914, the Clayton Act (amended by the Robinson-Patman Act of 1936 and the Cellar-Kefauver Act of 1950) attempted to correct publicly perceived flaws in the Sherman Act by clearly prescribing actions that were deemed 'anti-competitive'. These actions include price discrimination, exclusionary practices such as exclusive dealing contracts and tying arrangements (tie-in sales agreements), and mergers that may have the effect of reducing competition.[1] The Civil Aviation Act of 1938 applied anti-trust specifically to aviation.   Section 408 of the Civil Aviation Act, later recreated in virtually unchanged form in the Federal Aviation Act of 1958 and amended by the Airline Deregulation Act of 1978, made it unlawful for 1) two or more carriers to merge, 2) any carrier to control a substantial portion of the properties of another, or 3) any carrier to acquire control of another carrier. Section 414 provided the Civil Aviation Bureau (CAB) with the authority to grant limited immunity (exemption) from antitrust enforcement if it deemed the action to be 'in the public interest'. With the termination of the CAB in 1985, the Assistant Secretary for Policy and International Affairs in the Department of Transportation was given antitrust responsibility.

   Domestic alliances/mergers.   Following U.S. deregulation in 1978, twenty-four U.S carriers were allowed to merge 'in the public interest'. The rationale for some of the mergers was the *failing company doctrine*, however, Robert Pitofsky, formerly with the Federal Trade Commission, has told the Commerce, Science, and Transportation Committee of the U.S. Senate that some of these mergers were clearly 'anti-competitive'. He specifically cited the TWA-Ozark merger in his testimony (The impact, 1999). Alfred Kahn, the father of US deregulation, agrees and has commented that 'I said we should deregulate the airline industry. I didn't say we should abolish the antitrust laws' (Reno, 2000). The general attitude of the U.S. Republican party which was in power during much of this time was to view most business-related legislation as an interference in the workings of the free market (Clarkson, Miller, Jentz and Cross, 1992). This view was supported by the so-called Chicago School of anti-trust whose members argued that while monopoly pricing hurt consumers, it had little effect on overall economic growth and productivity (Mandel, France, and Carney, 2000). However, these political and economic arguments do not entirely account for the level of consolidation permitted during the 1980s. In an effort to ensure competition, the Federal Aviation Administration and the Department of Transportation became caught in their own trap. When they allowed United Airlines to acquire the Pacific routes of the failing Pan Am, they created a carrier whose large domestic base and extensive, profitable international route system placed domestic rivals with smaller geographic reach at a major disadvantage. So when Northwest petitioned the Department to purchase Republic citing the need to expand their geographic reach in order to counter the United threat, the DOT agreed and so it went as other carriers pressed similar arguments.[2]   In effect, the FAA created, somewhat reluctantly, a domestic market dominated by six or seven major carriers each possessing an extensive continental network (Oum and Park, 1997; Gesell, 1993).

The existence of these large, overlapping network competitors explains in part the failure of U.S. carriers to form the type of joint activity alliances common in Europe. Two cases, one old and the other still pending, explain the governments' view that such joint activities are on balance anti-competitive. The first case, *In Re Passenger Computer Reservation System Anti-trust Litigation CCH 21 AVI 17, 732*, was brought against U.S. carriers' use of computer reservation systems in booking and marketing. It was charged that these systems, created by individual carriers, restricted competition by 1) displaying flight information in a biased manner, 2) imposing discriminatory fees on competing carriers, 3) using the data to identify travel agents who could be persuaded to divert business to the carrier owning the CRS, and 4) delaying the entry of competitor data. Since the development of computer reservation systems is expensive and beyond the reach of many carriers such practices were considered an unfair use of market power and proprietary technology. In addition, the courts upheld the decision of the Civil Aviation Bureau in *Republic Airlines vs CAB 756 f.2d 1304 (1985)* to prohibit an exclusivity provision of joint operating agreements between carriers (Gesell, 1993). Most recently, the American Society of Travel Agents has asked the U.S. Department of Justice to take action against 27 U.S. and foreign carriers participating in the development of an industry web site for online booking. According to the chief executive of the ASTA the 'joint site is a clear attempt on the part of the airlines to lure consumers onto the Web with lower prices, and drive all their competitors out of business' (Carey, 2000).   The Federal Trade Commission and the Department of Justice have issued a joint policy statement (to be discussed later in the chapter) that attempts to consolidate and clarify policy regarding competitor collaboration.

The U.S. Federal Trade Commission and the Department of Justice have also begun to scrutinize airline mergers and alliances more closely. This does not mean that more consolidation is not likely. American Airlines was permitted to go ahead with its acquisition of Reno Air. The rationale behind this acquisition was that American had a very weak position in the California/West Coast market where Reno Airlines was relatively strong, thus, competition was not likely to be harmed. On the other hand, the Department of Justice filed suit when Northwest Airlines announced plans to acquire a controlling stake in Continental. While this case was recently settled when Northwest agreed to sell its Class A voting shares and retain only a 5 percent non-voting position, it should be noted that the Department of Justice did allow the two carriers to implement a number of their planned marketing activities (Carey and McCartney, 2000). UAL Corp, parent company of United Airlines, announced its proposed $11.6 billion deal to purchase US Airways with great fanfare, but ended its planned merger after consumer groups, fellow airlines, and local governments complained about the scope and nature of the acquisition which would have created an airline with a combined market share of over 30%, making it twice as large as its nearest US competitor (Hatch, 2000; Zellner, Carney and Arndt, 2000). This would have been the first merger between two major US airlines since 1987 when US Air (now US Airways) and Piedmont Aviation were consolidated. It should be noted that a study conducted by Lehn and Kole on 18 airline mergers from 1979-1991 found that most resulted in negative long-run stock returns for the acquiring airline, including the US Air/Piedmont merger (Lehn, 2000).

Since deregulation took effect in the U.S. over 200 airlines have started up and failed (Rosen, 1994). Start-ups contend that major carriers are unfairly using their market power advantages, specifically the ability to control price and capacity, to force them out of profitable markets. This is commonly called predatory behavior. Unfortunately for regional carriers, the record of antitrust cases in the U.S. courts, particularly those involving charges of predatory behavior, has been very poor. In *Brookes Group Ltd v Brown & Williamson Tobacco Corp* (1993), the U.S. Supreme Court ruled that aggressive cost-cutting (even selling below costs) benefited consumers. Of the 37 cases to reach the Supreme Court since this decision not one has prevailed (Carney and Zellner, 2000). The record for other cases of predatory behavior is equally poor (Walker, 1999). There is a renewed effort by the U.S. Department of Justice to enforce legislation relating to predatory behavior. As part of this new commitment, the U.S. Department of Transportation has issued the 'Proposed Statement on Enforcement Policy on Unfair Exclusionary Conduct by Airlines'. The statement outlines the following situations when the DOT is likely to act on predatory practice complaints: (1) a major airline adds seats and discounts fares reducing 'local revenue', or (2) a major airline carries more passengers at the new low fare than the new entrant has capacity, reducing the major's local revenue, or (3) a major airline carries more at the new low fare than the new entrant carries reducing the major's local revenue. This issue has a number of implications for domestic alliances. First, many regional U.S. carriers have decided to avoid direct competition by entering into franchise agreements with major carriers acting as a feeder service to their hubs. Second, regional carriers themselves have begun to consolidate either through merger or alliance (AvStat, 1998).

International alliances. As discussed in Chapter 5, the deregulation of the U.S. airline industry was accompanied by a renewed effort to liberalize international markets and anti-trust legislation had an important role to play in the U.S. strategy first as a means to attack the fare setting power of IATA and then to encourage the spread of open skies bilaterals through the promise of anti-trust immunity for alliance partners from open skies countries. To date, nine alliances have received anti-trust immunity. The first of these alliances was Northwest and KLM. Of the remaining eight, three are no longer in effect due to the failure of one or more of the carriers involved in the immunized alliance - American with Canadian International Airlines, Delta with Swiss Air, Sabena, and Austrian Airlines (formerly the Qualifyer group), and Swissair with American. The immunized alliances still in effect are United with Lufthansa, SAS, and Air Canada, Northwest with Malaysia Airlines, Delta with Air France, and American with LanChile (PRNewswire, 2000; OIG, 1999).

In December of 1999, the United States Department of Transportation released a report on the benefits of Open Skies. According to the report, fares in Open Skies markets dropped 17.5% between 1996 and 1998. Non-Open Skies markets experienced only a drop of 3.5 percent (DOT, 1999). Thus, the United States rationale for waiving anti-trust provisions in approved alliances between Open Skies market partners is that the pro-competitive benefits to consumers of open skies outweighs the possible anti-competitive harm.

Europe

While each individual European nation has its own legislation relating to competitive activity, we will address the development of antitrust or competitive policy as it is called in Europe from the perspective of European integration.[3] Although a common transport policy was one of the stated goals of the European Community, the Council of Ministers, under their authority to issue block exemptions, chose to exempt transportation from the enforcement of competition rules. In 1986 the Court of Justice ruled in the *Nouvelles Frontieres* case that the air transport sector was subject to the general rules of the EEC Treaty. In that same year, the Commission began proceedings against ten Community airlines for violation of various competition rules. The 'first package', adopted December 14, 1987, officially included an implementing regulation giving the Commission the authority to investigate alleged violations of the competition rules and fine violators.

Domestic alliances/ mergers. The Commission's policy toward airline mergers has been shaped in large part by what they perceive as failures in U.S. policy. According to many European aviation experts, 'the experience of deregulation combined with the lack of antitrust enforcement, destroyed many of the benefits of that deregulation' in the United States (Soames, 1990: 82). Mario Monti, the ECs anti-trust commissioner, has undertaken a concerted effort to crackdown on industries that attempt to set prices or divide markets. While there is a general feeling that cross-border ownership would benefit the system by reducing the tendency to favor 'local' firms and allow for more economies of scale, the Commission has also been cautious in approving mergers and acquisitions. The Commission's policy was questioned several years ago when Air France/UTA were allowed to merge, however, a series of Commission rulings, including one involving AirTours planned takeover of First Choice, appears to indicate that the Commission is prepared to take a tougher stance in aviation/aerospace mergers/acquisitions (Soames, 1990; Taverna, 1999). In aerospace, Monti did move to block the proposed GE/Honeywell merger, however, he has suffered several setbacks in 2002 as European courts have reversed his rulings on three cases of mergers (Reinhardt and Carney, 2002). This leaves the fate of the GE/Honeywell and Microsoft cases in some doubt. In aviation, the British Airways/KLM merger talks raised questions concerning the fact that any merger would place a single airline in control of two of Europe's most important airports – Heathrow and Schiphol. The stated reason for ending the talks was 'intractable commercial and regulatory issues', but clearly there were serious concerns over European Commission approval (Field, 2000).

While European officials have taken a hard line on the issue of mergers and acquisitions, they have tended to have a more favorable view of cooperative agreements between carriers involving fleet rationalization and network efficiencies. While EC competition rules do not explicitly consider 'the public interest', they have often held that these types of agreements 'contribute to the promotion of economic progress and to the interests of consumers' (AEA, 1999). Some of the allowed practices include consultation on and coordination of tariffs, joint operations, interline agreements, route planning, coordination of schedules, and linked frequent flyer programs. Perhaps signaling its limits, the European Commission recently conducted a raid on the offices of Scandinavian Airlines and Maersk Air to determine whether Maersk Air stopped operating between Stockholm and Copenhagen 'in concert with SAS' following their recent cooperation pact (Dow Jones Newswire, 2000). U.S. officials, on the other hand, have tended to view almost all actions relating to route planning, schedule coordination, and joint operations as violations of anti-trust law.

In an address at the 23rd Annual FAA Commercial Aviation Forecast Conference, Frederik Sorenson, Head of the Air Transport Policy Unit Directorate General of Transport, European Commission, addressed the issue of competitive behavior by stating that the EU did not agree with the U.S. 'free for all system depending on the good behavior of air carriers' (Sorensen, 1998: 125). The Commission has acted in several cases of alleged predatory behavior ruling in favor of plaintive airlines (easyJet-KLM, easyJet-BA Go). Most recently, BA's Go has lodged a complaint with the European Commission charging that Deutsche Lufthansa AG is selling tickets below cost (Independent, 2000). If these decisions are upheld by the High Court, it would be a major victory for European start-up carriers (IATA, 1999). Given sufficient protection, many of these carriers may opt to remain independent, niche players rather than franchising feeders for the major airlines.

International alliances. While the U.S. has chosen to tie alliance approval to Open Skies, European officials have tied alliance approval to domestic market development. A key issue in recent alliance approvals has been the willingness of potential partners to relinquish slots at congested European airports (United-Lufthansa and BA/AA, for example). These slots are deemed necessary to the development of viable start-up competitors. The European Commission has also argued for a multilateral approach to traffic rights negotiations on the basis of the one market concept. In 1991, the EU and the U.S. agreed to notify and give weight to the competition policies of the other party in instances where their own enterprises were concerned. Most of the notifications to date have involved proposed mergers. Unfortunately, the principle of positive comity has often merely served to highlight the differences between EU-US policy. In particular, U.S. authorities explicitly consider 'the public interest' when assessing the benefits of proposed action (AEA, 1999). We will discuss attempts to harmonize EU-US policies further under strategies for success.

Asia

There is no single legal framework for Asia, but most of its countries do have some kind of legislation dealing with monopoly and competition. The difficulty lies in understanding the degree to which these regulations are applied and/or enforced. In Japan, the Anti-Monopoly Act is intended 'to eliminate excessive concentrations of business power and to encourage fair and free competition' (Jetro, 1999). It prohibits holding companies and places restrictions on share holding, interlocking directorates, mergers and acquisitions. The Fair Trade Commission is responsible for enforcing the anti-monopoly guidelines. The Korean Fair Trade Commission is also charged with promulgating guidelines and enforcing policies of their Monopoly Regulation and Fair Trade Act. Like its Japanese counterpart, the Monopoly Regulation and Fair Trade Act is intended to prohibit excessive concentration, abuse of market power, and unfair business practices. To the outside observer, the Japanese Keiretsus and the Korean Chaebols, forms of tightly linked industrial groupings, appear to violate much of this legislation. Critics have often complained that the legislation is primarily directed at limiting foreign assess to domestic markets (Gibney, 1985; Prestowitz, 1988). The recent financial crisis in Asia has put a great deal of pressure on these structures. Indications are that Korea at least is willing to dismantle much of the chaebol structure to improve efficiency and transparency within their market.

Domestic alliances. Efforts were underway in a number of Asian countries to deregulate aspects of their air transport sectors before the Asian crisis. The Japanese government changed it policy in 1995 to make discounted fares easier and in 1996 created a zone-fare system. On December 5, 1996, the Japanese Ministry of Trade announced an end to the supply-demand balance clauses that had effectively blocked new entry. A recent study of the changes, however, has not found a significant shift in market share or reduction in airfares (Yamauchi, 1999). The Korean market continues to be heavily regulated. The domestic market is divided between Korean Airlines (KAL) and Asiana. Internationally, Asiana is primarily restricted to short-haul Asian routes while KAL flies Transatlantic and Transpacific Routes. Given the recent safety problems at KAL, it is possible that the Korean Civil Aviation Bureau will consider such options as allowing Asiana greater route authority and/or possible new entrants into the Korean market. To date, there is little evidence of domestic alliance development outside the traditional industrial grouping structure.

International alliances. As with aviation policy as a whole, there is no consistent 'Asian' strategy toward international alliances. Market access through code sharing has been the dominant form of alliance arrangement. The economic crisis that started in Thailand and spread throughout Asia affected all of the region's air carriers. Hardest hit were Thai Airlines, Philippines Airlines, Korean Airlines, Malaysian Airlines, and Garuda. High operating and financing costs have combined with outbound and inbound traffic decreases to place severe stress on these and other Asian carriers (Li, 1999). There have been talks of regional consolidation, but to date no actions have been taken. Many of these talks have included Singapore Airlines which has emerged as one of the strongest of the Asian carriers and has continued an aggressive campaign to improve its already impressive quality and position itself well in the mega-alliance world.

To Keep from Stumbling

A global alliance cannot succeed without a strategy for overcoming and/or avoiding antitrust issues. One means of doing this is to create competitive-related scenarios and responses for the major aviation regions of the world. The trend is clearest for the European Union whose Commission appears intent on maintaining a relatively hard line on mergers/acquisitions and predatory behavior. Several factors could slow this trend, but they are unlikely to reverse it. Perhaps the key factor will be the willingness of Europe's national governments and the people they represent to allow cross-border acquisitions. Consolidation is certainly a possibility in a deregulated market and more likely following September 11th. In fact, the Commission has indicated that it would like to see more consolidation in the relatively fragmented airline and aerospace industry (Sparaco, 1999). If, on the other hand, this consolidation is seen as destroying national flag carriers and/or eliminating jobs within certain countries, then there is likely to develop greater political opposition. This issue was already being hotly debated in the EU as national governments pondered the failure of Sabena and Swissair and efforts by their governments to salvage some part of these carriers.

As for predatory behavior, the EU has indicated that start-up carriers need greater protection than is typically afforded them in the U.S. market. This protection would help insure that deregulation increases competition at the route level within Europe. Recent alliances have found themselves caught up in the effort to promote start-up carriers as alliance approvals have hinged on carrier willingness to forfeit slot allocations. Still, a report by the British Civil Aviation Authority found that no more than 7% of intra-European city pairs are served by three or more competitors (Sparaco, 1998). The pool of start-ups in Europe remains relatively small and it is likely that many of the major European carriers have not felt the need to aggressively engage them. The events of 9/11 have also hit the major European carriers hard and regional European carriers appear poised to increase their 7% share of the intra-European market even more, possibly reaching the 25 percent share achieved by their U.S. cousins (Binggeli and Pompeo, 2002). With economic recovery, the European majors are likely to attempt to regain lost ground leading to an increase in predatory complaints.

The U.S., under the Clinton Administration, was moving toward stronger enforcement of its antitrust provisions. The Federal Trade Commission and the Department of Justice had jointly issued antitrust guidelines for collaboration among competitors which outlined those agreements that would be considered per se illegal from those that would be analyzed under the rule of reason to determine their effect on competition. According to these guidelines, any agreement addressing pricing or capacity is deemed per se illegal. All other agreements will be analyzed according to the rule of reason policy. The agencies will first define 'relevant markets', then calculate 'market shares' and concentrations to assess possible market power increases stemming from the agreement. If this raises concerns about anti-competitive harm, they will then assess the degree of independent decision making by partners to the agreement to determine the potential degree of collusion. They will be interested in the ability and incentives of partners to compete independently. According to the guidelines, the agencies will focus on six factors: (1) the degree of exclusivity in the agreement, (2) the extent of independent asset control, (3) the nature and extent of inter-partner financial interest, (4) the control of competitive decision making, (5) the degree of information sharing, and (6) the duration of the partnership. These guidelines are largely a consolidation and elaboration on existing law. A somewhat more problematic issue concerns weighing anti-competitive harm against collaborative efficiencies and whether these efficiencies are considered pro- or anti-competitive (Federal Trade Commission, 1999). Previous U.S. administrations have tended to accept the argument that pro-competitive benefits outweigh potential harm. In the area of predatory behavior, the failure of the U.S. government in the American Airlines case does not bode well for regional carriers seeking protection nor does the election of a new Republican president whose administration has already signaled its position on the excesses of anti-trust enforcement (France, 2002; Hamm, Greene, and Reinhardt, 2002). Three events that could significantly affect the course of EU-US antitrust policy both domestically and internationally are the proposed Trans-Atlantic Common Aviation Area (TCAA), the bilateral negotiations between the US and the UK, and the approval on either side of the Atlantic of one or more major carrier mergers. All of these issues will be discussed in more detail in Part III of the book, but suffice it to say at this point that these events would force parties on both sides of the Atlantic to re-examine the basic concepts and application of anti-trust legislation.[4]

From a planning perspective, the Asian region continues to be a question mark. It is possible that some Asian countries could retreat toward more protectionist policies in an effort to shelter their flag carriers. This isolation would provide short-term protection of domestic market, but these carriers could eventually face serious international problems on two fronts. First, the economic crisis has many Asian carriers, previous reluctant to join alliances, eager to sign on in the hope of improving traffic and increasing revenues. These carriers are likely to lock up the most desirable alliance partners and leave the stragglers with few choices (Thomas, 1999). Second, if the proposed U.S. legislation requiring airlines to monitor alliance partner safety passes and spreads to other countries, weak carriers may find international partners hesitant to take them on for fear of legal liability.

A second key step to surviving in the world of anti-trust and alliances is to develop clear guidelines for permissible alliance activities. Simply put, without anti-trust immunity alliance partners cannot discuss any issue relating to price or capacity. Since these are considered per se violations, a finding of fact is not required (i.e. proof that any such discussions have taken place). Therefore, alliance partners cannot even be seen to engage in activity that might have implications for pricing and capacity. This would include schedule coordination, CRS sharing or linkage, exclusive agreements, etc. Clearly, an alliance not enjoying anti-trust immunity is at a disadvantage in relation to its immune competition. Airlines in alliances without immunity should have clearly established guidelines for all inter-alliance discussions. All parties to such discussions should be pre-briefed on the guidelines.

Notes

1. Federal antitrust laws are enforced by the Department of Justice (DOJ) and the Federal Trade Commission (FTC). Violations of the Sherman Act fall under the jurisdiction of the DOJ and can be prosecuted as either a criminal or civil case. The Department can ask companies to divest certain holdings or dissolve a partnership. The FTC has the responsibility to enforce the Clayton Act through civil proceedings. In addition, private parties may sue for damages as a result of violation of the Sherman and Clayton Acts. Private parties may also seek an injunction to prevent antitrust violations. It should be noted that European law does not include possible criminal prosecution.
2. I am indebted to Paul V. Mifsud, Vice President, Government & Legal Affairs, US, for KLM Royal Dutch Airlines for his willingness to share his insight and experience.
3. Anti-trust legislation was first contained in Articles 4 and 65-67 of the European Coal and Steel Community Treaty. It is incorporated in Articles 85-86, 90, and 92-94 of the Treaty of European Union. The European Commission (Directorate-General IV) is responsible for implementing competitiveness policy.
4. It should be noted that allowing cabotage in the U.S. would require changes in US laws and would have to be approved by the U.S. Congress. There is also some question as to whether the EC can negotiate a multilateral agreement with the US.

References

AEA (1999), *Towards a Transatlantic Common Aviation Area*, Association of European Airlines, Brussels.

AvStat Associates Inc. (1998), Summary of passenger service by state. AvStat Associates.

'BA's Go Accuses Lufthansa of Unfair Competition, Paper Says' (2000, February 29), *Independent*, p. 17.

Carey, S. (2000), 'Travel Agents Ask the U.S. to Act Against Web-Site Plan', *The Wall Street Journal*, February 18.

Carey, S. and McCartney, S. (2000), 'Antitrust Trial Pressures Northwest Airlines to Cede Controlling Stake in Continental', *Wall Street Journal*, November 7.

Carney, D. and Zellner, W. (2000), 'Caveat Predator?', *Business Week*, May 22, pp. 116-118.

Clarkson, K.W., Miller, R.R., Jentz, G.A. and Cross, F.B. (1992), *West's Business Law: Text, Cases, Legal and regulatory Environment* (5th ed.), West Publishing Company, New York.

Department of Transportation (1999), 'International aviation developments: Global deregulation takes off', DOT:Washington, D.C. ostpxweb.dot.gov/aviation.

Dow Jones Newswire (2000), 'EU Raids Maersk, SAS In Connection with Cooperation Pact', June 21.

European Cockpit Association (2000), *From EASA to the TCAA: The flight crews view on the new regulatory framework in aviation*, ECA, Brussels.

Federal Trade Commission (1999), www.ftc.gov/opa/1999/9910/jointven.html.

Field, P. (2000), 'BA, KLM Ground Merger Plan. Airlines Faced Opposition from Government Which feared Massive Layoffs', *USA Today*, September 22, 1B.

France, M. (2002), 'Uncle Sam's Trustbusters: Outgunned and Outmoded', *Business Week*, November 18, pp. 44-45.

Gesell, L.E. (1993), 'Aviation and the Law' (2nd ed.), Coast Aire Publications, Chandler, AZ.

Gibney, F. (1985), *The Fragile Super-Power*, New American Library, New York.

Hamm, S., Greene, J. and Reinhardt, A. (2002), 'What's a Rival to do Now?', November 18, pp. 44-46.

Hatch, M. (2000), 'Minnesota Attorney General letter to the DOJ re US-UA', June 5.

Independent (2000), 'BA's GO accuses Lufthansa of unfair competition', London, February 28, p. 17.

International Air Transport Association (1999), 'Competition and Court Cases in Europe', *Airlines International*, vol. 4, p. 58.

JETRO (1999), www.jetro.go.jp.

Lehn, K.M. (2000), 'Why airline mergers are a disaster - Soaring labor costs may ground airline mergers', May 25.

Li, M.Z.F. (1999), 'Asia-Pacific Airlines amidst the Asian Economic Crisis', presented at the Air Transportation Research Group Conference, Hong Kong, June 1999.

Mandel, M.J., France, M. and Carney, D. (2000), 'The Great Antitrust Debate', June 26, pp. 40-42.

Merrill Lynch, Pierce, Fenner & Smith, Inc. (1998), *Global Airline Alliances: Why Alliances Really Matter from an Investment Perspective*, Merrill Lynch, Pierce, Fenner & Smith Inc., New York.

Oum, T.H. and Park, J. (1997), Airline Alliances: Current Status, Policy Issues, and Future Directions', *Journal of Air Transport Management*, vol. 3, pp. 133-144.

Phillips, E.D. (1999), 'Oneworld Late, But Powerful', *Aviation Week & Space Technology*, August 23, 62-64.

Prestowitz, C.V. (1988), *Trading Places: How We Are Giving Our Future to Japan and How to Reclaim it*, Basic Books, Inc, New York.

PRNewswire (2000), 'Northwest Airlines and Malaysia Airlines receive Antitrust Immunity; Approval Represents First Immunized Alliance Between a U.S. and Asian Carrier', November 21.

Reno, R. (2000), 'In several ways, United/US Airways merger might not fly', *STAR TRIBUNE*, June 1.

Rosen, S.D. (1995), 'Corporate restructuring: A labor perspective' in *Airline Labor Relations in the Global Era: The New Frontier*, P. Cappelli (ed.), ILR Press, Ithaca, NY.

Soames, T. (1990), 'Joint Ventures and Cooperation Agreements in the Air Transport Sector' in P.D. Dagtoglou and T. Soames (eds), *Airline Mergers and Cooperation in the European Community*, Kluwer Law and Taxation Publishers, Boston.

Sorensen, F. (1998), 'Open Skies in Europe' in *FAA Commercial Aviation Forecast Conference Proceedings*, U.S. Department of Transportation, Washington, D.C., pp. 125-131.

Sparaco, P. (1999), 'EC Pushes Quick Aviation Accord with U.S.', *Aviation Week & Space Technology*, November 29, pp. 40-41.

Sparaco, P. (1998), 'European Deregulation Still Lacks Substance', *Aviation Week & Space Technology*, November 9, 53-57.

Taverna, M.A. (1999), 'European Rulings Signal Tougher Antitrust Stance', *Aviation Week & Space Technology*, October 4, pp. 42-43.

The impact of recent alliances, international agreements, DOT actions, and pending legislation on air fares, air service, and competition in the airline industry, 10x Cong., 2nd Sess. (1999).

Thomas, G. (1999), 'Alliances make hubs more valuable in Asia', *Aviation Week & Space Technology*, October, 25, pp. 97-98.

Toh, R. (1998), 'Towards an International Open Skies Regime: Advances, Impediments, and Impacts', *Journal of Air Transportation World Wide*, vol. 3, pp. 61-70.

Walker, K. (1999), 'American Justice', *Airline Business*, July, pp. 66-67.

Yamauchi, H. (1999), 'Air Transport Policy in Japan: Policy Change and Market Competition', paper presented at the Air Transportation Research Group Conference, Hong Kong, April 1999.

Zellner, W., Carney, D. and Arndt, M. (2000), 'How many airlines will stay aloft', *Business Week*, June 19.

Chapter 11

Stumbling Blocks: The Quality Question

Changing Quality

While avoiding the legal stumbling block of anti-trust has been difficult for alliances, it has not been as visible a failure to consumers as the hurdle of achieving seamless service. Few businesses have escaped the need to change some structure or process in order to remain competitive. The litany of change techniques is legion - reengineering, restructuring, rightsizing, total quality control, process redesign, process management, total quality management, delayering, downsizing, rethinking, business process innovation, etc (Ashkenas, Ulrich, Jich and Kerr, 1995; Keidel, 1994). All of these techniques have two basic goals in common: 1) the desire to increase organizational flexibility and speed, and 2) the belief in the necessity of customer-focus. Achieving these goals requires businesses to reduce or eliminate organizational barriers. Some of these techniques have focused on eliminating vertical barriers (delayering, downsizing, etc) in order to improve the speed and flexibility of organizational decision making. This generally requires organizations to empower lower level employees with greater decision making authority and/or reducing the organizational levels of approval involved in the decision process. Other techniques are more focused on reducing the horizontal boundaries within organizations (process management, reengineering, etc). These boundaries between organizational units (usually functional units) have been blamed for slow development time, poor responsiveness to customer concerns and desires, and organizational conflict. A series of recent books have added two other boundaries that must be breached - external and geographic (Ashkenas, Ulrich, Jich and Kerr, 1995; Keidel, 1994; Davidow and Malone, 1992). These boundaries separate companies from their suppliers and regional, domestic business units from international business units. In large part, the alliance movement is about breaking down the barriers that separate companies from their suppliers, their customers, and, in many cases, their competitors. It is about creating linkages and networks. Alliances are 'about spinning a web to catch more customers' (Sparks, 1999: 106).

Whose Quality?

The term quality can be defined as excellence, value, conformance to specification, etc. The most commonly used definition comes to us from the total quality movement.   It defines quality as 'meeting and/or exceeding customer expectations'.   To comply with this definition of quality, companies must first know who their customers are and then continually strive to understand and meet their expectations (continuous improvement).   While this sounds simple on paper, many companies find it difficult to put into practice.   For airlines, revenue management systems that divided customers by their preferences on booking time, price, class, etc and frequent flyer surveys of services provided have often been considered sufficient to comply with this quality definition.   However, the growing movement to 'brand' airline and alliance service is focusing new attention on issues of quality.   This movement is fueled by the belief that 'a very real risk exists that the flight will be reduced to a commodity status, and that the individual choice of airlines will be factored out of the buying process' (Fraser, 1996: 61).   The answer, as we discussed in chapter 10, is to create products and services that send images and messages to the consumer that reassure them about quality, convenience, comfort... In short, the very name must separate one airline (one alliance) from another in terms of key consumer expectations whether they are 'global reach', 'superior service' or 'value for the money'.

For individual carriers, consumers have two basic sources of information on quality - personal experience or third-party surveys.   These surveys are typically conducted by such organizations as J.D. Powers and Conde Nast utilizing information from frequent flyers to rank or award airlines for quality.   J.D. Powers' 1997 survey found that there are ten factors that drive consumer satisfaction with airline quality: on-time performance, airport check-in, schedule/flight accommodations, seating comfort, gate location, aircraft interior, flight attendants, food service, post-flight services, and frequent flyer programs.   Specifics in the pre-flight categories include availability of flight when desired, helpfulness of reservations agents, ability to get seat preference, ability to get priority boarding, and frequent flyer qualification levels.   In-flight issues judged important by consumers include, effective communication on flight delays/cancellations, carry-on luggage space, seating comfort, and helpfulness of flight attendants.   In the area of airport activities, consumers want such things as speedy baggage delivery, good connecting flight information, short check-in times, and good airport lounges (Glab, 1997).

To date, there has been no attempt to comprehensively evaluate the quality of alliances from a consumer perspective, but many of the same issues cited in individual carrier surveys would apply.   In the following section, we will address some of the preliminary work on alliance quality and suggest other elements that should be considered.

Measuring Alliance Quality

Chapter 8 outlined four basic reasons that carriers form alliances: 1) to gain market access, 2) to build global seamless networks, 3) to reduce costs, and 4) to maintain market presence.   From a consumer perspective, airline cost reduction is only important if it allows the carrier or alliance to reduce consumer costs and/or improve other aspects of airline service valued by consumers.   Reasons 1 and 4 relate to the scope and/or depth of the alliances' coverage and the area of schedule/flight accommodation identified above for customer satisfaction with an individual carrier. From an alliance perspective, the more destinations they serve and the more frequently they serve them should be a quality issue for consumers.

This issue proved to be a key factor in the recently released Merrill Lynch (1999) report on alliances. In the report, Merrill Lynch rated the mega alliances in terms of geographical network, market size, network density, financial strength and regulatory freedom. This study drew a distinction between geographic scope (number of destinations/departures) and network density (utilization of network or extent of duplication). In this regard, an alliance such as Wings outscores the other mega-alliances on network density but ranked lowest on geographic scope. From an alliance point-of-view, less duplication of network lowers fears of anti-competitive outcomes and means more overall extension of geographic scope. From a consumer point-of-view, greater density means more frequency to desired destinations. Thus, the ideal alliance configuration would involve partners having extensive depth within their geographic scope but little network duplication of alliance partner networks. This is not always an easy combination to find. One of the major stumbling blocks to the proposed BA-AA alliance was the extent of network overlap and the fear that such overlap would encourage the alliance partners to 'rationalize' their networks (i.e. dividing markets between partners in such a way that only one partner would effectively serve a particular route).

While the Merrill Lynch Index does not provide a comprehensive overview of alliance quality, it is an important first step in the process of understanding alliance quality. From a consumer quality perspective, a more difficult area to address is the issue of 'global, seamless service'. 'Global' is a function of geographic reach, but 'seamless' suggests a great deal more. What does it mean to provide seamless service? How do independent airlines provide such service? Let us start at the airline level. Airlines are organized by function - flight operations, engineering and maintenance, marketing, and services. Under marketing, which composes approximately 50% of the workforce, there are units concerned with reservations and ticketing, cabin service, ground service, food service, etc (Wells, 1994). The consumer view, however, is not segmented into functions. Consumers experience airline service as a series of processes. The order fulfillment process begins with check-in and proceeds to final destination and baggage retrieval (Ekdahl, Gustafsson, and Edvardsson, 1999). When a problem arises during the travel experience, consumers are not interested in fixing the blame on a particular function and they certainly do not wish to stand around while the airline attempts to do so. Consumers want the issue resolved to their satisfaction as quickly as possible by their first contact point. They do not wish to be shuffled from department to department or supervisor to supervisor looking for resolution. One of the greatest drawbacks to a functional structure is that consumers often 'feel they are forced into a system characterized by contradictions, redundant or insufficient information, misguided authority, and confusion' (Ekdahl, Gustafsson, and Edvardsson, 1999). In other words, the traditional functional structure often finds it difficult to provide a seamless service. Many companies claim that 'quality is everyone's business', but they fail to realize that quality must also be 'someone's responsibility'.

There are basically two ways to approach the process quality issue. The most obvious way is to restructure the organization on a process basis - order fulfillment, new product development, customer acquisition, etc.   In a process-structured organization, coordination within the process eliminates the 'cracks' through which customers often fall.   This coordination is usually achieved through the establishment of cross-functional teams that include at least one member from each functional area involved in that process. All elements of the process become the responsibility of the process leader and his team. Their job is to 1) insure that all elements of the process are addressed, and 2) act as liaison to the functional departments, providing input from and guidance to the process. According to SAS, three principles should govern the design of the process: (1) give passengers control, (2) make the process transparent, and (3) empower the staff (Ekdahl, Gustafsson, and Edvardsson, 1999). A related option would be to institute a matrix structure that would in fact overlay the functional structure with a process structure. This type of organizational restructuring was popular in the 1980s but met with resistance from employees who in effect now had two bosses – the function leader and the process leader.

There are many personal and organizational barriers to process restructuring. At the personal level, teamwork requires good interpersonal skills and demands more emphasis on cross-functional skill development. Since many companies tie some portion of an individual's compensation to team results, individuals may also feel a loss of control in this important area of organizational life. If team results are not compensated in any way, then firms run the risk that team activities will not receive the necessary level of individual attention. Organizationally, team make-up and training are critical. Firms must decide on functional skill requirements for membership, number of representatives from each function, level of functional representatives (customer service manager, vice-president of customer relations, etc), leadership of groups, etc. These decisions can become very politicized. Functional conflicts over resource allocation and differing goals or objectives require the establishment of some process or procedure for conflict resolution. There are clearly costs associated with such a massive change in structure. There is also likely to be resistance from within the organization.

Quality Function Deployment (QFD) is one way to retain a functional structure while 'systematically deploying operations and functions that make up the quality into step-by-step detail' (Akao, 1999).   QFD requires companies to identify consumer desires, translate them into specific components, establish standards and procedures for delivery, and follow-up on delivery. For example, consumers want reliability in a number of company-provided areas. One such area is food service. They expect food to be consistent in quality, to taste and look good, to provide a good portion, and to be hot or cold (depending on the type of food). Companies must translate these desires into specific parameters (i.e. temperature of food, size of portions, etc). Then establish and enforce standards on the 'function' charged with delivering the item. Finally, there must be feedback and improvement (Barlow, 1999). While there is elaborate software to support the implementation of

QFD, it is still a complex process that has yet to be fully embraced outside Japan [see Akao (1990) for a fuller discussion of QFD].

As difficult as process quality can be for individual airlines, it is potentially nothing compared to the prospect of integrating the process across multiple carriers. As Deming and other have pointed out, no two processes are identical. Each process will invariably produce a certain amount of random variation (flaws or problems related to the nature of the system(s) in place). Special variations (flaws or problems related to a change in the system such as change in training procedures, receipt of a batch of faulty parts, etc) also occur from time to time. Management must understand their process well enough to distinguish between random and special variation. Management must act to identify the source of special variation and remove its cause. Random variation, on the other hand, can only be reduced by changing the process itself.

When attempting to integrate the processes of two or more carriers, there are two primary areas of concern. First, are the processes compatible? A case in point is the airline boarding pass. All carriers issue them and most require that they be run through an electronic device before boarding. However, if the size of these boarding passes differs between carriers such that the boarding pass issued by one carrier will not pass through the system of the other (and customers are required to check-in again at the second airline for a new pass), then some of the seamlessness of the process is lost. The same question applies for many other standards and procedures such as upgrade requirements, carry-on specifics, seating assignments, boarding procedures, etc. To the extent that these differences create snags in the seamless fabric of air travel for consumers, they will detract from perceived quality and can result in loss of business to higher quality alliances. We will discuss strategies for avoiding these snags later.

The second area of concern is potentially more serious and more difficult to resolve. It relates to differences in the quality level (or random variation) of alliance partners. Consumers who book a flight on one airline but find at least one leg of their journey flown by a carrier of lesser quality can develop a negative perception of the alliance as a whole. Obviously, the greater the difference in quality levels the more severe the problem becomes. In a truly seamless alliance, consumers should perceive no difference in quality levels. The most worrisome difficulty lies in equalizing the quality level of alliance partners. Again, there are no studies examining the overall quality levels of alliance partners or the effects of quality equalization, but a recent study suggests one possible scenario. Research on quality levels at major U.S. carriers indicates that over the last ten years quality levels have begun to converge and now show little variation across the major U.S. carriers (Rhoades and Waguespack, 2000). In statistical research, the term 'regressing to the mean' refers to the tendency for extremes at both ends of a particular phenomena to move over time toward the mean for that population. In the case of quality levels between alliance partners, there might be a similar tendency for quality levels to converge toward a mean. At the lower end, alliance partners quality will tend to rise. On the other hand, the alliance quality leaders could see declines in their quality toward the alliance mean. Singapore Airlines would likely find this prospect disturbing.

Of course, this is not the only possible scenario. However, an alliance seeking to brand itself as one of high quality must be aware of the fact that upward equalization of quality standards will not just happen. Higher quality standards will not just 'rub-off' on alliance partners. This is where 'cross-alliance' teams become important in insuring the quality of lateral/cross-airline processes. The Star alliance currently has 15 committees overseen by a policy group that reports directly to a board composed of alliance member chairmen. In addition, working groups are often formed to address specific problems. These groups report to an alliance development committee. Some of the results of this committee work have been manuals to explain members' products and services, common baggage tracking systems, common lounge access, linked frequent-flyer plans, etc. However, some issues have proved more problematic, such as joint facilities and integrated information systems (Feldman, 1998). As noted above, there are personal and organizational problems associated with the use of cross-functional, alliance teams. In the early years of their alliance United and Luftansa found it difficult to agree on something as seemingly simple as the joint purchase of airsick bags (Feldman, 1998). Imagine the potential for disagreement on an issue such as the operation of the Malpensa Airport or yield management integration. At the very least, alliances are finding that coordination takes time and effort. Jurgen Weber, Luftansa CEO, has estimated that alliances consume approximately one-third of his time (Feldman, 1998). The Wings alliance (NW/KLM) is moving toward eliminating some of the problems of cross-functional coordination by merging certain operations such as sales forces, but this too takes time and effort.

Strategies for Achieving Quality

There are two important steps in achieving and insuring overall alliance quality. The first factor is conducting pre- and post-alliance audits. In May 1999, U.S. Congressman James Oberstar introduced a bill that would require U.S. carriers to conduct safety audits of code share partners as a condition for approval of the code sharing agreement. Under the existing system, the Office of the Secretary (OST) of Transportation must approve all code share agreements. The OST has a statutory mandate to consider safety as 'the highest priority in authorizing air transportation services' (Title 49, section 40101(a)(1)), but has not required such assessments before. Under the guidelines recommended by the Office of the Inspector General, the safety audit 'must demonstrate that foreign carriers have implemented safety procedures in critical areas such as maintenance operations, aircraft airworthiness, crew qualifications, crew training, flight operations, en-route procedures, emergency response plans, security, and dangerous goods' (OIG, 1999: 12). The U.S. Department of Defense and six U.S. carriers have already put such systems in place, although there is as yet no standard process for such an audit.

Given government-mandated safety audits, carriers should establish a similar auditing procedure for the service quality aspects of potential partners. These audits would establish a baseline quality level for each partner. Assuming that each alliance partner understands the needs and expectations of its customers, the next step is to reach some consensus among alliance partners on the level of desired quality and the priority of service quality goals. Finally, a plan must be created that outlines the goals, objectives, and tactics to be used by each carrier to achieve the necessary changes.

The second step is to create a process that 'shows one face to the customer'. Alliances, like individual firms, are finding that it is essential 'to make it easy for the customer to access resources, products, and services across the horizontal spectrum' (Ashkenas et al, 1995: 128). When customers can enter into the company or alliance through multiple doors (or portals as they are sometimes called), there are several problems that can arise that have the potential to adversely affect process quality. Without careful coordination, customers may find that the point-of-entry changes the final destination. For example, if alliance members are not familiar with the products and services offered by their partners, then a customer accessing the alliance through one partner may receive different scheduling information, and service than another customer accessing the 'system' from a different partner. A related problem occurs when the parts of the system are not aware of the actions of each other and fail (or are unable) to take these differences into consideration when assisting customers.

In their book, *The Boundaryless Organization: Breaking the Chains of Organizational Structure*, Ashkenas, Ulrich, Jick, and Kerr (1995) outline five warning signs of disfunctional horizontal boundaries: '(1) slow, sequential cycle times, (2) protected turf, (3) suboptimization of organizational goals, (4) the enemy-within syndrome, and (5) customers doing their own integration' (115). Slow, sequential cycle times occur whenever multiple divisions, departments, units, etc must be consulted one by one to create new products or respond to customers demands. Whenever protecting one's own resources or power interfere with customer service, quality suffers. The same thing is true when members of a process come into decision making situations with different, often, conflicting goals such as cost reduction versus higher service level or higher yield versus higher load factor. One of the most damaging problems related to horizontal boundaries occurs when members of a process come to see each other as enemies. Ashkenas, Ulrich, Jick, and Kerr (1994) give an example of an airline where baggage handling at a particular airport was the responsibility of two separate teams. One team handled check-in and ticketing while the other was responsible for loading, transferring, and off-loading. Teams were reluctant to help each other, to accept advice from 'them', and frequently argued over which team was responsible for baggage handling errors. Finally, horizontal boundaries can also create problems if it forces customers to do their own integration of products and services. In the airline industry, there are customers who would prefer to customize their own bundle of products and services in order to accommodate special needs in terms of price, scheduling, and destination. On the other hand, there are customer groups that want a one-stop-shopping experience. They do not want to be handed from one airline to another because an airline cannot book to a code share partner directly or to be told that seats cannot be assigned through to final destination, etc.

There are a number of possible solutions to the problems of horizontal boundaries including the close, cross-alliance, cross-functional coordination already mentioned. These efforts need to encourage and teach teamwork, define measures of shared resources success, restructure quickly to meet changing customer needs, and create new mental models that do not see the world as divided by clearly defined borders between functions and companies (Ashkenas, Ulrich, Jick, and Kerr, 1995; Berardino and Frankel, 1998). In addition, many service organizations have created 'customer managers' who are responsible for coordinating all the needs of specific customers or specific customer groups. This approach clearly makes sense for major customers.

Several problems can arise on the way to upward equalization. The traditional customers of alliance partners may not have similar expectations. After over twenty years of deregulation, the expectations of many U.S. travelers in seating comfort, food, etc have declined below the expectations of many European and Asian travelers. This difference in expectations may make agreeing on a level of service more difficult. This is further complicated by airline cost, pricing structure, and available resources for quality improvements. Alliance partners may find it necessary to establish inter-alliance programs for training, cost sharing, and other quality improvements. Another stumbling block to success is the need to share more information between partners on service offerings, prices, and amenities. In short, partners may be called upon to share the revenue management information that has traditionally been treated as proprietary or share facilities that certain partners have spent years developing. Such attempts can create three problems for alliance members. The first problem is a legal one; without anti-trust immunity, this level of sharing would be deemed illegal in most regions of the world. The second problem relates to the technological difficulties of systems integration. The sheer size and cost of integrating information systems can be very daunting to alliance members. Finally, alliance members must perceive a benefit to such information sharing that is greater than the risk of 'giving up' the potentially valuable information on customers and operations. Alliances will need to find ways to track the costs and benefits of joint alliance activities and to maximize joint benefits (Beradino and Frankel, 1998).

In light of the events on September 11th, there are questions about the 'quality' of security at airlines and some implications for alliance members. In general, quality is a function of creating a process, standardizing it, and incrementally improving on the process. However, security is an exception in several ways. First, 'standardization' should not be the goal, even if the level of standardization is raised. Any 'established standard' makes it easier for acts of terror to occur because actions are predictable. The major concern for alliances is the overall 'quality' of security among all partners in order to prevent lax security in one partner from jeopardizing security within the alliance as a whole. Second, governments might be willing to relax some aspects of antitrust enforcement if it is perceived to impede the ability of airlines to coordinate on security efforts.

Catching Customers, Delivering Benefits

If alliances are all about catching more customers, then there are two basic approaches - weave and throw a wider web or throw a finer web over a smaller area. At the present time, the Star alliance appears to be striving to master the first approach, while the Wings alliance has focused more on the second approach. In fact, these approaches are not mutually exclusive. As competition increases, many of the alliances will seek to do both. Either way, the need for lateral, cross-alliance coordination exists. For this reason, antitrust legislation and enforcement is taking on new meaning in many regions of the world and the need for a coordinated international approach is gaining ground. While the events of September 11th have introduced some uncertainty as to the future of the airline industry and the direction of liberalization efforts, there is equally compelling reasons to suggest that in the long term liberalization may increase as nations struggle to stabilize a viable airline industry. In this vein, nations will be asked to rationalize and harmonize their respective policies. The success or failure of these efforts will have a profound effect on airlines and the alliances to which many belong. Understanding the potential benefits and dangers of antitrust policy is a necessary step in designing lasting, effective alliances. Airlines can not afford to be anything but proactive in their approach to antitrust issues because the alliance that can (given anti-trust immunity) and is willing to weave a finer network will be able to achieve the 'global, seamless service' that all alliances currently hold out as a goal of their partnership.

References

Akao, Y. (1999), 'ISO 900 and 14000 Systems Supported by QFD' in S.K.M. Ho (ed.), *Proceedings of the Fourth International Conference on ISO 900 and TQM*, pp. 325-331.

Akao, Y. (1990), *Introduction to Quality Function Deployment*, JUSE Press.

Ashkensas, R., Ulrich, D., Jick, T. and Kerr, S. (1995), *The Boundaryless Organization*, Jossey-Bass, San Francisco.

Barlow, G.L. (1999), 'QFD within the Service Sector - A Case Study on how the House of Quality was used within Service Operations', in S.K.M. Ho (ed.), *Proceedings of the Fourth International Conference on ISO 900 and TQM*, pp. 332-340.

Berardino, F. and Frankel, C. (1998), 'Keeping Score', *Airline Business*, September, pp. 82-87.

Binggeli, U. and Pompeo, L. (2002), 'Hyped Hopes for Europe's Low Cost Airlines', *McKinsey Quarterly*, online edition, www.mckinsey/quarterly.com.

Davidow, W.H. and Malone, M.S. (1992). *The Virtual Corporation*, HarperBusiness Press, New York.

Ekdahl, F., Gustafsson, A. and Edvardsson, B. (1999), 'Customer-oriented Service Development at SAS', *Managing Service Quality*, vol. 9, pp. 403-410.

Feldman, J.M. (1998), 'Making Alliances Work', *Air Transport World*, June, pp. 27-35.

Fraser, D. (1996), 'A Personal Approach', *Airline Business*, March, pp. 58-61.

Glab, J. (1997), 'The People's Choice', *Frequent Flyer*, June, pp. 24-28.

Keidel, R.W. (1994), 'Rethinking Organizational Design', *The Academy of Management Executive*, vol. 8, pp. 12-30.

Merrill Lynch, Pierce, Fenner & Smith, Inc. (1998), *Global Airline Alliances: Why Alliances Really Matter from an Investment Perspective*, Merrill Lynch, Pierce, Fenner & Smith Inc., New York.

Merrill Lynch, Pierce, Fenner & Smith (1999), *Global Airline Alliances: Global Alliance Brands*, Merrill Lynch, Pierce, Fenner & Smith Inc., New York.

Rhoades, D.L. and Waguespack, B. (2000), 'Service Quality in the U.S. Airline Industry: Variations in Performance Within and Between Firms', *Journal of Air Transportation World Wide*, vol. 5, pp. 60-77.

Sparks, D. (1999), 'Partners', *Business Week*, October 25, pp. 106-112.

Wells, A.T. (1994), *Air Transportation: A Management Perspective*, Wadsworth Publishing Company, Belmont.

Chapter 12

Strategic Actions

When 1 + 1 = Too Much

As mentioned in Chapter 8, the proposed British Airways-American Airlines alliance raised concerns on both sides of the Atlantic that the combination of these two giants was simply too much for consumers to bear and the politicians who represented them to accept. At issue was the fact that a BA-AA alliance would monopolize many Trans-Atlantic routes. Critics argued that the logical strategic response of an approved BA-AA alliance would be to rationalize their route structure, that is to say, allocate routes between themselves in such a way as to avoid direct competition. For consumers, restricted competition would mean higher fares. In an open market, the high profits accruing to BA-AA would encourage new entrants, thus reducing fares. However, such open competition does not yet exist in the arena of international aviation. This was the stated basis for U.S. government insistence on tying BA-AA approval to an open skies agreement with the United Kingdom. On the other side of the Atlantic, EU officials reasoned that an open Atlantic meant little without open landing slots and pressed for the BA surrender of Heathrow landing slots. In the United Kingdom, concern was being expressed that an open skies agreement would give U.S. carriers access to Europe while denying British carriers access to the North American market. Further complicating the matter, individual carriers within the US (US Airways) and the UK (British Midlands) argued that this high level wrangling was denying them the strategic opportunity to enter trans-Atlantic routes. Upping the ante, the Association of European Airlines (AEA) and the European Commission have increased their calls for an even broader change in the aviation landscape with the Trans-Atlantic Common Aviation Area. Now talk of further consolidation has aviation experts rewriting the alliance landscape.

At the heart of all this apparent chaos, airlines, alliances, and public officials are grappling with questions of strategic behavior and competitive advantage. How are alliances changing strategic choices? Would consolidation create more cost-effective competitors capable of meeting ever greater consumer needs or fewer choices and less competition? How will liberalization change airline and alliance behavior? The international aviation industry is facing a wide range of possible futures and it is probably too soon to provide definitive answers to all the questions these possibilities raise, but this chapter will address the emerging trends in alliance behavior and outline several possible scenarios for the future. Given the uncertainties, airlines and government officials should have contingency plans for each of these possible futures.

In the Beginning

Airlines that serve a large number of destinations tend to be preferred by consumers because such an airline can minimize their travel time and offer a higher quality of service (Tretheway and Oum, 1992). Responding to this preference, carriers have sought to develop extensive domestic, continental, and international service networks. In the US following deregulation, carriers consolidated and created hub-and-spoke networks to achieve continental coverage. Achieving international coverage, however, proved more difficult. American Airlines initially attempted to apply the domestic model of network coverage to foreign markets by creating foreign spokes to their US hubs. They encountered two problems: legal barriers created by the bilateral system and high financial costs. We have already discussed many of the legal barriers to establishing an efficient foreign network. In regard to the financial costs, Oum, Taylor, and Zhang (1993) have estimated that the potential revenues of a 'successful' global network would be more than $30 billion. This is at least twice the revenue level of the largest existing mega-carriers. They argued that a single carrier simply could not marshal the financial resources to establish such a network. Whether a single carrier could administer such a network is a matter we will address later.

Given these problems and the legal restrictions on international mergers and acquisitions, strategic alliances have become the method of choice in global network construction. They allow individual carriers to compensate for strategic weaknesses in their operations or route structure. The savings in cost and time over internal development can be substantial. In fact, outsourcing to alliance partners may be the easiest way to control costs, but there are additional problems with this approach. First, it is difficult to restart an activity once it is discontinued. So, if the alliance falls apart or the quality of the work does not meet standards, bringing that activity back in-house can be expensive. Second, such cost savings require more airline integration than many carriers are currently willing to accept (Feldman, 1999).

As far as route construction, Oum and Park (1997) envisioned the following future for airline alliances. First, global alliances would consist of a two-tier system of super-hub anchor carriers on each continent and junior spoke carriers feeding the continental super-hubs. Second, the number of major global alliances, constrained by the limited number of major continental carriers, would be no more than five or so. Finally, carriers left out of the 'system' would be forced to become niche players. By and large, these predictions are coming to pass with the formation of four major mega-alliances (Star, Oneworld, Wings, and SkyTeam) and the announcement of secondary and tertiary carriers (Merrill Lynch, 1999). Although further consolidation in the North American and European airline industry is also likely to result in shifts in current alliance partnerships, there will probably continue to be three to four mega-alliances in the future. What remains to be seen is the level of integration these mega-alliances will seek and achieve.

All in the Family

Anderson Consulting has identified three integration platforms in strategic alliances based on the level of control (degree of carrier control over resources) and degree of global coverage (Ott, 1999). Bilateral strings are essentially based on a series of international code shares between partners. These alliances string together a moderate number of international destinations. Andersen Consulting classified US Airways, Japan Airlines, and America West as string airlines. The Regional Cluster is the second type of integration platform. As the name implies, the backbone this platform is several regional airlines. The geographic coverage is approximately equivalent to the bilateral string, but the level of control is greater. Swissair and the Qualifier alliance were an example of this type of platform. The final integration platform is the global skeleton. This platform has greater coverage than the other two and slightly lower levels of control than the regional cluster. Andersen Consulting envisions all three platforms moving toward the Global Network with its maximum global coverage and balance between alliance control and member independence. Based on their analysis, the four mega-alliances are roughly equivalent in terms of global coverage while the ranking on control is as follows: Wings, Star, SkyTeam, and Oneworld. Comparing this to the Merrill Lynch report cited in Chapter 8, there are two areas of disagreement. The Merrill Lynch report ranked the Delta-led alliance well below Star and Oneworld in geographic reach and market size. Key weaknesses were the lower number of destinations (654 for Delta as compared to 974 for STAR and 745 for Oneworld) and the lack of major market presence. In another section, Merrill Lynch found that the Delta alliance had a dominant presence in only two of the top thirty international markets. (NOTE: Their report was released before the official announcement of the alliance with Air France and the collapse of Atlantic Excellence.) The second area of disagreement concerns the coverage of the Wings alliance. Merrill Lynch rated the geographic network of Wings low but the network density high. If the Anderson Consulting report is combining these two aspects of network coverage, then this discrepancy is understandable. This would also explain why the Wings alliance appears to be bypassing the global skeleton platform since it has already achieved a high level of network density and linkage. In short, both consulting companies are in general agreement on the direction and relative ranking of the mega-alliance groups. The push now is likely to be on putting meat on the bones of these alliances.

Where's the Beef?

There appear to be six key areas of development for alliance skeletons. The first area is route overlap or increasing 'unduplicated route miles/kilometers. Several studies have shown that complementary (non-overlapping) alliance networks increase overall demand and passenger volumes (Park, 1997; US GAO, 1995) while parallel alliances decrease demand (Park, 1997). The problem for airlines and regulators lies with addressing pre-existing alliance overlap. Airlines clearly have some incentives to reduce overlap, especially if the overlap results in decreased demand and/or lower fares. The degree of intra-alliance competition might also damage efforts to build a cooperative alliance arrangement. We will deal more with the problems of cooperating and competing in the chapter on alliance duration and stability. Regulators are also concerned with the degree of competition/cooperation and any action that might decrease capacity and increase fares. The second area of development involves 'filling the gaps' in overall global coverage and in specific destination departure levels. Given the stated consumer preference for airlines with wide coverage and increased connections, the goal of a superior global alliance would be to serve more destinations more frequently than their competitors. All the mega-alliance groups are looking to fill major gaps in Asia, the Middle East, and Africa (Merrill Lynch, 1999; Taverna, 1999). Wings is positioned to add Kenya Airways as a possible African partner (Hill, 1999a) and Malaysian Airlines as an Asian partner (Reuters, 2000). Other alliance groups are also active in courting prospective members (Flint, 1999). In line with this notion of a superior global alliance is the third key area of alliance branding. In addition to the sort of advertising employed by the Star alliance, alliances may seek other areas of alliance integration and standardization such as joint facilities, alliance terminal grouping, harmonized (merged) distribution networks including CRS systems and joint internet booking sites, and common service standards such as seat pitch and reclining angle. The Star alliance has announced their intention to pursue many of these areas, although they have encountered resistance to some of their plans, specifically alliance terminal grouping (Taverna, 1999). The Wings alliance is committed to a single yield and revenue-accounting system and uses a program called Interhost Through Check In to communicate essential passenger information between airlines (Feldman, 1998; Ott, 1999). Oneworld has yet to aggressively brand itself in part because of the BA-AA approval question while the Qualiflyer group in Europe has maintained separate names although they are combining lounges, check-in facilities, etc. Issues of integration and standardization are also important in the fourth key area of development - cost reduction. The major alliances have already begun to reduce operating costs through such actions as facility sharing and maintenance and other ground personnel utilization, but there are a number of other fruitful areas to explore including joint purchasing, combined cargo operations, wet-leasing, joint marketing, etc. Examples of such activities include the joint aircraft purchasing done within the Qualiflyer group (Swissair, Sabena, and Austrian), the widebody maintenance consortiums formed by two groups of European airlines in the early 1970s (KSSU-KLM, SAS, Swissair, UTA and Atlas Alitala, Lufthansa, Air France, and Sabena), the AirLiance Material joint venture formed by Star alliance partners Air Canada, Lufthansa, and United to reduce maintenance costs and improve parts provisioning, and the leasing of simulator time to alliance partners by American and United (Airlines International, 1999). There are obvious risks to the development of some types of joint activities. These efforts require more integration of operation, more information sharing, and greater trust. Given the current transient nature of alliance, this entails great risks. Efforts to untangle the already integrated aspects of the now defunct merger between KLM and Alitalia are a case-in-point. The fifth key area of development is the creation of the secondary and tertiary tiers of national/regional carriers whose job it will be to increase feed to alliance hubs. From an alliance perspective, the more developed and exclusive these arrangements the better they will be able to extract benefits (Berardino and Frankel, 1998). However, such exclusivity raises anti-competitive fears in many countries as we have already discussed in the chapter on anti-trust law. The final area of development, and probably the last to receive formal attention, is likely to be multipoint competition.

Research on competitive behavior suggests that it is driven by both the ability to compete and the motivation to engage in competition (Chen, 1996). Global networks give alliances the ability to compete in numerous markets. The motivation to compete (or not to compete) is based on other considerations including expected retaliation by competitors. Research at the firm level indicates that multi-market contact 'gives a firm the option to respond to an attack by a rival not only in the challenged market, but also in other markets in which both compete' (Gimeno, 1999: 102). In the United States, major airlines seek to maintain some presence in all their competitors' markets. Those that are successful 'are able to simultaneously: (a) enjoy lower intensity of price competition from their rivals, (b) display less intense competitive behavior of their own, and (c) maintain a higher equilibrium market share' (Gimeno, 1999: 122). Retaliation in an attacker's hub has been shown to be a powerful and effective response to attacks on one's own hub (Nomani, 1990a, 1990b). Assuming that competition eventually moves from the airline to the alliance level, then multipoint alliance contact will gain increasing importance. This also assumes that a liberalizing global aviation system allows for the development of such a framework. Merrill Lynch (1999) has examined the market presence of the mega-alliances in thirty world markets. Of these thirty markets, fifteen have an alliance with 50 percent or more market share. This indicates the basic framework of a multipoint system that, given regulatory freedom, would allow one alliance group to respond to an attack in their dominant market by acting in the attacker's market.

The Finer Points

The discussion of multipoint competition links structure to behavior. Research points to other behavioral possibilities in alliance strategic action. At the firm level, organizational size has been positively associated with economies of scale, experience, brand name recognition, and market power (Hambrick, MacMillan, and Day, 1982; Kelly and Amburgey, 1991). Small firms tend to be more flexible, faster, innovative, and risk-seeking. Such firms initiate more competitive moves and implement them quicker than their larger rivals (Chen and Hambrick, 1995; Fiegenbaum and Karnani, 1991; Hitt, Hoskisson, and Harrison, 1991; Katz, 1970). Large firms initiate fewer actions, tend to be slower to implement agreed upon actions, and are less likely to change core features (Chen and Hambrick, 1995; Kelly and Amburgey, 1991). However, as Chen and Hambrick (1995) found they respond quickly to perceived attack. This rapid response to attack may indicate a greater need to protect their reputation (Fombrun and Shanley, 1990), to signal stakeholders (Pfeffer, 1982) and competitors (Axelrod, 1984) that they are not passive, and to deter further attack (Chen and MacMillan, 1992).

As we have noted earlier, the size of an organization or alliance necessary to establish a successful global network is tremendous (Oum, Taylor, and Zhang, 1993). There are already signs that administering these networks is proving time consuming, frustrating, and cumbersome. British Airways has estimated that its alliance staff spends two-thirds of their time attending or traveling to meetings. The Star alliance reduced the number of alliance committees from 25 to 15 and is rethinking the overall alliance structure. Even apparently simple decision making such as joint airbag purchase has proved difficult (Feldman, 1998). Alliances run the risk that their alliance structure may in fact become too great a burden and allow quicker, more nimble competitors to overtake them.

Succeeding at Alliances

The rapidly changing aviation landscape will require successful alliances to address two key areas. The first key area is alliance structure; structures must be designed to increase the speed of action and reaction. As stated above, one of the major disadvantages of size is the drag it places on an organization's ability to act, react, and change. The joint decision making between multiple alliance partners exacerbates this problem. As noted in Chapter 8, the Star alliance is considering ways to strengthen its management board. A holding structure is one possibility. The SairGroup had a holding structure, but this arrangement may have had more to do with the fact that Swissair was a non European Common Market Carrier and was thus restricted in its European airline growth prospects. On the other hand, the potential for growth in related businesses in the structure (Technical Services, Catering, etc) was much better. Other options would include the creation of stand-alone joint ventures such as the AirLiance Material purchasing unit of Star. As a legally separate entity, decision making should be simplified over the currently cumbersome multi-level cross-functional team structure currently utilized by many alliances.

A second key to surviving in the current environment involves multiple scenarios and contingency plans for possible critical changes in the landscape. As the Anderson Consulting and Merrill Lynch reports suggest, the current trend in airline alliances appears to be toward global networks, mega-alliances with their continental anchors and secondary national and regional feeder structures, however, several factors could change the equation. As Craig Jenks, president of the Airline/Aircraft Projects consultancy has noted 'the global alliance model apparently makes fifth and seventh freedoms redundant due to the availability of a foreign partner through alliances and code sharing' but a number of carriers have the right to exercise such freedoms (Walker, 1998). In an increasingly liberalizing international aviation market, some carriers may decide to exercise this option rather than pursue alliances, particularly if time and coordination issues appear to make alliances 'not worth the trouble'. A second factor in the alliance equation is the establishment of a regime such as the proposed Transatlantic Common Aviation Area. If implemented in its fullest form to include cabotage and the right of establishment, then market access ceases to be a major driver of alliance formation. In addition, changes to existing laws regarding foreign ownership could lead to an increase in cross-border mergers and acquisitions. Julius Maldutis of CIBC Oppenheimer has suggested that alliances are merely poor substitutes for mergers (Flint, 1999). He has also pointed to signs that government regulators in the US and EU are prepared to rethink the issue of competitiveness and consumer benefits. Another possibility is that aviation will become included in the World Trade Organization/General Agreement on Trade and Tariffs framework, although this is not likely to occur anytime in the near future. This would hypothetically place aviation in the 'same boat' as other world industries. Not only would aviation become part of the multilateral trading system and subject to the rules set down in the 1994 multilateral trade treaty that resulted from the Uruguay Round of the GATT negotiations, but the World Trade Organization has enforcement mechanisms in place to handle country violations of fair trade and market access policies. Finally, it is not entirely clear what effect the events of September 11th will have on airlines or the alliances that they form. Widespread global bankruptcy and/or consolidation have the potential to change not only the membership of alliances but alter the competitive dynamics as well. Government actions to support failing airlines or require extensive new regulations will also affect the situation.

The Art of Maneuver

As this book goes to print, the international aviation landscape is in the process of redefining itself. This was true before September 11th and remains true today even though there is no clear direction for change. There is little question that those calling for liberalization are currently in the majority, but how fast and how far liberalization proceeds will be anyone's guess, particularly in light of the airline industry's current struggle to survive. In *The Art of War* Sun Tzu has said that 'nothing is more difficult than the art of maneuver. What is difficult is to make the devious route the most direct and to turn misfortune to advantage' (102). We are likely to see a great deal of maneuvering in the near future. Where it leads and who will achieve the advantage has yet to become clear.

References

Axelrod, R. (1984), *The Evolution of Cooperation*, Basic Books, New York.

Berardino, F. and Frankel. C. (1998). 'Keeping Score', *Airline Business*, September, pp. 82-87.

Chen, M.J. (1996), 'Competitor Analysis and Inter-firm Rivalry: Toward a Theoretical Integration', *Academy of Management Review*, vol. 21, pp. 100-134.

Chen, M.J. and Hambrick, D.C. (1995), 'Speed, Stealth, and Selective Attack: How Small Firms Differ from Large Firms in Competitive Behavior', *Academy of Management Journal*, vol. 38, pp. 453-482.

Chen, M.J. and MacMillan, I.C. (1992), 'Nonresponse and Delayed Response to Competitive Moves: The Role of Competitor Dependence and Action Irreversibility', *Academy of Management Journal*, vol. 35, pp. 359-370.

Feldman, J.M. (1998), 'Making Alliances Work', *Air Transport World*, June, pp. 27-35.

Feldman, J.M. (1999), 'Disappearing act', *Air Transport World*, February, pp. 25-30.

Fiegenbaum, A. and Karnani, A. (1991), 'Output Flexibility - A Competitive Advantage for Small Firms', *Strategic Management Journal*, vol. 12, pp. 101-124.

Flint, P. (1999), 'Alliance Paradox', *Air Transport World*, April, pp. 33-36.

Fombrun, C. and Shanley, M. (1990), 'What's in a name? Reputation Building and Corporate Strategy', *Academy of Management Journal*, vol. 33, pp. 233-258.

Gimeno, J. (1999), 'Reciprocal Threats in Multimarket Rivalry: Staking Out Spheres of Influence in the U.S. Airline Industry', *Strategic Management Journal*, vol. 20, pp. 101-128.

Griggin, S.B. (ed.) (1963), *The Art of War*, Oxford Press, New York.

Hambrick, D.C., MacMillan, I.C. and Day, D.L. (1982), 'Strategic Attributes and Performance in the BCG Matrix-A PIMS-based Analysis of Industrial Product Businesses', *Academy of Management Journal*, vol. 25, pp. 510-531.

Hill, L. (1999a), 'Out of (East) Africa', *Air Transport World*, August, pp. 95-97.

Hill, L. (1999b), 'Global Challenger', *Air Transport World*, December, pp. 52-54.

Hitt, M.A., Hoskisson, R.E. and Harrison, J.S. (1991), 'Strategic Competitiveness in the 1990s Challenges and Opportunities for U.S. Executives', *Academy of Management Executive*, vol. 5, pp. 7-22.

Katz, R.L. (1970), *Cases and Concepts in Corporate Strategy*, Prentice-Hall, Englewood Cliffs.

Kelly, D. and Amburgey, T.L. (1991), 'Organizational Inertia and Momentum: A Dynamic Model of Strategic Change', *Academy of Management Journal*, vol. 34, pp. 591-612.

Merrill Lynch, Pierce, Fenner & Smith (1999), *Global Airline Alliances: Global Alliance Brands Create Value*, Merrill Lynch, New York.

Nomani, A.Q. (1990a), 'Fare Games: Airlines May be Using a Price-data Network to Lessen Competition', *Wall Street Journal*, June 28, pp. A1-A8.

Nomani, A.Q. (1990b), 'Fare Warning: How Airlines Trade Price Plans', *Wall Street Journal*, October 9, pp. B1-B10.

Ott, J. (1999), 'Alliances Spawn a Web of Global Networks', *Airline Business*, August 23, pp. 52-53.

Ott, J. (1999), 'Wings Partners Seek Ways to Maintain Alliance Edge', *Airline Business*, August 23, pp. 61-62.

Oum, T.H., Taylor, A.J. and Zhang, A. (1993), 'Strategic Airline Policy in the Globalizing Airline Network', *Transportation Journal*, vol. 32, pp. 14-30.

Oum, T.H. and Park, J.H. (1997), 'Airline Alliances: Current Status, Policy Issues, and Future Directions', *Journal of Air Transport Management*, vol. 3, pp. 133-144.

Park, J.H. (1997), *Strategic Airline Alliance: Modeling and Empirical Analysis*, Ph.D. dissertation, Faculty of Commerce and Business Administration, University of British Colombia.

Pfeffer, J. (1982), *Organizations and Organizational Theory*, Pitman, Boston.

Reuters (2000), 'KLM, MAS in quite intensive Wings Talks', March 15.

Taverna, M.A. (1999), 'Star Alliance Approaches Next Phase of Collaboration', *Airline Business*, August 23, pp. 58-60.

Tretheway, M.W. and Oum, T.H. (1992), *Airline Economics: Foundation for Strategy and Policy*, The Centre for Transportation Studies, University of British Colombia.
US General Accounting Office (US GAO) (1995), 'Airline Alliances Product Benefits, but Effect on Competition is Uncertain', *GAO/RCED-95*, April.
Walker, K. (1998), 'Lifting the 7th Veil', *Airline Business*, October, pp. 73-76.

Part III
Future Possibilities

Chapter 13

Pause to Reflect

Images

The images of 9/11 have been forever etched into the memory of the world and the individuals who lived through them. To ask someone where they were when the events took place and what they remembered of those first moments will become a new ritual marking one generation from the next. What will fade are the details of these events. It is important for this book, the aviation industry, and all those interested in the future of aviation that these 'details' remain firmly in the foreground. The purpose of this chapter is to set these events in order beginning with September 11th itself and progressing through the ground stop and the immediate events afterwards that impacted aviation and will continue to influence the course of events.

September 11, 2001

8:45 a.m. - American Airlines Flight 11 from Boston to Los Angeles crashes into the north tower of the World Trade Center in New York City with 92 people onboard.

9:03 a.m. - United Airlines Flight 175 from Boston to Los Angeles crashes into the south tower of the World Trade Center with 65 people onboard.

9:06 a.m. - The Air Traffic Control System Communication Center sends a verbal notice of suspected hijacking out through the system.

9:08 a.m. - Written advisory issued to 'sterilize' the airspace surrounding New York City. No aircraft operations permitted.

9:26 a.m. - A national ground stop is ordered for all aircraft in U.S. airspace.

9:40 a.m. - American Airlines Flight 77 from Washington, D.C. to Los Angeles crashes into the Pentagon with 64 people onboard.

9:45 a.m. - All airborne aircraft are ordered to land at the nearest available airfield.

9:48 a.m. - The U.S. Capitol and the West Wing of the White House are evacuated.

9:49 a.m. - All aircraft banned from taking off in the United States.

9:50 a.m. - The south tower of the World Trade Center collapses.

9:58 a.m. - Emergency operator in Pennsylvania receives a call from a passenger on United Airlines Flight 93 from Newark to San Francisco stating that the plane has been hijacked.

10:00 a.m. - United Flight 93 crashes eighty miles southeast of Pittsburgh with 45 people onboard.

10:29 a.m. - The north tower of the World Trade Center collapses.

10:39 a.m. - A Notice to Airmen (NOTAM) is issued closing all U.S. airports.

11:00 a.m. - New York City Mayor Rudolph Giuilani orders lower Manhattan evacuated.

11:40 a.m. - U.S. military placed on alert and President George Bush taken to Barksdale Air Force Base in Louisiana.

1:20 p.m. - President Bush boards Air Force One for Offutt Air Force Base in Nebraska, the headquarters of the U.S. Strategic Air Command.

2:51 p.m. - U.S. military deploys destroyers and other equipment in New York and Washington.

5:20 p.m. - Building 7 of the World Trade Center collapses.

7:00 p.m. - President Bush arrives in Washington, D.C.

8:31 p.m. - President Bush addresses the nation.

September 12, 2001

• NATO invokes Article V (which states that an armed attack on one member shall be considered an attack on all members) for the first time.

- FAA allows a limited reopening of U.S. airspace to allow flights diverted the prior day to continue to their original destination. Only passengers on the original flights are permitted to board.

- FAA allows airlines to reposition empty aircraft.

- Curbside and off-airport check-in discontinued.

- Reserve boarding areas declared off-limits to all but ticketed passengers.

- Vehicles near terminal areas closely monitored.

- Canadian and Mexican airspace reopened.

September 13, 2001

- U.S. airspace reopened to commercial aviation effective 11:00 a.m.

- Boston's Logan airport and Washington, D.C.'s Reagan airport remain closed.

- U.S. bond markets open.

September 14, 2001

- General aviation aircraft operating under Instrument Flight Rules (IFR) allowed to resume operations.

- European Union day of mourning observed.

- President Bush activates 50,000 national guard and reserve members to help with recovery and security.

- The U.S. Congress unanimously approves $40 billion for emergency aid.

- The U.S. Security and Exchange Commission (SEC) relaxes rules on company buybacks.

September 15, 2001

- Some commercial and general aviation aircraft at Reagan National Airport moved to other airports without passengers and under IFR rules.

- Continental announces 12,000 layoffs.   Continental, American, United, and Northwest announce schedule cuts.

September 17, 2001

- Airlines begin receiving notice from their insurers that the seven-day cancellation clauses are being activated.

September 18, 2001

- United Airlines announces layoff of 20,000.

- Secretary of Transportation, Norman Mineta meets with airline executives and discusses financial aid to the airlines.

September 21, 2001

- The FAA lifted many of the restrictions on flight training operations allowing such operations to be conducted in single- and multi-engine, non-turbojet aircraft of less than 12,500 pounds maximum gross takeoff weight.

- Other restriction on general aviation under Visual Flight Rules (VFR) permitted outside Class B airspace.

- Sightseeing flights allowed to resume outside enhanced Class B airspace with the exception of Washington, D.C. and New York.

- VFR operations for banner towing, news reporting, traffic watch and airship/blimps remain restricted.

- The Air Transportation Safety and System Stabilization Act is passed.

September 23, 2001

- FAA begins issuing government-backed insurance.

September 28, 2001

- FAA distributes a Notice to Airmen (NOTAM) on their responsibility to avoid restricted airspace and the procedures to follow if intercepted. Additional airspace barred from civilian aircraft.

October 12, 2001

- The FAA announced that private aircraft would be allowed to resume flying in the airspace around 15 major metropolitan areas - Houston, Kansas City, Memphis, New Orleans, St. Louis, Cleveland, Dallas-Ft. Worth, Honolulu, Minneapolis, Phoenix, Charlotte, Cincinnati, Salt Lake City, Seattle, and Tampa.

October 21, 2001

- The FAA announced that private aircraft would be allowed to resume flying around 12 more metropolitan areas - Atlanta, Las Vegas, Los Angeles, Miami, San Francisco, Denver, Detroit, Philadelphia, Pittsburg, San Diego, Chicago, and Orlando.

November 19, 2001

- The Aviation and Transportation Security Act is passed establishing the Transportation Security Administration.

Where Are We Going?

In his November 10, 2001 address to the General Assembly of the United Nations, President Bush compared the situation of post 9/11 with World War II saying 'in the Second World War, we learned there is no isolation from evil. We affirmed that some crimes are so terrible they offend humanity itself, and we resolved that the aggressions and ambitions of the wicked must be opposed early, decisively, and collectively before they threaten us all. That evil has returned, and the cause is renewed.' The international aviation system of today was born in the events of the Second World War. The international aviation system of tomorrow is being shaped by the events of 9/11 and is waiting to be born. The succeeding chapters will examine the forces that are shaping the 'new' international aviation system. The final outcome has yet to be decided but all the elements are present to suggest what some of the possible paths to recovery will be.

References

FAA Office of Public Affairs (2001), 'FAA Restores General Aviation in 12 More Major Metropolitan Areas', Press release, October 21.

FAA Office of Public Affairs (2001), 'Airports to Remain Closed, Mineta Says', Press Release, September 12.

FAA Office of Public Affairs (2001), 'Statement of U.S. Secretary of Transportation Norman Y. Mineta', Press Release, September 13.

FAA Office of Public Affairs (2001), 'Some Aircraft to Move from Reagan National', Press Release, September 15.

FAA Office of Public Affairs (2001), 'Secretary Mineta Re-opens Skies to General Aviation', Press Release, September 14.

FAA Office of Public Affairs (2001), 'VFR Flight Training', Press Release, September 21.

FAA Office of Public Affairs (2001), 'Pilots Notified of Restricted Airspace; Violators Face Military Action', Press Release, September 28.

FAA Office of Public Affairs (2001), 'FAA Restores Private Flying in 15 Major Metropolitan Areas', Press Release, October 12.

Family Education Network (2002), 'Time Line of Events: September 11-18, 2001', www.teachervision.com.

Chapter 14

Counting the Costs

Coming to Terms

The scenes of 9/11 have been replayed in many forums and for many purposes since those events. Still, the world has only begun to come to terms with the magnitude of the losses suffered that day. It is very likely that we will be counting the costs for many years to come. The purpose of this chapter is to look at the economic costs of 9/11 for the airline industry, the network of industries associated with it, and the broader economy. These are certainly not the only costs of these acts of terror and they may prove to be the easiest to overcome, however, this book must leave to social and political scientists, ethicists, and theologians the work of sorting out these greater costs and helping us to understand and cope with them.

For the world aviation community, it will be difficult enough to deal with the magnitude of its losses and the possible implication of those events for the future of international aviation. This is not the first time that the industry has experienced a period of turmoil, but these events were so unexpected and devastating that few in the industry have yet come to terms with the long term possibilities and challenges. As mentioned in the introduction, 9/11 may well prove in retrospect to be one of those moments of discontinuous change that signals a radical shift in the environment and the organisms (firms) that inhabit it. Before looking at the future possibilities of the industry, it is important to understand the nature of the current discontinuity - the changes, the challenges, and the new contenders.

Examining the Overall Effects

The U.S. Congressional Joint Economic Committee has estimated that the first year costs of 9/11 and the War on Terror could reach US$41 billion for the U.S alone. This includes the estimated costs to civil aviation and air travelers from new security measures and increased waiting times. In addition to this figure, the new Transportation Security Administration has received US$1.35 billion already and is requesting an additional US$4.4 billion in order to carry out its mandate to take over passenger and baggage screening at U.S. airports. In the broader economy, it is estimated that increased travel expenses, workplace security, and information technology (primarily for tracking and security) have added as much as US$151 billion to the general cost of businesses. Businesses now struggle under the burden of 'longer cross-border transfers, heavier demand for information and data, intelligence agency upgrades, higher construction costs, more government regulation, costlier shipping, slower mails, and a myriad of other costs' (Mann, 2002: 37). The Joint Economic Committee report goes on to suggest that their figures might considerably underestimate the economic damage since they did not 'take into account the multiple forms of terrorism, the difficulty of measuring intangible economic effects like the crowding out of productive capital, and the ways in which terrorists will revamp their tactics in response to the government's reinforcement of homeland security' (Mann, 2002: 37). Clearly, the overall economic costs of 9/11 are only beginning to be realized in the broader economy. For many industries and businesses, the costs were immediate and alarming.

Airline Effects

The world airline industry had been predicted to lose almost US$2 billion dollars in 2001 before the events of 9/11 due to the industry's longtime enemy-economic downturn. After 9/11, the losses mounted rapidly. According to the Air Transport Association (ATA), the U.S. industry losses for 2001 totaled US$7.7 billion and estimated 2002 losses are expected to top US$9 billion (ATA, 2002). The International Air Transport Association (IATA) reported losses on international scheduled service of US$12 billion for 2001, making it the worst single year loss in the industry's history. The 2002 projections call for losses of only US$5 to US$7 billion (BBC News, 2002).

Aviation losses fall into several categories. The most obvious losses are in the area of airline revenues. The first revenue losses were incurred during the shutdown of the U.S. aviation system immediately after the attacks of 9/11. IATA has estimated that approximately 4,000 aircraft around the world were grounded in the days immediately following 9/11. The U.S. shutdown from September 11-15 is estimated to have cost world airlines US$1 billion per day (M2 Communications LTD, 2001). While these costs were borne primarily by the U.S. carriers, foreign carriers with significant traffic to the U.S. were also impacted by the shutdown and grounding of their fleet (Flottau, 2001). Slowdowns were also experienced in the Canadian and Mexican market as a result of the shutdown (M2 Communications, LTD, 2001). Transport Canada has estimated that the shutdown and gradual return to service cost Canadian airlines roughly C$150 million (Fiorino, 2002). Estimates from Europe suggest that carriers may have lost up to US$171.4 million during the shutdown with Lufthansa and British Airways taking the greater hit (Sparaco, 2001).

In general, revenues in the airline industry are closely tied to passenger and cargo traffic numbers, load factors and yields. Worldwide monthly traffic figures (passenger and cargo) prior to 9/11 had shown little change over the same period in 2000 despite the economic slowdown. While passenger numbers were down slightly, the numbers for cargo traffic were up sufficiently to offset passenger declines. When the traffic figures for all of 2001 are examined, however, there is a 3 percent decrease in passenger traffic and a 5 percent drop in cargo traffic. Passenger load factors fell from 72% in 2000 to 70 percent in 2001. The numbers internationally indicate a decline from 71 percent in 2000 to 69 percent in 2001 (ICAO, 2002). Operating expenses declined about 0.5% due to somewhat lower fuel prices over all of 2001, but this was not enough to offset an estimated 7.1% decline in operating revenues. The net results i.e. after non-operating items and taxes were an operating loss of 3.9% (ICAO, 2002).

Yield which is a measure of the passenger revenue per mile has dropped sharply at many carriers as the traditional, high-yield business traveler failed to return to the airline travel market. The Air Transport Association estimates that business revenue decreased 22% for the period January-September 2002 (ATA, 2002). Since business fares typically account for about 60% of airline revenues and most of their profits, the traditional carriers have begun to experience sizable losses (Velocci, 2002). At carriers such as American Airlines, domestic yields were down 18 percent while international yields declined by 11% (Phillips, Fiorino, Velocci, and Smith, 2002).

Revenues were also affected by the imposition of additional costs following 9/11. For U.S. carriers, these costs include the US$2.50 per-segment ticket tax imposed in November 2001 to pay for aviation security and the so-called 'hassle factor' costs of airport security. Taxes on a U.S. ticket now account for 26% of the ticket price (ATA, 2002). Leo Mullin, CEO of Delta Airlines, has estimated that the tax will cost Delta alone approximately US$265 in 2002 while the 'hassle factor' could add billions of additional dollars to airline costs (Bond, 2002). Insurance costs also raised post-9/11. Many insurers fearful of further losses either revoked coverage for war risk and terrorism, requiring a separate, very expensive policy to cover these risks, or capped coverage at US$50 million. To aid struggling carriers, the FAA agreed to back war risk insurance policies (Bond, 2002). Likewise, European governments have stepped in to cover roughly US$1 billion in war risk for their carriers (Flottau, 2001). These costs are now estimated to average 0.8% of European airlines' direct costs, twice the level of 2001 (Sparaco, 2002). In Japan, the government has agreed to pay premiums of an additional US$0.35 per passenger. In the wake of 9/11, credit rating agencies imposed a further cost to airlines by downgrading their debt or placing them on credit watch. Several U.S. carriers already have debt equated with junk-bond status (Isidore, 2001).

The second category of losses relate to the reduction in flight schedules and routes. Following the passage of the Air Transportation Safety and System Stabilization Act, the Department of Transportation issued orders requiring airlines to provide detailed information on service reductions. The notices must be filed if a carrier plans to drop all scheduled flights to a U.S. community, leave a domestic market without nonstop service or reduce seats or flights to hubs by 33 percent or more during a 90-day period. United Airlines, Atlantic Coast, SkyWest, and Air Wisconsin (all of whom fly express service for United in designated areas) were among the first to file notices of service reductions (Bond, 2001). Since 9/11, the top five U.S. carriers, American, Delta, Continental, Northwest, and United, have all instituted schedule reductions of roughly 20%. In addition, a number of airlines have begun pulling out of marginal markets entirely. This has been a boon for lower cost carriers who have expanded into these markets attempting to gain permanent market share. The only major carriers in the U.S. to increase their number of departures during 2001 were Southwest and ATA (Rhoades and Waguespack, 2002).

Over in Europe, transatlantic traffic dropped 36.3% in the five week period immediately following 9/11 (Sparaco, 2001). As a consequence of the reduced demand, European airlines began to reduce their own schedules. British Airways announced a 10% reduction in schedule while Iberia instituted an 11 percent reduction (BBC News, 2001). The restructuring plan of British Airways has also called for the carrier to relinquish five long- and five short-haul routes (Barrie, 2002). Smaller European carriers such as Finnair have cut routes as well in an effort to improve profitability. As in the U.S. market, the primary beneficiary of these reductions has been low-cost carriers such as EasyJet and Ryanair (Milner and Osborn, 2002). These reductions in flight frequency and routes have allowed the industry to retire aircraft, reducing aircraft age and lowering operating costs (Mecham, 2002; Sparaco, 2002). Overall, world airlines grounded roughly 8% of their fleet and delayed or cancelled orders for new aircraft as part of an effort to reduce capacity (BBC News, 2002).

Table 14.1: Job Losses at Major International Carriers as of November 2001

Airline	Losses
Aer Lingus	2,500
Air Canada	5,000
Alitalia	2,500
American Airlines	20,000
All-Nippon Airways	1,080
Austrian Airlines	800
Braathens	800
British Airways	5,200
British Midlands	600
Continental Airlines	12,000
Delta	13,000
Iberia	3,000
KLM	2,500
Northwest Airlines	10,000
SAS	1,100
United Airlines	20,000
US Airways	11,000
Virgin Atlantic	1,200

Source: Adapted from BBC News, 'Round-up: Aviation in Crisis'.

The fourth category of losses reflects the impact of 9/11 on labor in the airline sector. Moving quickly, world airlines had already announced major cuts in their labor force two months after 9/11. Table 14.1 lists some of these job losses. The International Labor Organization (ILO) has suggested that job losses could total more than 200,000 for the aviation industry (Lubetkin, 2001). These job losses reflect not only the retirement of aircraft but the reduction in flight schedules instituted by many carriers. In many cases, these job cuts were not enough to improve the financial outlook of many of the carriers. British Airways' recently announced restructuring plan has recommended an additional cut of 5,800 jobs. This plan calls for a 23 percent workforce reduction by March 2004 which roughly equates to 43,700 jobs (Barrie, 2002). The economic turmoil has been reflected in the stock value of international carriers as well, leading to further losses by airline shareholders. Shares of the top eight U.S. carriers lost US$11.8 billion on the first day of trading following the attacks. This was roughly 41 percent of their combined market capitalization (Isidore, 2001). As Figure 14.1 indicates, share prices for the largest U.S. carriers have fallen to new lows. All of the major U.S. carriers with the exception of Southwest now carry bond ratings below BBB giving them the dubious label of junk bonds (ATA, 2002).

Figure 14.1: Stock Values at Top Five U.S. Carriers

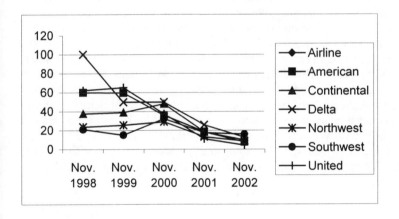

General Aviation

General aviation is defined as 'aviation other than military and commercial common carriage, including business flying, instructional flying, personal flying, and commercial flying such as agricultural spraying and aerial photography' (Wells, 1994). General aviation covers a very diverse group of firms ranging from large operators of flexible jet leasing to small flight schools operated out of regional airports. Estimating the costs to this segment of the industry is extremely difficult, however, the General Aviation Manufacturers Association (GAMA), a trade association representing U.S. manufacturers of general aviation aircraft and related equipment, was a key supporter of a bill before the U.S. House of Representative's Committee on Transportation and Infrastructure entitled the General Aviation Industry Reparations Act. This bill called for the establishment of US$2.5 billion in grants and loans for general aviation entities that incurred direct losses as a result of 9/11 and an additional US$5 billion for indirect small business losses (GAMA, 2002).

Tourism Effects

The World Tourism Organization has reported that international tourists' arrivals in 2001 fell by 1.3% to 688 million. While this does not sound like a significant drop, it is in fact the first decline in international arrivals since World War II (World Tourism Organizations, 2002). The Travel Business Roundtable/World Travel and Tourism Council Index of Leading Economic Indicators showed a decline in seven of its eight indicators: hotel/motel occupancy rates, hotel/motel room revenue, revenue passenger miles, employment for air transportation and transportation service industries, rental car travel and mileage per-day index, total travel agent sales, retail sales in eating and drinking establishments, and consumer confidence index. Their index declined 8.4% for September 2001 alone. For this period hotel/motel revenue fell 19.4% while travel agent sales dropped 8.9%. According to their latest study, an estimated US$76.7 billion in traveler spending could be lost in the 16 months following 9/11 (U.S. Newswire, 2001). Losses related to reduced travel hit almost every region of the world. Britain's tourism industry suffered losses of nearly 2.5 billion pounds in 2001, mainly due to a decline of between 15-25 percent on their long-haul visitors from the U.S., Canada, Australia, and Singapore (Northern Leisure, 2002). In Ireland, losses from U.S. visitors alone could total more 23 million pounds (Walsh, 2001). In the U.S., Pacific and South Atlantic regions are considered at high risk for tourism declines. This includes such popular destinations as Orlando, Florida, host not only to Disney World but Universal Studios and Sea World (PR Newswire, 2001). The International Labor Organization has estimated job losses in the tourism industry worldwide could exceed 8.8 million (International Labor Organization, 2001).

Aircraft Manufacturers

The slowdown in international aviation and efforts by carriers to reduce capacity and cut costs impacted operations and forecasts at the two largest aircraft manufacturers, Boeing and Airbus. The intense competition between these rivals coupled with the economic slowdown and the parking or retirement of aircraft that took place after 9/11 have resulted in 'rolling deferrals' by many carriers. Their best customers, large leasing companies, have for the most part deferred orders until 2005 (Mecham, 2002). While Boeing predicts that many of the retired aircraft will never return to service, estimating the number of returning aircraft and their impact on long-term orders is difficult. Boeing has announced that it is cutting aircraft deliveries for 2002 from 510-520 to about 380 and expects to deliver between 275-300 aircraft for 2003 (Smith, 2002). Meanwhile, rival Airbus expects to deliver no more than 300 in 2002, roughly 100 less than expected and could deliver fewer than 280 in 2003 (Sparaco, 2002). Analysts at Credit Suisse First Boston have suggested that the numbers for both carriers may prove optimistic and Standard & Poor's analysts do not see improvement in the market until 2004-2005 (Sparaco, 2002). At Boeing, reduced orders and deliver delays have led to job cuts of up to 30,000 (BBC News, 2001). In an attempt to sell new aircraft, Boeing is also expected to increase its exposure to customer financing about 43 percent over 2001 (Velocci, 2002a). Unfortunately, analysts fear that this strategy which started three years ago with the establishment of Boeing Capital Corp. has already placed Boeing at risk due to the very real possibility that financially strapped companies might file bankruptcy and return jets back to Boeing forcing Boeing to attempt to return the jets to service with other carriers at much lower rates (Holmes and Matlack, 2002).

Makers of regional jet aircraft are expected to fare better in the current crisis. As major carriers reduce schedule or eliminate routes, smaller, regional carriers are moving into vacated markets. Departures by regional jet worldwide have actually increased 42% since 9/11. In the U.S. alone, regional airlines have added more than 100 new routes (Ott, 2002). Several U.S. regional carriers are planning to use the current crisis among major carriers to increase capacity and market share. AirTrans plans to accelerate its fleet modernization plans and expand into several key markets such as Baltimore-Washington International. JetBlue plans to increase capacity 97% in 2002 and achieve load factors of 78% (Bond, 2002). Some of this expansion in fleets is likely to come at the expense of Boeing and Airbus as carriers replace larger aircraft with smaller, regional versions and major carriers leave marginal markets to affiliated regional carriers. Deliveries of regional jets are expected to reach 385 by 2003 (Ott, 2002). Despite this relatively rosy picture, Bombardier, maker of the Canadair Regional Jet, has called for a slight reduction in its production (Ott, 2002) and announced layoffs of 3,800 employees (BBC News, 2001).

Manufacturers of business jets also do not expect to see a major slump in activity for several reasons. First, the fractional ownership market is continuing to grow at about 15% a year. The 'hassle factor' and high business fares have made this an attractive alternative for U.S. businesses (Velocci, 2002). The fractional ownership option is also gaining markets in Europe (Sparaco, 1999). Second, there was a backlog in the industry overall and potential pent-up demand (Velocci, 2002b). The general aviation market has reported better than expected results with record sales in 2001 (GA Recovery, 2002).

These gloomy predictions on aircraft sales also affect the engine and avionics industry where Rolls-Royce expects deliveries to fall by 30% in 2002 and General Electric/Snecma where they anticipate a delivery reduction of 25% (Sparaco, 2002). At Honeywell, a major supplier of avionics to the airline industry, job losses are expected to reach 16,000 based on declining demand (BBC News, 2001).

Air Cargo

In the accounting period following 9/11, the two major U.S. air express carriers, UPS and FedEx, reported declines in revenue of 7.7 and 5.8% respectively. UPS, the world's largest parcel carrier, has estimated the direct losses from September

11 at US$130 million and saw net profit drop 19%. FedEx saw net profit fall by 35% in its first quarter, reflecting its greater dependence on pure express mail traffic. Both carriers anticipate continued erosion in the highly profitable over night market (Page, 2002). In their 2002 World Air Cargo Forecast, Boeing does expect to see an average annual growth in air cargo traffic of 6.4% over the next 20 year in part due to growth in China and the rest of Asia. This is good news for an industry that posted negative numbers for traffic growth for almost a year. However, industry experts are concerned that added security measures such as universal screening could cause as much as 76% of shipments to miss their intended flights, increasing delays and costs. Added screening devices could also add US$7.4 billion to industry costs in the U.S. alone (Air Cargo World, 2002).

Insurance

The insured losses for the 9/11 attacks have been projected at $40.2 billion making them the single largest economic loss in U.S. history. For U.S. insurers, 2001 was already shaping up to be a difficult year because of natural disaster losses. With an estimated loss of US$16.6 billion in property and business interruption losses associated with 9/11, the industry set a new record for 2001 with losses of US$24.1 billion (Hartwig, 2002). Munich Re, the world's largest reinsurance company has reported that it expects claims of as much as $1 billion euros from the attacks in New York and Washington (Financial Times, 2001). While many companies are pulling back or raising premiums for war and terrorism risk, Berkshire Hathaway has seen opportunity in a market where companies are paying 5-30% of the policy's face value, however, even risk taking entrepreneurs in the insurance industry are now carefully crafting policies to define and limit liability (Bianco, 2002).

Still Counting

The above list of industries and economic losses is not intended to be exhaustive. In fact, it will likely be several years before a reasonable estimate of total losses from 9/11 can be made with any degree of certainty. Still, this chapter has attempted to outline the magnitude of the losses, as we currently know them, for airlines and related industries in order to lay the groundwork for Chapters 15-17 which will explore the possible futures for international aviation and the firms that work and struggle in an environment that is forever changed in the aftermath of 9/11.

References

Air Cargo World (2002), 'Cargo's Security Phases', *Air Cargo World Online*, October 15.
Air Transport Association (2002), 'State of the U.S. Airline Industry: A Report on Recent Trends for U.S. Air Carriers, 2002-2003', Air Transport Association.

Barrie, D. (2002), 'British Airways Seeks Billion-Dollar Savings', *Aviation Week and Space Technology*, February 18, p. 43.

BBC News (2002), 'Airlines Still Facing Big Losses', September 16.

BBC News (2001), 'Round-up: Aviation in Crisis', November 22.

Bianco, A. (2002), 'Buffet Jumps in Where Other Fear to Tread', *Business Week*, July 15, pp. 120-121.

Bond, D. (2002), 'Back to Capital Hill: Airlines Seek More Relief', *Aviation Week and Space Technology*, September 30, pp. 38-47.

Bond, D. (2001), 'With Airlines on Relief, The Feds Demand Data', *Aviation Week and Space Technology*, October 8, pp. 31-32.

Financial Times (2001), 'Munich Re Faces Liabilities of 1 billion euros', *Financial Times*, September 12.

Fiorino, F. (2001), 'Canada and Japan Seek to Ease Impact of Terrorism', *Aviation Week and Space Technology*, October 8, pp. 33-31.

Flottau, J. (2001), 'Europeans Take Aim at U.S. Carrier Bailout', *Aviation Week and Space Technology*, October 5, p. 66.

Foss, B. (2002), 'Airlines Expect to Lose $8 Billion', *AP Wire Service*, New York, September 26.

GAMA (2002), 'GAMA Urges Congress to Pass GA Relief Bill', *GAMA News 02-5*, February 26.

Hartwig, R.P. (2002), 'Industry Financials and Outlook: 2001-Year End Results', *Insurance Information Institute*, Online Edition, October 16.

Holmes, S. and Matlack, C. (2002), 'Caught in United's Downdraft: How will Boeing's Finance and Leasing Business be Affected?', *Business Week*, December 23, p. 35.

ICAO (2002), 'Events of 11 September Had Strong Negative Impact on Airline Financial Results for 2001', Press Release, May 28.

International Labor Organization (2001), 'ILO Meeting on Hotels, Tourism Endorses Action to Combat Crisis', *Press Release*, October 26.

Isidore, C. (2001), 'Economy Down in the Air', *CNNMoney* Internet Edition, September 21.

Lubetkin, W. (2001), 'ILO Meetings Examine September 11 Impact on Tourism and Aviation', *Washington File*, Office of International Information Programs, U.S. Department of State, Washington, D.C., October 25.

M2 Communications Ltd (2001), 'Airline Industry Information', Internet edition.

Mann, P. (2002), 'Terrorism Cost Estimates Understate Total Damage', *Aviation Week and Space Technology*, May 13, pp. 36-37.

Mecham, M. (2002), 'Are There Too Many Aircraft Even with the Desert Full?', *Aviation Week and Space Technology*, April 22, pp. 40-41.

Milner, M. and Osborn, A. (2002), 'September 11 adds $10bn to Airline Losses', *The Guardian*, Internet Edition, January 16.

Ott, J. (2002), 'Roles for Regional Aircraft Expand Through Troubles', *Aviation Week and Space Technology*, March 18, pp. 63-64.

Page, P. (2002), 'Rating Express', *Air Cargo World Online*, October 15.

Phillips, E.H., Fiorino, F., Velocci, A.L., and Smith, B.A. (2002), 'From Big Losses to a Small Profit, Airlines Report Rocky Quarter', *Aviation Week and Space Technology*, April 22, pp. 42-43.

PR Newswire (2001), 'DRI-WEFA Study Finds Two Million Jobs Related to Tourism May Be Lost Due to the Attack', *PR Newswire*, October 19.

Sparaco, P. (2002a), 'EasyJet's Shopping Spree Signals That Size Matters', *Aviation Week and Space Technology*, May 13, pp. 36-37.

Sparaco, P. (2002b), 'European Air Insurers Face Sea of Red Ink', *Aviation Week and Space Technology*, July 8, p. 43.

Sparaco, P. and Wall, R. (2001), 'Europeans Map Airline Survival', *Aviation Week and Space Technology*, September 24, p. 35.

The Northern Echo (2001), 'Tourism Losses to hit 2.5 billion', *Northern Leisure*, September 27.

Velocci, A. (2002a), 'Manufacturer-as-lender Role Could Have Unhappy Ending', *Aviation Week and Space Technology*, September 30, p. 50.

Velocci, A.L. (2002b), 'Analysts Take Cautious Measure of Near-Term Uncertainties', *Aviation Week and Space Technology*, March 18, pp. 65-66.

Walsh, D. (2001), 'Tourism Fight Back to Plug 23 Million Losses', *Clare Champion*, December 1.

World Tourism Organization (2002), 'Latest Data, 2001', internet edition, www.world-tourism.org/market-research/facts&figures.

Chapter 15

Exploring the Future:
Searching for Profits

Old Dogs

In an industry notorious for 'boom-or-bust' and 'no stranger to bankruptcy court', the post 9/11 situation should look strikingly familiar (Arndt and Woellert, 2001). If the losses are higher or the causes not entirely the same, still the basic issues remain: consumers are increasingly price sensitive, overexpansion in the boom led to overcapacity in the bust, costs are too high, labor problems are too contentious, and competition from low-cost and foreign carriers is high (Costa, Harned, and Lunquist, 2002; Derchin, 1995; Wolf, 1995). These issues were identified as key components of the financial crisis of the 1990s when the losses in the U.S. reached a new record of US$13.1 billion for the period 1990-1994 (Bond, 2002). In response to past crises, the industry has created the hub-and-spoke system as a means of funneling and managing traffic, developed complex holding structures to manage debt, renegotiated labor contracts to manage wages and benefits, retired fleets and cut marginal routes to reduce capacity, merged and consolidated as weaker players faltered and stronger ones strived to position themselves for the next boom, and looked for marginal ways to reduce costs. Then the boom comes again and the dominant logic of the industry becomes expand and spend (Rosen, 1995).

What may be very different this time around is that the core, high yield business traveler may never come back to the carriers in their former numbers. According to the Business Travel Coalition, many corporations intend to make travel cuts permanent (Mecham, 2002). This trend began before 9/11 with business traveler complaints that fares were too high, restrictions too confining, and service too low, but the events of 9/11 and the 'hassle factor' of additional security has accelerated the exodus from traditional carriers. Many business travelers have switched to one of the low cost carriers or discovered the benefits of flexjet and leasing options. The second difference may be in the size of gains that low-cost carriers will make on their more traditional brethren during this downturn. Some projections suggest that the low cost market share will rise in the near future from 20 to 40% of the U.S. national market (Velocci, 2002; Haddad and Zellner, 2002). Europe's low cost carriers also appear to be on a path to gain up to 25% of their markets, up from a mere 7% at present (Binggeli and Pompeo, 2002). Estimates vary concerning the length of the current crisis, but traffic levels are not predicted to recover until the 2003-2006 time period, depending on the region, and profitability will likely occur only sometime after traffic returns (Bond, 2002; Sparaco, 2002). To date, carriers around the world appear to be pursuing the same strategies that 'worked' in the past. The problem, of course, is whether you believe that they worked. An increasing number of individuals and organizations are beginning to question the old strategies and ask themselves if it is possible to teach an old dog new tricks.

Old Tricks Under Fire

The events of 9/11 and the possibility that this crisis will truly be different from early industry trials have caused many to raise serious questions about the old model of doing business in the airline industry. Does size really matter? If so, is it the scale of the operations or the scope? Is size important for some factors of production but not others? What exactly does an airline produce? Is there such a thing as too big? Where does an airline add value and how can this value be enhanced and captured? What should an airline 'look' like and what should it do? Answering these questions is the topic of this chapter and must begin with a little lesson in economics.

One of the arguments presented in the debate over deregulation of the U.S. airline industry was that regulation prevented carriers from developing economies of scale. Economies of scale occur when average costs decline as the production of a good or service goes up. These economies can derive from several sources: technological, managerial, financial, marketing, commercial, and research and development. Technological economies may result when a larger firm is able to employ more expensive machinery and use it more intensively. Managerial economies arise when a firm is able to divide tasks and employ specialists. Financial economies result when a firm is able to borrow money at lower rates (primarily because size is usually associated with greater assets, age, credit record, etc). Marketing economies occur when firms are able to spread the high cost of advertising across a larger level of output. Commercial economies are gained from buying supplies in bulk and receiving larger discounts. R&D economies may appear when developing new or better products if basic research can give rise to multiple applications (Bized, 2002). From this breakdown, it is obvious that a firm, industry, or strategic group within an industry may enjoy economies in one area and not in another. Technologically, the new generation of aircraft tend to be more economical and efficient, however, the hub-and-spoke system employed by the major carriers limits the utilization of aircraft that must sit and wait for banks of smaller airplanes to feed passengers into the system nor does it seem economical for larger carriers to operate these smaller aircraft themselves since higher wage scales make them less productive. Currently, it is hard to argue that the major carriers enjoy financial economies over their smaller competitors given their low stock prices, high leverage, and negative growth. While major carriers may continue to enjoy economies in marketing, commercial, and R&D development, the level of this advantage is probably declining as technology, market fragmentation, and other factors come into play in the airline industry.

Since economies of scale are concerned with unit costs, it is important to define the unit of production in airlines. In other words, what does an airline produce? Does it produce a seat, a trip from point A to point B (called a leg) or an end-to-end experience i.e. many consumers connect from A to B to C as the final destination? The answer to this question may well matter since not all seats or trips are equal. The proverbial widget factory of business lore mass produces a product that is assumed to be the same - widgets. Economies of scale exist if the unit cost of the 10,000th widget are lower than the 1,000th. In the case of an airline, the seat on an aircraft from Atlanta to Boston is not necessarily the same as a seat from Atlanta to Denver or Denver to Chicago nor are the costs involved of producing these seats since they involve different lengths, flight crews, landing fees, aircraft types, passenger facilities charges, etc. Sophisticated systems can be employed to analyze costs by route, but this unit of analysis problem greatly complicates the economies argument for carriers. In part, this focus on unit costs is driven by the traditional approach to accounting which basically adds direct material costs, direct labor costs, and overhead (rent, utilities, insurance, etc) then divides by the unit of output to determine per unit costs. Activity based costing looks at costs from an activity standpoint. Business activities includes 'all of the processes that a company uses in order to conduct its business: order processing, procurement, engineering, production set-up, quality inspection, warehousing and material movement'. Under this approach, firms would determine the activities it performs and analyze them to determine the cost drivers within that activity. Costs to products are assigned based on how often they require inputs from that particular activity. The benefits of activity costing are found in the detailed cost information it provides and the focus on cost drivers within activities.

The notion of increasing scale leads to the question of whether a carrier can be too big. With size comes complexity - vertically, horizontally, and geographically. Large firms have more layers of management separating the top where 'decisions' get made from the bottom where 'decisions' and the actual work of the organization gets carried out. These layers often mean that actions are delayed and communications are poor, leading to misdiagnosis of problems or misapplication of solutions. Horizontal complexity occurs when firms become increasingly divided into ever finer units of specialized individuals who lose touch with the work (and importance) of other units as well as the overall goals of the organization. Geographic complexity occurs when firms spread across time zones and cultures making collaboration difficult and product and managerial decisions culture-specific. A further complexity, external boundaries, is becoming more common as firms outsource functions and blur the lines between the firm and its external environment. In fact, each of these areas creates its own boundary within the firm. In many large (old) firms, these boundaries are clear and impermeable; what is inside stays inside and what is out can not get in! Such organizations are slow to act, rigid in response, and poor in adaptation. Size becomes a disadvantage if the firm lives in a rapidly changing environment with younger, faster competitors (Ashkenas, Ulrich, Jick, and Kerr, 1995; Galbraith, 1995).

Economies of scope differ from those of scale in that they are not derived from increases in volume, but occur as the result of circumstances that allow firms to achieve synergy in production, product development, and distribution. Economies of scope can occur in production when firms are able to lower the cost of producing one product by producing other i.e. an airline flying both passengers and cargo. Economies of scope in product development arise when common knowledge or equipment is used to produce more than one product i.e. laser technology can be used in many applications from surgery to metal cutting. An infrastructure system capable of distributing one type of product may be able to distribute others.

If size is creating diseconomies of scale or scope, the firm has several options in downsizing: retrenchment, downscaling, or downscoping (DeWitt, 1998). Retrenchment attempts to maintain scope and often even increase output by centralizing certain firm functions, changing supplier relationships, and realigning managerial functions. For example, firms may re-engineer processes to improve productivity or eliminate redundant facilities (Hammer and Champy, 1993). Downscaling operations entails the permanent reduction of human and physical resources to bring supply in line with demand (Harrigan, 1983, 1985; Mahoney, 1992). Downscoping involves efforts to actually shrink the boundaries of the firm by effecting permanent cuts in human and physical resources as well as simplifying the organization's structure by reducing vertical, horizontal, or product diversity (DeWitt, 1993). The path a firm takes to downsizing is a function of many factors, but one factor is clearly the barriers to exit and mobility. Exit barriers create an impediment to the removal of excess resources (Caves and Porter, 1976) while mobility barriers affect the ability of firms to move between segments in an industry (Caves and Porter, 1977). Firms make certain industry-specific investments that may make exit difficult or very costly. For example, labor contracts may lock a firm into maintaining certain levels of operation. Fleet acquisitions may mean that cutbacks will lead to underutilization in the short-run, raising costs, and fleet sales may take time and not generate enough in certain market conditions to recoup costs. Likewise, a high-cost labor force with rigid work rules may prohibit a firm from shifting to a lower costs segment of the industry. The task ahead for airlines is figuring out how economies and value-adding activities can be used to shape a profitable airline in the new environment.

Searching for Profits

In the introduction to this book, Warren Buffet noted that the total money made in the airline industry since the time of the Wright brothers was zero (Loomis and Buffet, 1999). Clearly, one challenge ahead for the airline industry in general is proving this wrong. There are few that would question the air transport industry's status as a mature industry. It is true that in some countries in the developing world growth rates are relatively high due to the prior lack of aviation infrastructure, but the rate of development in even these countries is far faster than the early development of air transport in general. In the lifecycle of industries, emerging industries are characterized by uncertainty about products, markets, and standards. Companies compete on functional performance with little concern for cost and greater concern for user needs. In the second stage of life, demand increases attracting new competitors and competition centers on product types leading to efforts to standardize products. Organizations begin to segment the market based on costs or product differences. Rivalry is usually not as intense in the early stages of this phase because the market is growing faster than demand; companies can grow without taking the customers of other firms, thus limiting direct competition. In the mature phase, demand levels off or even drops. Competition often becomes intensive and is based on cost, increasing efficiencies, and incremental innovations in products and processes (Nadler and Tushman, 1997). Profitability is a function of these cost reductions, efficiencies, and standardized but incrementally improved products or services. Firms in a mature industry are generally large, functionally organized, and bureaucratic. They are not known for radical product innovation, preferring to emphasize stability, formality, and cost reduction (Nadler and Tushman, 1997).

Don Carty, CEO of American Airlines, told a Congressional panel that American's main objective in the post-9/11 environment was to achieve permanent structural cost reductions of at least US$3 billion within next several years in order to return costs to more competitive levels (Fiorino, 2002). He singled out three factors for special attention - fuel, distribution, and labor. Fuel prices represent roughly 10-15% of airlines costs and are largely a function of macroeconomic conditions (Zellner, 2002). There are things that airlines can do to reduce costs or stabilize them. Newer, more fuel efficient aircraft are one means of reducing fuel costs as well as overall maintenance costs. Many of the aircraft 'retired' since 9/11 fall into the less efficient category. Another means of reducing and/or at least stabilizing fuel costs is hedging, although this is not guaranteed to save costs since it depends on the financial and forecasting skill of the airline.

Distribution systems are areas over which carriers have greater control, however, the issues are more complex. In its formative years, air transport growth and profit was driven by airmail revenues. As passenger traffic increased in importance, airlines needed a process to track seat sales on flights. Without such a system, two problems can occur. First, an airline may sell more tickets than it has available seats on a given flight. This overbooking leads to disgruntled passengers who will have to be placated in some way (free tickets, discounts, frequent flyer mile, upgrades, etc) or potentially lost to another airline. Placating costs money, however, the second problem also costs money, namely not selling all available seats. Airlines need to return cancelled seats as quickly as possible to the available pool or risk losing the opportunity to maximize revenue. Airline seats, like cabbage, are perishable goods, meaning that at some point in time they become unusable and unsellable; once a flight takes off, the seat has perished.

The saga of airline distribution systems is a fascinating one and illustrates some of the potential issues facing airlines today. One of the earliest systems for tracking reservations was the Request and Reply system that required customers to contact ticket agents at the point of departure and wait for a reply confirming seat availability. The explosion in traffic following World War II, however, made this centralized point of departure system unwieldy. Agents in reservations offices soon used availability display boards to scan for seat openings and alternative flights.

At the Chicago office of American Airlines, an observer would have been confronted by a wall covered with a large cross-hatched board filled with cryptic notes. Men and women sitting in row upon row of desks would continually check this board, compare it to thick reference books all the while talking on the telephone to potential customers and filling out cards. Clerks and messengers scurried around between the desks with cards and sheets of papers as the chatter of teletypes and card sorting equipment filled the air (McKenney, Copeland, and Mason, 1967). American Airlines would replace this scene of mayhem with a machine called the Reservisor System which used a matrix of relays in which the columns represented dates and rows represented flights. Shorting plugs were inserted in the matrix to indicate a sellout. The system permitted fewer agents to book more flights, but maintenance of the system proved expensive. The next innovation introduced into the system was a magnetic drum computer memory to store data. By 1956, the Reserwriter, a computer that read punch cards of passenger data, converted them to tape, and telexed the data was in operation. However, even with these improvements, an estimated 8 percent of all transactions were incorrect and the process required 12 people, fifteen steps, and three hours. To remedy these problems, American worked with IBM to produce the SABRE system. The Computerized Reservation System (CRS) was born (McKenney, Copeland, and Mason, 1967).

The CRS was originally intended for use by travel agents and large corporate clients. By 1990, 93 percent of travel agencies were plugged into one of the major CRS systems (Bartimo, 1990). Not all carriers had their own CRS system and eventually began to accept the services of other carriers with CRS systems, however, since the CRS was initially developed by specific airlines, the systems that they each developed tended to favor their own flights. CRS systems also required a specialized knowledge of codes and procedures which made it profitable for many agencies to develop interfacing software that allowed them to use the system more efficiently and perform operations that their own customers wanted such as searching for best price (McKenney, Copeland, and Mason, 1967; Davidow and Malone, 1992). The relationship between airlines and travel agents began to change in the mid-1990s as airlines began their next major assault on distribution costs. This time the focus was reducing the travel agents' commissions on domestic and international ticket sales which had been as high as 10 percent for domestic and 15 percent for international sales. By 1997, the number of agencies in the U.S. had declined for the first time and the industry began to witness a wave of consolidation (Cook, Goff, Yale, and Wolverton, 1999).

The popularity of the internet opened up new possibilities for carriers to further cut distribution costs by selling directly to consumers. E-business became a new airline strategy. Orbitz was founded in 1999 by United, Delta, Continental, Northwest, and American as an on-line travel agent providing direct booking with the participating airlines. Newer entrants such as JetBlue and EasyJet are making extensive use of e-booking and seat assignments via the World Wide Web (Methner and Rospenda, 2001). American CEO Carty envisions greater use of a system called EasyFare that enables customers to receive web-based fares through travel agents. The internet has allowed carriers to reduce the fees to travel agents as well as to computer reservation systems which have now by-and-large been spun-off by the carriers into separate operating companies.   Carty estimated that American alone paid over US$400 in CRS charges in 2001 (Fiorino, 2002).   The fact that American is currently targeting a system to travel agents, however, points up at least one problem with the latest drive to reduce distribution costs, namely the growth of internet use.   Traffic on the internet itself 'was supposed to double every three months, but it's growing at just a quarter of that pace' (Rosenbush, Crockett, Haddad, and Ewing, 2002).   The dream of eliminating major costs by shifting a significant portion of customers to a system whereby they book their own flight over the internet, print out their own boarding pass and baggage tags, and deposit their own bags at a designated airport conveyor belt has not yet arrived.

It would seem that for the foreseeable future the internet will not be the answer to the distribution question, at least for the major carriers.   Reducing distribution costs in any significant way may require more radical solutions requiring extensive investment in new equipment and software, money which most of the major carriers do not currently have and can not likely raise in the current environment. The truth of the matter is that the distribution systems of many large carriers are still heavily mainframe-based, using PCs as dumb terminals whose sole function is inputting data into archaic programs that have been grown internally through haphazard means.   The industry that represents 'high tech' to many outsiders is in fact using old hardware and bad software to link to the high tech internet.

The third area of costs targeted for savings by American Airlines CEO Don Carty was labor, however, little or nothing was mentioned specifically in regard to how these costs would be cut (Fiorino, 2002).   Labor is the single largest cost of major carriers at roughly 40% and many experts suggest that labor costs need to drop by 20% to return the airline industry to profitability.   Unfortunately, in the absence of a major crisis there is little probability of gaining union agreement to these reductions.   There are still things that airlines could do to improve productivity such as changing work rules or investing in additional information technology, but these are unlikely to achieve the level of cuts that many consider essential.   Some have suggested that labor costs will need to come down at least 20% for the industry to return to financial health.   While productivity is up about 36% since 1990, compensation has risen by 46% (Zellner, 2002).   This fact may place greater stress on airline management to consider more radical measures to reduce costs and raise productivity.

More Radical Approaches

Every industry can be said to have a value chain or a sequence of activities (processes) that create value.   In a total quality sense, the value created is from the consumer's perspective and consumer's determine the value (price) placed on these activities.   The analysis of value-chain activities is based on the work of Michael Porter (1985).   Once the value-chain is examined, firms use it to develop strategies to 'create additional value' for their consumers.   It can also be the basis for the decoupling of an industry.   Decoupling is the reverse of the vertically integrated model that firms once pursued (referred to as the GM model in Chapter 8). Rather than perform all of the activities necessary to produce a good or service, firms outsource activities to other firms that specialize in that activity. In essence, firms choose an activity to perform based on their expertise, knowledge, or strategic vision. Figure 15.1 presents one model of a value-chain for airlines.

Figure 15.1: Airline Value-Chain

Raw Materials	Maintenance	Fleet Planning	Distribution	Service

At the end of this process is the consumer of airline services. Given this value-chain, it is conceivable that the industry could become increasingly decoupled. There has already been a move among a number of carriers to outsource maintenance to other airlines or companies. Decoupling would also seem to encourage a shift in accounting toward activity-based costing. This shift could enable the decoupled segments to focus more on cost reduction in activities, increasing the cost competitiveness of the segment as a whole. Within airline alliances, carriers have begun to shift some of these roles as well (Feldman, 1999). However, the extent to which decoupling can take place in alliances is constrained at the present time by anti-trust/competitive rules, national laws on related issues i.e. labor, safety, etc, and general trust issues within alliances themselves.

The decoupling of an industry raises a number of other questions as well. First, where does the most value get added in the process. This is obviously the site of greatest profit and the most desirable location to be for prospective firms. Galbraith (1995) has suggested that the firm that performs the integrator role would benefit from the highest profit. The integrator is the firm that coordinates the decisions and actions of the many companies making up the network. It is responsible for overall strategy, member firm selection, and network linkages. Boeing performs this role for the multitude of firms involved in the 'creation' of the 'Boeing aircraft'. In addition, the integrator decides on which function or functions it will perform and which will be outsourced. Again, these decisions are based on the integrator's perception of its own strengths, expertise, and role. In addition to answering the questions of where value lies and who integrates, there is a third question - is there enough value in each of the decoupled segments to attract sufficient numbers of firms to insure a competitive segment? Given that not all steps in the process generate the same level of value, and hence, profits, they should at least generate enough profits to attract firms into them and/or the decoupling should allow firms to find ways to increase profits through economies of scale, etc. In a decoupling industry, there is also the possibility of gaining economies of scope by using the same knowledge, machinery, and systems in other industries. The same system that distributes airline tickets could conceivably distribute cruise ship rooms or concert tickets. The firm that manages one type of fleet could conceivably manage another.

On the topic of 'enough profits', Chrysler, the integrator for its value chain, has an expression: 'My enemy is my supplier's cost, not my supplier's margins. Therefore, what can I do to help my suppliers reduce their (and ultimately my) costs' (Galbraith, 1995: 127). This comment brings up one key pitfall of decoupling, namely the ability and willingness of network partners to work together in a non-adversarial way. There is ample evidence from research in Western firms that the objective of traditional supplier relations was to minimize vulnerability to supplier opportunism. This lack of trust leads to problems in attempting to increase informal i.e. non-contractual ties within networks (Mudambi and Helper, 1998; Spekman, 1985, 1988a, 1988b; Sako, 1992). This distrust will also tend to affect the strategic decisions of firms on the question of what gets outsourced to whom; technologically complex or proprietary-knowledge-based activities will tend to be kept in-house rather than outsourced for fear of losing these assets to others (Monteverde and Teece, 1982; Morten, 1984). This obvious lack of trust has broader implications for the ability of the network to operate as a 'well-oiled machine'.

The decoupling of the aviation industry also creates the possibility of a virtual airline. During the May 1997 meeting for the International Civil Aviation Organization, Dr. Kotaite described the virtual airline as follows:

> The Virtual Airline owns no aircraft - they are leased.

> The Virtual Airline employs no cockpit or cabin crew - they too are leased.

> The Virtual Airline has no engineering facility - maintenance is contracted out.

> The Virtual Airline does no ground handling - that too is contracted out.

> The Virtual Airline also contracts out accounting and reservations, and may use electronic ticketing (ICAO, 1997).

In a decoupling world, the virtual airline becomes a possibility. What is left of the 'airline' may well be nothing more than a small corporate office that retains some small equity as assets of the Virtual Airline. The chief concern of ICAO, of course, is safety and security because 'regulation of safety and security is the responsibility of individual States and, while Article 83bis of the Chicago Convention will provide for the transfer of responsibility in the case of lease, charter and interchange of aircraft among States, national reach beyond international borders is in practice limited, particularly where airlines are privately owned and national human, technical and financial resources for regulatory activities are frugal.

Fully effective assurance of many aspects of safety and security can only be achieved by reciprocal arrangements or joint agreements, which only exist in certain areas of the world, or by world-wide co-operation' (ICAO, 1997). Lyle (1997) has offered the following example of a decoupled, virtual world in which 'an airline from country A operating code-shared flights to country B on behalf of an airline from country C, which is in turn a franchisee of an airline from country D...uses leased aircraft which are on the register of country E and for which the maintenance is carried out in country F' (6).

This globalization of aviation creates a host of safety, security, and political issues that have yet to be resolved. It can, however, create opportunities for improvement as well. For example, in the area of outsourced maintenance, many carriers already consider it a non-core activity and have outsourced to other maintenance facilities or original equipment manufacturers. With greater oversight by firms, these outsourcers may in fact be able to create economies and competencies that will improve the quality of maintenance and in a concentrated industry this could improve the ability of national aviation authorities to oversee the process (Ebbs, 1997; Smith and Culley, 1997). Greater economies of scale on the part of maintenance facilities can also reduce the price of maintenance (Seidenman and Spanovich, 1997).

Aside from the issues of safety and security, there are further problems with decoupling and virtual airlines, namely the transition. It is relatively easy to imagine a start-up carrier with a small, limited market pursuing a virtual airline as a way to overcome some of the capital and labor costs inherent in the industry, however, it is much more difficult to imagine a path that would take a United toward virtual status. The coordination needs of such a vast network would be immense, although the network of a Boeing or Airbus is probably no less complex. Even if this problem can be surmounted, there is likely to be tremendous resistance from labor organizations. In general, labor has opposed any efforts to outsource jobs including the wet leasing. There has also been substantial resistance in recent years to two-tier wage agreements i.e. agreements that create a separate, lower wage scale for certain groups of employees. These agreement were relatively popular in the U.S. in the years immediately following the financial crisis on the early 1980s, but evidence from the American Airlines acquisition of Reno Air and negotiations between American and American Eagle unions indicates resistance to any type of system that creates pay inequity or creates the possibility of substituting lower wage employees for higher wage employees as a means of reducing labor costs.

Studies of wage levels in the airline industry indicate that by far, pilots have the highest level of wages among non-management employee groups and are most likely to 'hold on' to wage gains in tough times (Johnson, 1995). In a decoupled industry, there would have to be some segment that handled labor for other firms to outsource this resource. This would appear to be the least attractive (possibly most costly) segment of a decoupled industry. Labor in the airline industry is highly unionized and labor-management relations highly polarized. Decoupling at this time does not seem to offer a solution, at least for the likes of United. A small, virtual carrier can find firms from which to outsource their labor needs, in many cases at a reduced cost since these pilots would not be paid benefits by the airline itself and are more likely to work for a lower wage. Outsourcing the total labor needs of United does not appear possible at this time. It is also not clear how such an outsourcing company would acquire a labor pool of this size willing to work for a wage likely to make it attractive for this firm's operating margins or interested outsourcers. Of course, the bankruptcy of one or several large carriers could free up a sizable pool of labor that might be available for outsourcing, but this assumes that governments would be willing to accept not merely bankruptcy but the possibility of liquidation. As noted in Chapter 1 by Wolf (1995), liberal bankruptcy laws in the U.S. certainly have allowed carriers to continue operating without shedding sizable portions of their labor force.

Basic strategic logic suggests that any effort to reduce costs should first focus on those factors representing the highest levels of expenditure. For airlines, this would be labor costs, particularly pilots. Clearly, the incentives exist to find ways to reduce these costs either by reducing the overall numbers of workers employed, increasing the utilization of the labor force, improving the productivity of labor, or reducing the wages of existing labor. Given the power of airline labor, particularly pilots, there is certainly an incentive to deskill the laborer as a means of reducing the wages of existing labor. Adam Smith in the work that established the field of economics and defines the general terms of capitalism offers the classic example of the pin factory where:

> A workman not educated to this business (which the division of labor has rendered a distinct trade, nor acquainted with the use of machinery employed in it (to the invention of which the same division of labor has probably given occasion), could scarce, perhaps with his utmost industry, make one pin in a day, and certainly could not make twenty. But, it is [now] divided into a number of branches, of which the greater parts are likewise peculiar trades. One man draws out the wire, another straights it, a third cuts it, a fourth points it, a fifth grinds it to the top for receiving the head (Smith, 1776. Reprinted in 1952 edition, R. Hutchins (ed.): 3).

Smith goes on to discuss how this division allows fewer men to do more work by specializing in a single task. While this is true, the process of division of labor also takes a skilled craftsman and deskills him. In the process, the value of his labor is decreased; skilled trades command higher wages, whereas the unskilled grinder of the pin above does not warrant such wages. New technology, like the machines that Smith spoke of in the pin factory, have been replacing workers for years by increasing the productivity of fewer workers or eliminating them entirely. These machines have reduced the skilled craftsman to a low wage operator. One of the key issues behind the longshoreman's strike on the U.S. West Coast is the computerized technology that would replace hundreds of workers. Ironically, both sides in the dispute agreed that this new technology would increase the efficiency of port operations and allow for greater volumes of traffic with higher quality in handling (The Mercury News, 2002). While there is currently no accepted technology to replace pilots, many aircraft do operate on a fly-by-wire technology that is computer based and recent events have led to suggestions for systems that would allow ground operators to override an aircraft in flight (in the case of hijacking, for example) and land it safely.

Of course, there are more traditional ways to reduce the power of labor groups as witness the bankruptcy of Continental and, more recently, US Airways, however, these means have provided only short-term relief from high labor costs. If the industry were to decouple by spinning off units like what occurred in the auto industry, old labor contracts could be rewritten and additional changes in work rules and environments could be instituted. After the union experience in the auto industry, this is not likely to go unnoticed in the airlines and would likely provoke labor unrest. In short, while a decoupled industry with virtual airlines may be a sound concept theoretically, there are major impediments to creating this future in the airline industry.

Looking Ahead

In a 1988 book on international aviation, Taneja described the 'prevailing attitude' of the North American airline industry as one that forced a carrier to choose one of three options- (1) become a megacarrier; (2) become a feeder to a megacarrier; or (3) fill a small niche in the marketplace. With the exception of carriers such as Southwest, the answer of the other major carriers was to become a megacarrier. A megacarrier, according to Taneja, has five key attributes. First, it has a large national and international route network. Second, it maintains a sufficient number of strategically located hubs with cost-effective feeder systems. Third, labor agreements are designed to provide low costs and high productivity in the long run. Fourth, an in-house automation system provides computerized reservations and the capability to manage yield and capacity cost-effectively. Finally, it possesses an attractive frequent flyer program. The events of 9/11 and the questions that it has given rise to be now challenging these attitudes and demanding that carriers in North America and around the world rethink the way they do business. The growing success of low-cost carriers is also challenging the great international carriers to redefine their place in the market and the ways that they generate value for consumers.

The questions have been asked, but there are as yet no clear answers. In fact, there is no 'one right answer' to the questions posed here in this chapter. Each airline and region may arrive at their own solution to these challenges and it will remain for the marketplace to determine the 'winners and losers'. Whether the great names of airline history will be able to meet the challenges facing them or fall to the younger, smaller, faster competitors rising up before them has yet to be determined. They clearly face some very difficult choices and their 'normal' options are constrained by an inability to quickly adjust capacity, lower labor costs, and readjust route networks. While bankruptcy does increase the range of options for carriers in some ways, it also carries definite risks. In the absence of government intervention, some carriers may simply not survive the process. While the 'death' of one or two carriers in certain markets might actually benefit the industry overall by reducing capacity, freeing up valued resources, and opening opportunities into new markets, the widespread loss of carriers can lead to serious economic problems in the broader economy. As if the problem of profitability were not enough for carriers to face in the new environment, there is another question that is waiting to be asked, namely - what is the future of global aviation liberalization? The industry before 9/11 was on a steady path toward greater freedom to enter, exit, set prices, and establish capacity based on market forces. This trend is now in question as we will see in Chapter 16.

References

Arndt, M. and Woellert, L. (2001), 'What Kind of Rescue: Cash won't Solve Air Carriers' Long-term Woes', *Business Week*, October 1, pp. 36-37.

Ashkenas, R. Ulrich, D., Jick, T. and Kerr, S. (1995), *The Boundaryless Organizations: Breaking the Chains of Organizational Structure*, Jossey-Bass Publishers, San Francisco.

Bain, J.S. (1956), *Barriers to New Competition*, Harvard University Press, Cambridge, MA.

Bartimo, J. (1990), 'Wanted: Co-Pilots for Reservation Systems', *Business Week*, April 9, p. 79.

Binggeli, U. and Pompeo, L. (2002), 'Hyped Hopes for Europe's Low-cost Airlines', *The McKinsey Quarterly*, Number 4.

Biz/ed (2002), 'Economies of Scale', www.bized.ac.uk.

Bond, D. (2002), 'Back to Capital Hill: Airlines Seek More Relief', *Aviation Week and Space Technology*, September 30, pp. 38-47.

Caves, R.E. and Porter, M.E. (1976), 'Barriers to Exit' in D.P. Qualls and R.T. Masson (eds), *Essays in Industrial Organization in Honor of Joe S. Bain*, Ballinger, Cambridge, MA, pp. 39-69.

Caves, R.E. and Porter, M.E. (1977), 'From Entry Barriers to Mobility Barriers: Conjectural Decisions and Contrived Deterrence to New Competition', *Quarterly Journal of Economics*, vol. 91, pp. 241-261.

Cook, R.A., Goff, J.L., Yale, L.J. and Wolverton, J.B. (2000), 'Fasten Your Seat Belts: Turbulence Ahead for Travel Agencies' in M.L. Taylor (ed.), *Case Set A to Accompany Dess & Lumpkin Strategic Management*, McGraw-Hill/Irwin, Boston, MA, pp. 32-41.

Costa, P.R., Harned, D.S. and Lunquist, J.T. (2002), 'Rethinking the Aviation Industry', *The McKinsey Quarterly*, Number 2: Risk and Resilience.

Davidow, W.H. and Malone, M.S. (1992), *The Virtual Corporation: Structuring and Revitalizing the Corporation for the 21st Century*, HarperCollins Publishing, New York.

Derchin, M. (1995), 'What went Wrong?' in P. Cappelli (ed.) *Airline Labor Relations in the Global Era: The New Frontier*, ILR Press, Ithaca.

DeWitt, R.L. (1998), 'Firm, Industry, and Strategy Influences on Choice of Downsizing Approach', *Strategic Management Journal*, vol. 19, pp. 59-79.

DeWitt, R.L. (1993), 'The Structural Consequences of Downsizing', *Organization Science*, vol. 4, pp. 30-40.

Ebbs, G. (1997), 'Supporting Roles', *Airline Business*, April, pp. 58-60.

Feldman, J.M. (1999), 'Disappearing Act', *Air Transport World*, February, pp. 25-30.

Fiorino, F. (2002), 'Carty to Analysts: AA Aims to Survive', *Aviation Week and Space Technology*, September 20, pp. 47-48.

Galbraith, J.R. (1995), *Designing Organizations: An Executive Briefing on Strategy, Structure, and Process*, Jossey-Bass Publishers, San Francisco.

Haddad, C. and Zellner, W. (2002), 'Getting Down and Dirty with the Discounters', *Business Week*, October 28, pp. 76-77.

Hammer, M. and Champy, J.S. (1993), *Reengineering the Corporation: A Manifesto for Business Revolution*, HarperBusiness, New York.

Harrigan, K.R. (1983), *Strategies for Vertical Integration*, Lexington Books, Lexington, MA.

Harrigan, K.R. (1985), *Strategic Flexibility*, Lexington Books, Lexington, MA.

International Civil Aviation Organization (2002), *Launch of the Strategic Action Plan-1997*, ICAO, May 22, pp. 1-9.

Johnson, N.B. (1995), 'Pay Levels in the Airline Since deregulation' in Peter Cappelli (ed.), *Airline Labor Relations in the Global Era: The New Frontier*, ILR Press, Cornell, pp. 101-115.

Loomis, C. and Buffet, W. (1999), 'Mr. Buffet on the Stock Market' in *Businessman of the Century*, Fortune, vol. 140.

Lyle, C. (1997), 'Global Safety: Can Advice Overcome Diplomatic Caution?' Presentation at the European Air Transport Conference on Airline Globalization, Brussels, BE, October 8.

Mahoney, J.T. (1992), 'The Choice of Organizational Form and Vertical Financial Ownership versus Other methods of Vertical Integration', *Strategic Management Journal*, vol. 13, pp. 559-584.

McKenney, L., Copeland, D.G., Mason, R.O. (1967), 'American Airlines SABRE System', Harvard Business School Case No. EA-C.

Methner, B.E. and Rospenda, C.J. (2001), 'Airline Strategy in a Digital Age: What Does "e" Mean to Me?' in Gail F. Butler and Martin R. Keller (eds), *Handbook of Airline Strategy*, McGraw-Hill Companies, New York, pp. 389-406.

Monteverde, K. and Teece, D. (1982), 'Supplier Switching Costs and Vertical Integration in the Automobile Industry', *Bell Journal of Economics*, vol. 13, pp. 206-213.

Morten, S. (1984), 'The Organization of Production: Evidence from the Aerospace Industry', *Journal of Law and Economics*, vol. 27, pp. 403-417.

Mudambi, R. and Helper, S. (1998), 'The "Close But Adversarial" Model in the U.S. Auto Industry', *Strategic Management Journal*, vol. 19, pp. 775-792.

Nadler, D.A. and Tushman, M.L. (1997), *Competing By Design: The Power of Organizational Architecture*, Oxford University Press, Oxford.

Porter, M. (1985), *Competitive Advantage*, Free Press, New York.

Rosen, S.D. (1995), 'Corporate Restructuring: A Labor Perspective' in P. Cappelli (ed.), *Airline Labor Relations in the Global Era: The New Frontier*, ILR Press, Ithaca.

Rosenbush, S., Crockett, R.O., Haddad, C. and Ewing, J. (2002), 'The Telecom Depression: When Will It End', *Business Week*, October 7, pp. 66-74.

Sako, M. (1992), *Prices, Quality and Trust: Inter-Firm Relations in Britain and Japan*, Cambridge University Press, Cambridge.

Seidenman, P. and Spanovich, D. (1997), 'Global Competition Drives Maintenance Market', *Aviation Maintenance*, January, pp. 8-14.

Smith, A. (1952), *An Inquiry into the Nature and Causes of the Wealth of Nations*, in Robert Maynard Hutchins (ed.), *Great Books of the Western World* series, no. 39.

Smith, T.W. and Culley, J. (1997), 'Gently Down Stream', *Airline Business*, October, pp. 2-55.

Spekman, R.E. (1985), 'Competitive Procurements Strategies: Building Strength and Reducing Vulnerability', *Long Range Planning*, vol. 18, pp. 75-81.

Spekman, R.E. (1988a), 'Strategic Supplier Selection: Understanding long-term Buyer Relationships', *Business Horizons*, vol. 31, pp. 75-81.

Spekman, R.E. (1988b), 'Perceptions of Strategic Vulnerability Among Industrial Buyers and its Effects on Information Search and Supplier Evaluation', *Journal of Business Research*, vol. 17, pp. 313-326.

Taneja, N.K. (1988), *The International Airline Industry*, Lexington Books, Lexington, MA.

The Mercury News (2002), 'Longshoremen's Union Pitches Adding Tech Workers', *The Mercury* News, October 9.

Velocci, A.L. (2002), 'Can Majors Shift Focus Fast Enough to Survive?', *Aviation Week and Space Technology*, November 18, pp. 52-54.

Wolf, S.M. (1995), 'Where Do We Go from Here: A Management Perspective' in Peter Cappelli (ed.), *Airline Labor Relations in the Global Era: The New Frontier*, ILR Press, Cornell, pp. 18-23.

Zellner, W. (2002), 'What's Weighing Down the Big Carriers', *Business Week*, April 29, p. 91.

Chapter 16

Exploring the Future:
Seeking Liberal Markets

Truly Open Skies

To the Europeans, open skies is an 'American term' that does not in fact truly involve open markets, but represents an extension of what bilateral air service agreements have always been about, namely negotiating to achieve maximum national benefit (Lobbenberg, 1994; Sorenson, 1998). In other words, they do not believe the rhetoric of open skies; they see open skies bilateral as another attempt by the U.S. to dominate their aviation systems without allowing them an equal opportunity to compete (Wallerstein, 1991). In the aftermath of World War II, the inequality was largely due to external factors relating to the destruction of commercial aircraft and aviation infrastructure. Today, the inequality is created by a bilateral system that grants U.S. carriers greater access to European markets than European airlines receive into the U.S. or even into their own markets. For example, the European Cockpit Association contends that the existing system prevents European companies from taking full advantage of the European market, but allows U.S carriers to string together the fifth freedom (beyond) rights included in open skies agreements to serve the European market in a more profitable way (European Cockpit Association, 2000).

Given these obvious disparities in access, it is not surprising that the shoe is now on the other foot in international aviation circles; the Europeans are calling for more liberal markets in aviation. They believe that issues of ownership and domestic market access should be addressed to eliminate any remaining barriers within the aviation market place (Sorenson, 1998). They are seeking to extend the single aviation market created by the 15-nation European Union across the Atlantic. They are calling for a Transatlantic Common Aviation Area (TCAA) that would create a single aviation market across the Atlantic that included North America. Clearly, the rhetoric of liberalization is now in the 'best interest' of European carriers. The question is does it benefit U.S. and Canadian carriers and individual consumers and local communities on both sides of the Atlantic. The first step is to understand the proposal itself.

A Common Market

In a 1995 policy paper on European Union (EU) external aviation relations, the Association of European Airlines (AEA) put forth a proposal for a new regulatory framework between Europe and the U.S. The following year the Council of Ministers for the European Union issued a mandate to the Commissions stating to establish a 'Common Aviation Area'. This Common Aviation Area would allow air carriers from both sides of the Atlantic to provide their services within it based on common commercial principles that would ensure competition on a fair and equal basis within an equivalent regulatory framework (AEA, 1999). Under a TCAA, the U.S. and Europe would have to 'harmonize' the following key areas: (1) rules governing market entry, access, and pricing, (2) rules governing airline ownership and the right of establishment, (3) rules governing competitive behavior and policies, and (4) rules governing leased aircraft.

Entry, Access and Pricing

The basic objective of a TCAA would be to insure unrestricted commercial opportunities allowing carriers (and market forces) to determine routes, markets, capacity, and pricing without discrimination anywhere within the countries party to a TCAA agreement. A distinction would then be made between TCAA countries as a group and third parties with whom the traditional bilateral air service agreements would apply. In other words, the two parties to the bilateral would be the TCAA (as a single unit) and the third party. This is a general principle behind economic integration. One of the problems of a free trade area (the first step in economic integration) is that although members of the FTA have eliminated internal barriers to the movement of goods, the external tariff barriers to third party goods remain in place and may vary in such a way that third parties can benefit by selectively entering the FTA country with the most favorable tariff conditions and then gaining access from there to other member states (Hill, 2002). The AEA has suggested a phased approach to establishing this new single aviation area that is similar to the EU liberalization that took place through a series of three packages (Chapter 6). The approach would allow EU countries flexibility to negotiate with the U.S. subject to achieving some minimum standards set by the overall parties (AEA, 1999).

Ownership and Right of Establishment

The right of establishment is a legal term relating to the national control of companies. In other words, TCAA should grant firms that are 1) majority owned or controlled by nationals of any of the TCAA parties or their governments or 2) incorporated and have their principle place of business within the territory of a TCAA country the same rights and recognition. With the right of establishment would come the end of 'foreign national' restrictions on cross-border mergers, acquisitions, and entry. Under the second definition, airlines from third party countries could begin operations in a TCAA country and then gain the right to operate throughout TCAA airspace. It would, of course, be possible under option one for a country to apply for membership into the TCAA, thus opening up their aviation system to all TCAA members in the process.

Competition Policy

In Chapter 10, the issue of anti-trust or competitiveness policy was discussed as it related to strategic alliances. From that discussion, it should be clear that although the basic concepts underlying both the U.S. and EU policies are similar, the application of these policies has differed in a number of significant ways. The Association of European Airlines (1999) has suggested that common standards should be developed in the following areas:

(a) Basic criteria for granting exemptions, and in particular means of reconciling the relevant criteria of the EC competition rules and the U.S. concept of the 'public interest';
(b) The definition of the 'relevant market';
(c) The concept of 'market power' as distinct from 'market share';
(d) The notion of 'predatory behavior';
(e) The question what 'essential facilities' airlines would have to share with each other;
(f) The treatment of airline cooperative arrangements;
(g) The nature of remedies and sanctions to be applied (AEA, 1999).

The AEA argues in their proposal that strategic alliances whose objective is to create TCAA airlines that are competitive in world markets should be considered by both EU and U.S. standards to contribute to economic progress, the interests of consumers, and the interest of the public at large (AEA, 1999). Further, they believe that code sharing, blocked space, franchising, and other cooperative agreements including activities involving tariff (fare) consultation for interline purposes should be considered indispensable to the operation of strategic networks.

Leasing Aircraft

There are differences between the U.S. and Europe over the question of wet leasing aircraft. U.S. rules prevent U.S. airlines from wet leasing non-U.S. registered aircraft from other airlines and requires non-U.S. leasers to have route authority for the operation concerned. EU rules require registration in a member state but permit this to be waived for short-term lease arrangements or other exceptional circumstances. The Association recommends that the U.S.-EU rules be modified to allow any TCAA carrier to lease from or to any other TCAA carrier and that if third party leasing is permitted a maximum percentage of fleet standard be set. These rules would be contingent upon all parties complying with established safety standards.

Raising Objections

The European Cockpit Association which represents over 2,600 pilots from EU countries has endorsed TCAA with several reservations. First, there is concern that relaxing ownership and leasing rules might create 'Flags of Convenience' in aviation similar to those existing in the maritime industry. In the United States, for example, the Jones Act requires that ships carrying cargo from one domestic port to another be built, maintained, and operated (and flagged) in the U.S., but does not have such a requirement for ships coming from a foreign port. There are a number of countries that allow open registries whereby ships owned by individuals or corporations in other countries may be flagged in their country rather than the country of the ship's owner. Critics charge that the practice of open registries allows owners to avoid the fees, taxes, safety requirements, and manning rules of their home country and poses a risk to crews, the marine environment, and the ports into which they enter (Morris, 1996; Ryan, 1996). If TCAA included countries with safety and social standards below the norm of EU/US standards, there would be a cost incentive to flag aircraft in that country leading to lowered safety standards for airline operations and the shifting of operations to common aviation areas offering lower taxes, wages, benefits, etc. This would obviously affect employment opportunities, local tax bases, and merchants in affected areas. The ECA also expressed concern that liberalized ownership could result in the conversion or merging of alliances into mega-airlines dominated by U.S. carriers and that route structures and associated carriers could be manipulated for cost-cutting purposes (ECA, 2000).

U.S. Reaction

There has not yet been a significant reaction from U.S. aviation groups to TCAA. Labor delegates at a 1999 aviation summit in the U.S. cautioned against rapid change and any liberalization that failed 'to maintain the integrity of companies and to protect jobs' (Ott, 1999: 45). Their reasoning and concerns are very similar to the position stated by the ECA, although they have not indicated even a conditional endorsement of TCAA. By and large, U.S. airlines have cautiously ignored the proposal. In light of these reactions, the U.S. government has been lukewarm to TCAA. At the 1999 aviation summit mentioned above, Rodney Slater, then U.S. Secretary of Transportation, committed the U.S. to examining the TCAA proposal. This U.S. reaction of 'committing to study the issues' was repeated recently when the President and CEO of Air Canada, Robert Milton, proposed a single aviation market for North America saying that he 'urged the two governments to build on the success story of the 1995 Canada-U.S. Open Skies Agreement by progressively removing all restrictions in order to arrive at a fully integrated, common air transport market with the United States' (Melnbardis, 2001: 1). Reacting to the Canadian Proposal, American Airlines and United Airlines have indicated that they support the principle of liberalized air policy, but need time to study the specifics (Chase and McArthur, 2001).

In the Balance

Before looking specifically at the possible winners and losers in a TCAA environment, it is important to examine several broader issues relating to TCAA. First, TCAA is the first time that the United States has been asked (or is considering) trading roughly equivalent domestic markets. A quick look at Table 5.1 will show that the Open Skies Agreements of the past have essentially involved countries with small domestic markets. Ideology aside, it has never made 'economic sense' for the United States to trade access to its large domestic market for the domestic markets of Singapore, The Netherlands, or even Germany. The size differences were simply too great. The population of the United States was estimated at 280,562,489 as of July 2002. Calculating the estimated 2002 population from Table 6.1 yields a total EU population of 379,590,000 (CIA Factbook, 2002). Given some of the differences between U.S. and EU transportation markets noted in Chapter 6, namely more developed EU inter-modal competition and charter market and the higher domestic departures of the U.S (Sinha, 2001), these markets appear to be roughly similar in size, particularly if we add in the estimated 31,902,268 population of Canada (CIA Factbook, 2002). This 'equivalent markets' argument raises a question about the proposed single North American market proposed by Air Canada. While the two countries have roughly equal land masses (9,976,140 square kilometers for Canada and 9,629,091 for the U.S.), there is a major difference in the population size (CIA Factbook, 2002). Much of the Canadian land mass is in the far north where the Canadian government has declared many communities in need of essential services, particularly in winter months when air service is a vital link to the outside world. U.S. carriers would have little interest in gaining access to these markets and under open skies have already gained access to the southern Canadian markets. Air Canada, on the other hand, would seem to have a great deal to gain from single markets. The Air Transport Association of Canada which represents a number of Canadian carriers has said that it supports the idea of 'modified sixth-freedom rights' between the U.S. and Canada, but this wording appears to be only a limited endorsement of the single market concept. The chairman of WestJet Airlines has gone on record as opposing the concept of a single market arguing that it would do nothing to lessen the grip of Air Canada on the domestic market and would put Canadian carriers at a disadvantage since they pay much more for fuel than their U.S. counterparts (Chase and McAuthur, 2001). In short, it does not appear that any North American carrier has anything to gain except Air Canada. The Canadian government might pursue single markets as a way to deflect consumer complaints over the decision to allow Air Canada to become a monopoly, but the U.S. government may receive a great deal of pressure from the U.S. airline industry to oppose a deal.

A second issue that argues in favor of TCAA is that the safety and security levels of European carriers are equal, if not higher, than their U.S. counterparts. European airports have historically incorporated security designs and policies that limited access in gate areas to ticketed passengers, encouraged bag matching, and other sophisticated screening techniques. In a post-9/11 environment, this is an important consideration and TCAA could facilitate closer cooperation on improving these areas.

Finally, the European Commission is committed to implementing a multilateral aviation approach for the EU that would end the current system of bilateral air service agreements. In January 2002, the European Court of Justice ruled that countries had broken EU laws in signing such bilateral. The key issue is the nationality requirements (contained in Article 52) and Article 307 of the EC treaty that requires states to make every effort to amend international agreements that violate EC law. The Commission brought the current case against Austria, Belgium, Denmark, Finland, Germany, Luxembourg, and Sweden for signing open skies agreements with the U.S. that infringed the Community principle of right of establishment as well as the rules on the division of powers between the community and member states (Zuckert, Scoutt, and Rasenberger, 2002). In short, the Commission contends that it is the right of the Commission to negotiate in matters relating to the external aviation relations of member states. The Commission has indicated that it would pursue this role with the goal of correcting the unequal access issues that exist between U.S.-EU carriers. If the EU continues on this path, the EU would declare the 15-nations to be a single market for external purposes and would then be in a position to undermine the extensive fifth freedom rights exercised by U.S. carriers. In a single market, these rights would be considered cabotage and the Commission would demand reciprocal access to the U.S. for their carriers.

Winners and Losers

At this point, it is important to note that TCAA and/or the single aviation market with Canada is like any other economic issue in that there are likely to be winners and losers emerging from implementation of the system. Calculations will be made on both sides of the Atlantic of the costs and benefits of single markets. These calculations will be made by consumer groups, airlines, employee organizations, local communities, and national governments. In this section, the issues relating to these group-specific calculations will be discussed.

Consumers

General economic theory suggests that consumers benefit from having more choices of products, services, and firms. Single aviation markets do promise to broaden the choices of consumers. However, the same problems may arise in this next phase of liberalization that occurred in earlier deregulation efforts. First, the heightened competition of the early period could be jeopardized by failures to enforce laws on predatory behavior and merger/acquisition leading to high failure rates of 'new entrants' and mergers that result in the concentration of the market in a few select carriers. Second, consumers in some markets may lose service as U.S.-EU carriers re-deploy their fleets to new, more lucrative markets. Given the cost structure of the entering international carriers, they would likely concentrate on higher yield markets with the all-important business travelers. Markets vacated by these carriers would be open for low-cost carrier entry and both the U.S. and EU now have stable, viable carriers that could fill these openings. In any event, neither the North Americans nor Europeans are likely to drop their right to insure that essential services are provided to local communities. The difficulty lies in harmonizing the implementation of the rules and policies that define the relevant markets, frequency requirements, carrier types, etc in the determination of essential services.

Airlines

Sorting out the potential winners and losers among the airlines is in large part of function of two factors - relative costs and relative service levels. The last major study to examine the cost competitiveness of international airlines was conducted by Oum and Yu (1998). They examined the cost of airline inputs (labor, fuel, aircraft, capital, and materials) and the revenue of airlines (outputs) from passengers, freight, and mail to determine the efficiency of carriers and their cost competitiveness. As mentioned briefly in Chapter 5, almost thirty years of deregulation in U.S. markets has created carriers with much lower costs and higher levels of productivity and cost competitiveness. In the Oum and Yu (1998) study, only British Airways and KLM were close to achieving a level of cost competitiveness comparable to their U.S. counterparts. Of course, if many of the European carriers began operating in the U.S. they would likely be able to reduce many of these costs, at least in U.S. operations, since fuel prices, the benefits component of labor costs, and many related fees tend to be lower in the U.S. The Oum and Yu (1998) study also did not consider the low-cost European carriers such as Ryanair and EasyJet who may well have costs structures more comparable to Southwest in the U.S. From a firm point-of-view, single markets also increase strategic flexibility by allowing firms to move assets as well as perform work where it makes the most sense to do so from a cost and logistical standpoint. This flexibility is precisely the concern of labor groups, as we will see in a minute.

The second issue is relative service levels between U.S. and European carriers. At least some of the cost differences between U.S.-EU carriers may be attributed to the generally higher levels of service provided by EU carriers ranking. In an environment where carriers are free to operate anywhere within the single market, there are some carriers that may clearly be disadvantaged by high cost structures and poor quality. At the margin, consumers will decide the issue of price and service level. In general, the trend in the U.S. has been toward viewing air transportation as a basic commodity that is cheap and relatively indistinguishable from one provider to another. Indications are that European markets are beginning to move more in this direction with the success of their own low-cost carriers. Nationality issues aside, single markets would increase the competition on international routes where service level issues are considered more important and would tend to favor the European carriers.

Labor Groups

Single markets open up the very real possibility that firms will shift operations from one region to another or utilize labor from one area over another as a means of reducing costs. This shift has occurred in other liberalizing industries and would very likely occur in aviation. Most at risk would probably be pilots who account for more labor costs than do mechanics and flight attendants. With or without single markets, however, the losses of recent years will force carriers and labor groups to make some very hard choices in their efforts to bring costs and capacity down to competitive levels. It should be noted that the cost of labor is not the only issue that managers should consider; the productivity of labor can balance this cost in the long run. Oum and Yu (1998) found that while Thai Airways had input costs that were 52.1% lower (22.4% of which were attributable to labor) than American Airlines, however, in terms of overall efficiency (outputs to inputs) Thai was 42.9% less efficient. A higher cost but more efficient labor force can still be cost competitive. In many western countries, productivity gains have been achieved through the adoption of improved information systems, but productivity can also be improved through more flexible work rules, attention to work flows, cross-functional team implementation, and other redesign options.

Local Communities

If we define local communities broadly as nations, then there are clearly risks involved in single markets. High cost, low productivity, low service carriers will probably not survive without government assistance. As we discussed in Chapter 1, airlines have historically been closely associated with national pride, power, and prestige. The EU is currently struggling with this issue as we speak and the debate over whether the Sabena's of aviation should be allowed to continue to serve 'their communities'. More narrowly defined, there may be some city and city-pair markets that will see reduced service as carriers adjust their route structure toward higher margin routes. Many of these markets will continue to receive service from the entrance of low-cost carriers, but the quality and frequency of service is likely to change for some communities.

National Governments

There is a saying that 'all politics is local'. Given the historic attachment of localities to their airlines and the strategic flexibility that single markets give to airlines, there will be pressure on governments to intervene in the process to influence local outcomes. Economists talk about long run equilibriums and structural adjustments; politicians are concerned about the next election. Predicting the outcome of this political wrangling is far more difficult, particularly when questions of local, national, and supranational jurisdiction, responsibilities, and calculations come into play.

Moving Ahead

Political rhetoric aside, neither the U.S. nor the EU are likely to consider a 'Big Bang' approach to transatlantic liberalization. The Europeans have already clearly indicated their belief that such an approach in the 1978 U.S. domestic deregulation was disastrous. The U.S. also appears reluctant to move quickly on the issue given the lukewarm reception in the industry and broader security and terrorism concerns. Therefore, a gradual approach seems most likely to gain support. The issues of harmonizing policies on predatory behavior and merger/acquisition could take a number of years to resolve and would likely require all parties to agree on some mechanism for mediation and reconciliation. Ironically, the events of 9/11 may have helped to push both sides closer to single markets. Unless consumers and taxpayers on both sides of the Atlantic are willing to accept costly and wholesale bailouts of failing carriers, the airline industry is not likely to achieve stability again until 2005 when profitability is predicted to return (ICAO, 2002). Rising consumer complaints about service, security, and other airlines issues could help the cause of single markets just as it has in the Canadian market following the merger of Air Canada and Canadian Airlines. A move toward single markets would also send an important political message as well. If the terrorists have any agenda other than chaos, it is a desire to halt the progress of globalization and free markets, both of which they blame on the U.S. Movement toward single markets would signal in no uncertain terms the commitment of the Western world to greater global economic integration.

References

Association of European Airlines (1999), *Towards a Transatlantic Common Aviation Area: AEA Policy Statement*, September.

Chase, S. and McAuthur, K. (2001), 'U.S. Warm to Proposed Increased Air Competition', *Global Interactive*, December 8.

CIA Factbook (2002), www.odci.goc/cia/publications/factbook.

European Cockpit Association (2000), *From EASA to TCAA: The Flight Crews View on a New Regulatory Framework in Aviation*, ECA, Brussels, BE.

Hill, C.W. (2001), *Global Business*, 2nd edition, Irwin-McGraw-Hill, Boston.

ICAO (2002), *One Year After 11 September Events ICAO forecasts World Air Passenger Traffic will Exceed 2000 Levels in 2003*, Press Release. October 2.

Lobbenberg, A. (1994), 'Government relations on the North Atlantic: A Case Study of Five Europe-USA Relationships', *Journal of Air Transport Management*, vol. 1, pp. 47-62.

Melnbardis, R. (2001), 'Air Canada Wants Open U.S.-Canada Air Market', Reuters Newswire, December 6.

Morris, J. (1996), 'Flags of Convenience give Owners a Paper Refuge', *Houston Chronicle online edition, www.chron.com*.

Ott, J. (1999), 'Aviation Summit Yields EU Plan for Open Market', *Aviation Week and Space Technology*, December 13, pp. 43-45.

Oum, T.H. and Yu, C. (1998), *Winning Airlines: Productivity and Cost Competitiveness of the World's Major Airlines*, Kluwer Academic Publishers, Boston.

Ryan, G.J. (1996), 'Testimony by George J. Ryan, President-Lake Carriers' Association', Presented before the House Subcommittee on Coast Guard and Maritime Transportation, June 12, Washington, D.C.

Sorenson, F. (1998), 'Open Skies in Europe', *FAA Commercial Aviation Forecast Conference Proceedings: Overcoming Barriers to World Competition and Growth*, March 12-13, Washington, D.C., pp. 125-131.

Wallerstein, I. (1991), *Geopolitics and Geoculture: Essays on the Changing World-system*, Cambridge University Press, Cambridge.

Zuckert, Scoutt and Rasenberger (2002), 'European Court Says "Bye Bye Bermuda"', *Aviation Advisor*, Special Edition, November 6.

Chapter 17

Exploring the Future:
Spreading the Promise

Problems and Promises

Aviation and the globalization movement of which it is an integral part promised to transform domestic and global economies by linking distant communities in an ever shrinking, complex web of interaction. Along these links flow a vast variety of goods, services, and people. As the flow increases, so does the income, standard of living, and general welfare of the people connected to this great web. This is the promise of globalization and aviation, but the reality is that there are a number of countries and regions around the world that have yet to collect on the promise. Three areas in particular have yet to experience the full benefits of this transformation: Africa, the Middle East, and Latin America. The purpose of this chapter is to explore the reasons why these areas have not yet benefited from civil aviation and to address various means by which the world community and national governments can work to spread the promise.

Africa - Understanding the Problems

Africa is the second largest continent in the world and possesses the population base and the geographically challenging terrain to make it ideal for air transportation. Unfortunately, these advantages are outweighed by a number of factors that have prevented the development of a viable civil aviation industry in Africa. The first factor is the underdeveloped state of the national economies of most of Africa (Graham, 1995; Taneja, 1988). As Table 17.1 demonstrates, the majority of the nations in Africa are poor. According to the World Bank Group, over 50% of the population in all of the 18 nations for which data was available were living on US$2 or less a day (World Bank Group, 2002). While the gross domestic product of Africa rose 3.2% in 2000, African economies will need to grow at an average of 7% a year to halve the poverty level by 2015. This may be difficult for a region heavily dependent on foreign aid and investment. At the 2002 Financing for Development conference, the World Bank released its annual report on African Development Indicators showing that development aid to Africa dropped from US$17.2 billion in 1990 to US$12.3 billion in 1999 (World Bank Group, 2002). The level of poverty in Africa means that most of these nations cannot afford the necessary level of investment in aviation infrastructure to create an aviation system competitive on the international level.

Table 17.1: Information on Selected African Countries

Country	Area*	Population**	Airports (paved)***	GDP****
Angola	1,246,700	10,593,171	244 (32)	$1,330
Cameroon	475,440	16,184,748	49 (11)	$1,700
Cape Verde	4,033	408,760	9 (3)	$1,500
Chad	1,284,000	8,797,237	49 (7)	$1,030
Kenya	582,650	31,138,735	231 (20)	$1,000
Liberia	111,370	3,288,198	47 (2)	$1,100
Madagascar	587,040	16,473,477	130 (29)	$870
Mauritius	2,040	1,200,206	5 (2)	$10,800
Namibia	825,418	1,820,916	137 (22)	$4,500
Nigeria	923,768	129,934,911	70 (35)	$840
Senegal	196,190	10,589,571	49 (7)	$1,700
South Africa	1,219,912	43,647,658	740 (144)	$9,400
Sudan	2,505,810	37,090,298	65 (12)	$1,360
Zambia	752,614	9,959,037	11 (11)	$870
Zimbabwe	390,580	11,376,676	454 (17)	$2,450

Source: CIA Factbook.
* Square Km. **Estimated July 2002 figures ***Data from 2001****Estimated 2001.

This lack of aviation infrastructure is reflected in a number of ways. First, the recently released report by the Flight Safety Foundation reported that Africa had the highest level of accidents per departure of any region in the world at 9.8

accidents per 1 million departures, compared to a world average was 1.2 accidents per 1 million departures. This rate of accidents is attributed to poor training for pilots, controllers, and regulatory officials, poor to non-existent radar coverage, high numbers of non-precision approaches, and non-enforced or nonexistent legislation (Phillips, 2002). In many developed nations, revenues generated by aviation activity are placed in designated funds for the upgrade infrastructure, however, in Africa this is generally not true; aviation revenues go into the general coffers and are spent on other needs (Phillips, 2002).

Second, there is not a substantial internal demand for air transportation due to the general level of poverty and the increasingly competitive global market has not been kind to African airlines. Almost all of Africa's airlines remain wholly or partly state-owned. The traffic patterns of these carriers reflect Africa's colonial past running north to south, unfortunately placing African airlines at the wrong end of the route i.e. principal flows originate in the northern, wealthy nations of Europe where passengers tend to fly on European national carriers (Graham, 1995). In order for African carriers to compete effectively with these European carriers they must provide equal or superior service in a number of areas including flight punctuality, in-flight service, superior aircraft, comfortable seats, clean cabin, seats, and washrooms, good food, efficient reservation systems, competitive pricing, good check-in, attractive frequent flyer programs, and superior first and business class accommodations. At least seven of these areas are heavily dependent on the quality of the aircraft. Unfortunately, the aircraft of many African airlines are aging and investment for new aircraft is often nonexistent. These aging aircraft also do not meet the noise restrictions imposed by many countries and are, therefore, not eligible to land at many international airports. Aircraft leasing is not well developed in Africa, making the acquisition of new aircraft difficult for many carriers who might find this a preferred way to modernize their fleets (Abeyratne, 1998).

Addressing the Issues

Given the lack of domestic demand, the need to compete globally with larger, better established carriers, and the limited funding for aviation development, African nations have attempted to join together. In 1961, ten African nations signed the Treaty on Air Transport in Africa, popularly known as the Yaounde Treaty. Under Article 77 and 79 of the Chicago Convention which provides for joint or international operating organizations, these nations established Air Afrique to operate international service between contracting states and other nations and to provide domestic service within the territories of contracting states. The second major event in African aviation was the Yamoussoukro Declaration on a New African Air Transport Policy (1988). The Yamoussoukro Declaration committed African States to achieving the total integration of their airlines through the liberal exchange of air traffic rights, use of an unbiased computer reservations system, and other joint aviation infrastructure developments. The first phase of the Declaration was expected to last two years and result in recommendations for integrating African airlines with the rest of the world. Phase two was to be a three year effort dedicated to the commercial aspects of aviation including the integration of CRS, joint purchasing of spare parts, maintenance, and overhaul equipment, training of personnel, etc. In Phase three, African carriers were to be integrated into a consortium of competitive entities that would bring about sustained progress in air transport in Africa (Abeyratne, 1998: 34). Progress has been made in a number of areas including the development of the Gabriel Extended Travel Service (GETS) CRS, the establishment of the Air Tariff Coordination Forum of Africa to assist airlines in adapting to international air tariff policies, the opening up of South Africa to intra-African aviation, and efforts to establish an African financing and leasing company (Abeyratne, 1998).

Challenging the Promise in Africa

Unfortunately, one area in which Africa has not made significant progress is the integration of airlines. Air Afrique, one of the oldest jointly owned airlines, declared bankruptcy in 2002 after years of financial crisis. The company's troubles have been blamed on 1) the difficulty of managing an airline owned by 11 states, and 2) Air Afrique mismanagement (BBC News, 2002a). One area of mismanagement cited by critics was the fact that many people with family links to government members and senior officials were allowed to travel free (BBC News 2002b). Other efforts at joint ownership include East African Airlines, a joint venture between the governments of Kenya, Tanzania, and Uganda, which dissolved in the 1970's and Alliance Air, jointly owned by South Africa, Uganda, and Tanzania, which ceased operations in 2000 (BBC News, 2002e). A joint service agreement between Air Mali and Cameroon Airlines also ended in 2001 (BBC News, 2002e). These failures should not be attributed solely to the joint nature of the airlines. Like young, small market carriers around the world, African airlines have often struggled. In 2000, Uganda Airlines went into liquidation after South African Airways withdrew its bid (M2 Communications Ltd, 2000). Nigeria Airways announced a cut of 1,000 employees in January 2002 in a 'right-sizing exercise' (BBC News, 2002c). Ghana Airways announced in June 2002 that its debt had risen to US$160 million and creditors were threatening to seize assets (BBC News, 2002d).

Several recent events have raised hopes that Africa may finally begin to emerge from the old pattern of tightly restricted air service agreements and government ownership that have plagued them in the past. Two new airlines have recently been formed; both are privately owned and financed by groups of African entrepreneurs, Afrinet and AfricaOne. Both carriers cite the collapse of Air Afrique, Sabena, and general reductions in service following 9/11 for creating a vacuum in air transport service that they believe can support new carrier entry (BBC News, 2002b; BBC News, 2002g; BBC News, 2002f). In addition, Afrinet has announced its intention to overthrow the old north-south colonial traffic patterns and focus on direct connections between West Africa and the United States (BBC News, 2002g). Another sign of the changing times in Africa is a growing movement toward privatization with carriers such as Air Tanzania, Kenya Airways, and Air Mali opening up to private investment (BBC News, 2002e; BBC

News, 2002g; Godwin, 2002). Liberalization in bilateral service agreements is also taking hold in Africa. As of the end of 2001, 10 of the 56 nations signing open skies agreements with the United States were from Africa.

Prospects for the Future

The latest traffic forecasts issued by the International Civil Aviation Organization offer encouraging news for Africa in general. While traffic growth for the world as a whole declined 2.9% in 2001, Africa posted a 1.4% gain. Future prospects offer even more reason for optimism as traffic is expected to increase 3.0% in 2002, 6.5% in 2003, and 4.8% in 2004 (ICAO, 2002). Several developments are essential if Africa is to take advantage of the current growth in traffic and increasing liberalization in international markets. First, the continent must make a commitment to improving aviation safety. Projects are underway with the U.S. Federal Aviation Administration, the American Association of Airport Executives, and the U.S. Trade & Development Agency. The goal of these efforts is 'to provide the full universe of what they need, a road map to upgrade safety and security and ATC and to put them in touch with funding sources' (Ott, 2001: 108). The International Federation of Air Line Pilots Associations (IFALPA) is working to document deficiencies in the aviation system and suggest remedies. ICAO funding is being provided to eight African nations through their Technical Cooperation Program (Ott, 2001). The extent to which African nations can find funding for and participate in aviation safety programs will clearly help the continent integrate into the international aviation system. Second, African nations need to continue the privatization of airlines. This privatization not only has the potential to create viable, competitive airlines, but removes the government incentives to offer preferential treatment to the state's flag carrier. Third, African nations need to continue to sign liberal bilateral agreements within Africa and with the outside world. The newly created carriers of Africa cannot survive if they are not granted access to outside markets.

Latin America and U.S. Challenge

ICAO groups 32 nations into the Latin American region. This region covers approximately 15% of the earth's landmass and accounted for roughly 5% of world passenger traffic in 2001 (ICAO, 2002). Compared to Africa, Latin America and the Caribbean are more affluent (Table 17.2), support larger domestic markets, attract more tourists, and possess larger, more modern fleets of aircraft. Like Africa, the transportation network tends to be dominated by colonial and imperialist forces with international traffic focused primarily on North-South U.S. routes and European links funneled through former imperial capitals (Graham, 1995). Latin America also tends to be far more urbanized than is true for Africa (Taneja, 1988).

Nuutinen (1993) has identified three key problems facing Latin American carriers. First, they compete directly with the aggressive US mega-carriers. With

Table 17.2: Information on Selected Latin American Countries

Country	Area*	Population**	Airports (paved)***	GDP****
Argentina	2,766,890	37,812,817	1,369 (144)	$12,000
Bolivia	1,098,580	8,445,134	1,109 (13)	$2,600
Brazil	8,511,965	176,029,560	3,365 (627)	$7,400
Chile	756,950	15,498,930	363 (70)	$10,000
Colombia	1,138,910	41,008,227	1,066 (93)	$6,300
Costa Rica	51,100	3,834,934	152 (29)	$8,500
Cuba	110,860	11,224,321	172 (78)	$2,300
Guatemala	108,890	13,314,079	475 (11)	$3,700
Honduras	112,090	6,560,608	117 (12)	$2,600
Jamaica	10,991	2,680,029	35 (11)	$3,700
Mexico	1,972,550	103,400,165	1,852 (235)	$9,000
Nicaragua	129,494	5,023,818	182 (11)	$2,500
St. Kitts & Nevis	261	38,736	2 (2)	$8,700
Suriname	163,270	436,494	46 (5)	$3,500
Venezuela	912,050	41,008,227	1,066 (93)	$6,300

Source: CIA Factbook.
* Square Km. **Estimated July 2002 figures ***Data from 2001****Estimated 2001.

their large domestic base, highly sophisticated yield management systems, and lower cost structures, these mega-carriers have presented their Latin American counterparts with a very difficult challenge.

Second, the terms of U.S. bilateral agreements are heavily biased in favor of U.S. interests. Ten Latin American nations have now signed open skies treaties with the United States (Table 5.1), while many others have liberalized their bilateral air service agreements in recent years. The experience with liberalized markets has not been kind to many Latin American carriers. In Chile, the first Latin country to sign an open skies agreement in 1997, LAN-Chile and Ladeco suffered heavily at the hands of U.S. competitors, American and United Airlines (Graham, 1995). Roughly 14% of American's operating revenue comes from Latin America which is currently the highest level for a U.S. carrier (American Airlines, 2001). This clearly makes them a serious challenger, however, LAN-Chile has recovered well since 1995 posting the third highest growth rate of any carrier in the world with a 44.8% increase in sales. They posted record profits in 1997 and 1998 entering into an alliance with American Airlines (LAN-Chile, 2002). In November 2001, they opened a new cargo terminal in Miami. Cutbacks by U.S. carriers on marginal routes are likely to open up even more opportunities after 9/11. While the more liberal bilateral between the US and Mexico has increased the number of tourists traveling between the two countries and lowered fares, it has also decreased airline yields.   Both Aeromexico and Mexicana have suffered, experiencing a combined loss of US$371.5 million in 1992-1993 (Graham, 1995). The 1994 Mexican financial crisis almost brought both carriers to bankruptcy before they were purchased by CINTRA, a consortium of banks. The two carriers have since agreed to cooperate on ground handling, training, and computer reservation systems which have allowed them to improve service and lower costs. Aeromexico has since joined the SkyTeam alliance while Mexicana is a member of STAR (Moody's Transportation Manual, 2000). Third, less than one-third of Latin America's carriers are now state-owned. While this is generally a good trend, the fact that many Latin American governments rushed into the sale of loss-making carriers as part of the general shift toward market economies in the 1990s did nothing to help these carriers adjust to the new realities of industry deregulation and liberalized international operations. In fact, this rush to privatize and throw open markets may have done as much or more to destabilize the Latin American carriers as US mega-carrier competition. Cross-border consolidation of some of Latin America's carriers could create a core of airlines capable of withstanding US carrier pressure. Greater economic ties between the countries of the Americas also promise to increase passenger and cargo traffic.

Caribbean nations in particular have struggled in international aviation. Of the 44 developing nations identified by the Commonwealth Secretariat/World Bank Joint Task Force (2000) as vulnerable small states i.e. population below 1.5 million people, thirty-three are in the Caribbean region. The United Nations Conference on Trade and Development has also addressed the problem of small island developing states (SIDS). Although these two lists are not identical, both reports cited similar concerns and issues for these nations. According to the U.N. report, SIDS not only face problems associated with their smallness but are 1) more susceptible and vulnerable to natural disasters, 2) geographically remote and dispersed, 3) ecologically fragile, and 4) constrained in terms of transportation and communication infrastructure (Abeyratne, 1999; UN General Assemby, 1993). Tourism is a key component in the economy of most of these nations. Given the generally inaccessible nature of SIDS, air transportation is vital in developing tourism. Many of these nations would benefit from direct nonstop service from major tourist markets, however, these nations tend to lack the fleet or market access to offer these services necessitating island hopping (Abeyratne, 1999; Antoniou, 2001). Abeyratne (1999) has suggested that air services in these regions may qualify as natural monopolies and would, therefore, not benefit from the effects of competition i.e. improving efficiency, lowering costs etc. Caribbean nations could, however, benefit from a greater focus on regional cooperation and/or integration in a number of areas like aviation.

Turbulence in the Middle East

The Middle East is composed of 14 nations that accounted for roughly 3% of the world scheduled passenger traffic in 2001. These 14 countries range widely in size and income (Table 17.3). Like the region of Africa, most aviation activities are focused on international travel rather than domestic service which accounts for less than 20% for the region as a whole (Feiler and Goodovitch, 1994). This figure actually hides a great deal of variation; Saudi Arabia has a domestic market that has increased at an average annual rate of 15% from 1970 to 1994 carrying over 1.6 million passengers (Ba-Fail, Abed, and Jasimuddin, 2000) while the Gulf States and Kuwait have essentially no domestic air services (Taneja, 1988). In 1982 ICAO identified three attributes of the Middle East that affected the demand for air travel. First, there is a relatively large movement of people to, from, and within the area. Second, the population density of the area is comparable to North and Latin America. Third, two-thirds of the area's population lives in oil producing nations. In fact, oil and tourism have been key factors in the traffic growth in the Middle East (Graham, 1995; Taneja, 1998).

Many Middle Eastern nations have invested heavily in infrastructure improvements in recent years, particularly airport expansion and fleet renewal. Dubai International Airport, located in the UAE, served over 12 million passengers in 2000, making it the busiest airport in the region. King Abdulaziz International Airport in Saudi Arabia served over 10 million in that same year (Ferry, 2002). Emirates Airline, based out of Dubai, has been one of the fastest growing and highest quality rated carriers in the world. El Al, the Israeli carrier, is considered one of the most efficient carriers in the world. In short, as a whole, the Middle East enjoys a number of advantages over the other two regions discussed in this chapter. While the wealth is still unevenly distributed in the region, efforts have been made by richer nations to assist the neighbors. The single greatest factor limiting the ability of the region to prosper has been the instability and conflicts that seem to be endemic (Graham, 1995).

Table 17.3: Information on Selected Middle Eastern Countries

Country	Area*	Population**	Airports (paved)***	GDP****
Egypt	1,001,450	70,712,345	92 (72)	$3,700
Iran	1,648,000	66,622,704	322 (118)	$6,400
Iraq	437,072	24,001,816	108 (73)	$2,500
Israel	20,770	6,029,529	54 (29)	$20,000
Jordan	92,300	5,368,585	136 (58)	$4,200
Kuwait	17,820	2,111,561	7 (3)	$15,100
Libya	1,759,540	5,368,585	136 (58)	$7,600
Saudi Arabia	1,960,582	23,513,330	209 (71)	$10,600
Syria	185,180	17,155,814	99 (24)	$3,200
UAE	82,880	2,445,989	38 (19)	$21,100
Yemen	527,970	18,701,257	49 (14)	$820

Source: CIA Factbook.
* Square Km. **Estimated July 2002 figures ***Data from 2001****Estimated 2001.

Helping the Developing World

In addition to providing funding and technical advice, developed nations can also contribute to the success of civil aviation in these regions by considering the adoption of a number of recommendations by international agencies and scholars. ICAO addressed these issues in a 1996 report on preferential treatment for member States who are at a competitive disadvantage in international markets. The following is a list of their recommendations for preferential treatment:

1.   The asymmetric liberalization of market access in bilaterals with developed countries, including access to more cities and greater fifth freedom rights.
2.   More flexibility for air carriers in changing capacity and gauge between routes in bilaterals.

3. Trial periods for carriers of developing nations to operate under liberal arrangements for an agreed period of time.
4. Gradual introduction of more liberal market access over longer periods of time for developing country carriers.
5. Use of liberalized arrangements.
6. Waiver of nationality requirements for ownership.
7. Special allowances for developing nation carriers to use more modern, leased aircraft.
8. Preferential treatment for the purpose of slot allocation.
9. More liberal policies for ground handling, conversion of currency, and employment of foreign personnel (ICAO, 1996).

Several scholars have also made some additional recommendations. Abeyratne (1998) has suggested that developed nations consider allowing an air carrier from one country to exercise the air traffic rights on behalf of another carrier in the event that no carrier from that country were able to launch service to that route for economic reasons. Other recommendations by aviation scholars in Findlay, Sein, and Singh's (1997) book on policy reforms in Asian markets include opening freight and charter markets between countries in a region, relaxing code sharing and ownership rules, liberalizing markets before airline privatization, and expanding multilateral agreements with regional neighbors. Longer term, these expanded multilateral agreements could become regional open skies and general trade agreements, even inclusion in GATS (these ideas summarize the recommendations of Oum, Forsyth, and Trethaway in Findley et al, 1997).

References

Abeyratne, R.I.R. (1998), 'The Future of African Civil Aviation', *Journal of Transportation World Wide*, vol. 3, pp. 30-48.

Abeyratne, R.I.R. (1999), 'The Environmental Impact of Tourism and Air Transport on the Sustainable Development of Small Island Developing States', *Journal of Transportation World Wide*, vol. 4, pp. 55-66.

American Airlines (2001), 'Annual Report-2001', www.sec.gov.

Antoniou, A. (2001), 'The Air Transportation Policy of Small States: Meeting the Challenges of Globalization', *Journal of Transportation World Wide*, vol. 6, pp. 65-92.

Ba-Fail, A.O., Abed, S.Y. and Jasimuddin, S.M. (2000), 'The Determinants of Domestic Air Travel Demand in the Kingdom of Saudi Arabia', *Journal of Air Transportation World Wide*, vol. 5, pp. 72-86.

BBC News (2002a), 'Air Afrique Finally Goes Bust', www.bbc.co.uk, February 7.

BBC News (2002b), 'Pan-African Airline Takes off', www.bbc.co.uk, April 29.

BBC News (2002c), 'Nigeria Airways Halves Workforce', www.bbc.co.uk, January 4.

BBC News (2002d), 'Ghana Airways Seeks Outside Help', www.bbc.co.uk, June 13.

BBC News (2002e), 'Air Mali Strikes Egyptian Alliance', www.bbc.co.uk, May 8.

BBC News (2002f), 'New Airline for West Africa', www.bbc.co.uk, September 6.

BBC News (2002g), 'Air Tanzania Sell-off Delayed', www.bbc.co.uk, August 5.

CIA Factbook (2002), www.odci.gov/cia/publications/factbook.

Commonwealth Secretariat/World Bank (2000), *Small States: Meeting the Challenges in the Global Economy*, A Report of the Commonwealth Secretariat/World Bank Joint Task Force on Small States, London, March.

Feiler, G. and Goodovitch, T. (1994), 'Decline and Growth, Privatization and Protectionism in the Middle East Airline Industry', *Journal of Transport Geography*, vol. 2, pp. 55-64.

Findlay, C., Sein, C.L. and Singh, K. (eds) (1997), *Asian Pacific Air Transport: Challenges and Policy Reform*, Institute of Southeast Asian Studies, Singapore.

Godwin, N. (2002), 'Kenya Airways Comes to N. America to "do Business"', *Boston Ventures Management, Inc.*, June 17.

Graham, B. (1995), *Geography and Air Transport*, John Wiley and Sons, New York.

ICAO (1996), *Study on Preferential Measures for Developing Countries*, ICAO Doc AT-WP/1789, August 22.

ICAO (2002), 'Press Release: One Year After 11 September Events ICAO Forecasts World Air Passenger Traffic will Exceed 2000 levels in 2003', October 2.

LAN-Chile (2002), 'Our History', www.lanchile.com.

M2 Communications Ltd. (2000), 'Uganda Airlines Corporation to go into Liquidation', www.findarticles.com, March 31.

Moody's Transportation Manual, Mergent FIS, New York.

Nuutinen, H. (1993), 'Fighting to Beat Back the US Majors', *Avmark Aviation Economist*, vol. 10, pp. 11-18.

Ott, J. (2001), 'Rising African Safety Culture Paves Way for New Projects', *Aviation Week and Space Technology*, March 19, pp. 106-109.

Phillips, E.H. (2002), 'Africa Leads in Hull Losses: FSF Cites Challenges to Flying', *Aviation Week and Space Technology*, April 22, pp. 44-45.

Taneja, N.K. (1988), *The International Airline Industry: Trends, Issues, and Challenges*, Lexington Books, Lexington.

United Nations General Assemby (1993), Resolution 47/186, A/RES/47/186, February.

World Bank Group (2002), 'Making Monterrey Work for Africa: New Study Highlights Dwindling Aid Flows, Mounting Challenges', Press Release no. 2002/273/S.

Chapter 18

Wave of the Future

Waves of Change

In *The Third Wave*, Alvin Toffler, noted futurist, talks about wave-front analysis or the examination of history as a succession of waves of change that represent the discontinuities or breakpoints in the pattern. The goal of the futurist or forecaster is, of course, to identify the wave-front, the leading edge of the approaching wave; the goal of the firm is to position itself to ride the 'wave of the future'. Unfortunately, the present sometimes resides between two waves of change or, worse still, the trailing wave has begun to overtake the earlier wave creating a clash of currents that makes it difficult to catch the wave-front. In the 1960s an observant watcher of aviation might have detected the rolling motion that would eventually become the breaking wave of change once the bottom began to shallow. On this wave, among other things, rode the principle of deregulation. Even as this wave approached the shore in the early 1990s, another wave was forming that carries with it the possibility to change the way we see aviation. The international airline industry was already riding between these wave fronts before 9/11 but those events have accelerated the trailing wave. It is now overtaking the earlier wave causing the raging ocean that we see today.

Before the ink was dry on the manuscript for this book another airline was swamped by the turbulent seas - United Air Lines. United became the second U.S. carrier to file for bankruptcy since 9/11. The world's second largest airline with 1,700 flights a day and 20 percent of the total flights in the U.S. is now facing the prospect of a major downsizing which is likely to include labor cuts of up to US$2 billion, fleet reductions of possibly a dozen or more planes, and another round of schedule cutbacks. Worse still, many industry experts give the company less than a 50 percent chance of avoiding Chapter 7 liquidation (Arndt and Zellner, 2002; Holmes and Matlack, 2002). If this bankruptcy is allowed to drag on beyond the Spring of 2003, it is likely to spread the 'bankruptcy virus' to other U.S. carriers (Wolf, 1995).

Forecasting is a dangerous and thankless job, however, the purpose of this final chapter is to summarize what 'we think we know' about what is happening in the airline industry and where 'we think it is going'. There are no certainties and miraculous turnarounds do occasionally happen, but the odds-makers in Las Vegas and the hindsighters in industry and academia will have to deal with these issues when the future becomes the past and 'prediction' becomes easy.

What We Think We Know

At this stage it does not seem premature to declare that the mega-carrier concept in North America is dead. As discussed in Chapter 15, the mega-carrier pursued by the large U.S. carriers demanded the creation of a large domestic and international route network linked at key hubs to a low cost feeder system. The system was managed by an automation system designed to maximize revenues (yields) and manage capacity (Taneja, 1988). Carriers consolidated their hold on these strategic hubs utilizing large aircraft that waited at the gates for banks of smaller feeder aircraft to arrive with passengers to fill the available seats. These large aircraft allowed carriers to spread their higher cost worker salaries over more passengers, giving them a somewhat better productivity per worker. On the other hand, these crews waited at the gates, often for extended periods, for the arriving bank of passengers. The revenue system which 'managed' these passengers often had as many as 10 different fare classes with attached rules and restrictions. The system could, and often was, run daily to determine if the pre-assigned number of seats in each class were filling up to expectations. If not, adjustments could be made in fares to achieve maximum yield. These two factors created conflicting demands on the mega-carrier. First, the pressure of low-cost price competition necessitated cuts in airline spending, many in the visible area of service quality, fare restrictions, meal quality, etc. Second, the revenue system placed consumers in the same cabin who were receiving the same service but at very different fare levels. This gave rise to the ultimate airline shopper, the individual whose mission in life was to shop until they had achieved the lowest fare possible and 'beat the system'. In the past, these 'shoppers' were primarily leisure travelers who could, and did, arrange their travel around deals. Business passengers continued to pay higher fares in exchange for the ability to book with little notice and travel at certain times of the day or week.

The events of 9/11 have accelerated two trailing waves that were already rapidly overtaking the mega-carrier concept. The first overtaking change is the growth of low-cost carriers who are likely to double their market share in the U.S. (and Europe) in the next decade. As major carriers around the world pull out of marginal markets in an effort to improve profitability, low-cost carriers will move in to fill the gaps. These carriers offer simplified fare structures, few restrictions, and, in many cases, reliable, consistent basic service. The second change is the flight of the traditional business traveler away from the high fare-high restriction traditional carriers and toward either less travel overall or lower costs carriers. These travelers have subsidized the cost-minded leisure traveler for years and have accumulated more frequent flyer miles than they could ever use. They have sat in lounges around the world drinking little bottles of wine while reading the financial publications of a dozen nations. They do not need any more gifts from the frequent flyer magazine or little salt-and-pepper shakers with their meals. Worse still, their companies are beginning to wonder if they can afford their travel budgets anymore.

If the U.S. mega-carrier is dying, then it won't die alone. Over the next two years, a number of the world's carriers will die, unless governments intervene in a major, and costly, way. Some of these carriers will come from small market nations where they were unable to generate enough long-term traffic to survive, particularly in the face of greater competition coming in the wake of international liberalization. Other carriers will fall victim to more efficient, low-cost carriers or to their own mistakes - overexpansion of routes, industry high labor costs, uncompetitive route structures, etc. Even more damning, carriers may fall victim to the harsh realities of the industry itself. Robert Crandall, former CEO of American Airlines, has said that '[i]f some of the steps that have been proposed to restore the industry's health are implemented, such as reducing labor costs and rationalizing fleets, U.S. carriers would stop hemorrhaging cash. But that's different from saying [the industry] can be economically and financially successful - which is to say, earn its cost of capital' (Crandall's Rx for Airlines, 2002). In a free market system, it seems inconceivable that firms could continue to exist without the ability to earn the cost of their own capital. Yet, as noted in Chapter 14, the stock value of the major U.S. carriers has dropped sharply, many into the single digits. With the exception of Southwest, these carriers have been downgraded below the junk bond level of BBB. The industry's debt leverage rate has risen to almost 93%, meaning that 93 cents on the dollar is now borrowed at a rate of interest that is above the current returns to assets and equity earned by the industry (ATA, 2002). Neither an individual firm nor an industry can survive for long under these conditions.

If the mega-carrier is on its way out, then so is sitting and waiting; carriers can no longer afford to have high-priced flight crews waiting at gate hubs for the next bank of flights to arrive. There is an old adage in the airline industry that 'if a plane is not flying, it is not making money' and these planes are not making money. To add to the problem, flights were often held waiting for arrivals which had a negative impact on the all-important on-time-arrival figures. After all, it is more difficult to arrive on time if you leave late. Arrivals and departures were also 'peaked' around customer preferences. Unfortunately, when everyone wants to leave at the same time, no one can because the airport capacity is not there nor can it be added if this capacity sits idle during 'non-peak' times.

What We Think We'll Try

Airlines around the world are being forced to make changes in many areas including labor contracts, employee benefits, hub-and-spoke systems, and fare structures. American Airlines has announced a new 'rolling hub' system that includes spreading flights out during the day to increase the utilization of planes and flight crews. In addition, they are planning to institute some changes to the fare structure that are similar, if not as broad, as those initiated by some of the European carriers (Arndt and Zellner, 2002). In the area of labor costs and benefits, carriers are moving to reduce these levels, but since contracts tend to call for the layoff of junior employees first average costs per employee are rising. This fact coupled with a system of rigid work rules means that productivity is declining (Velocci, 2002a, 2002b).

In one of the boldest moves yet, Delta Air Lines has announced its decision to expand its low-cost operations (Haddad and Zellner, 2002). Theoretically, it makes sense to focus on the segment of the industry that is growing, particularly when your carrier is facing some of the stiffest competition from this group of carriers. What remains to be seen is whether Delta and successfully run a 'carrier within a carrier'. Few if any carriers have been able to match the success of the Southwest low-cost, no-frills strategy even when they start out with the concept. It appears even more difficult for a traditional full-service, high-cost carrier to achieve success as the United Shuttle, USAirways MetroJet, Continental's Lite, and British Airways' Go tend to show. Aside from the very real difference in mindset inherent in a cost-focus strategy, there are two other significant problems. First, in order to be successful the low-cost unit needs low cost labor. Differences in wage scales tend to create dissension among employees of 'one company'. Any reasonable thinking employee of the low cost unit has to at least consider strategies for moving up in the company world. Second, if the two units are set up to run independently, then competition is likely to arise between the two units as both attempt to appeal to the same customer groups to 'grow their market share'. Again, any 'right-minded' low-cost unit of 'one company' would have to be considering how best to lure the dissatisfied business traveler to their operation. While it would be nice to think that they were luring these passengers away from the competition, some will inevitably come from their higher-cost, traditional operations. The answer to this problem might be to establish some artificial competitive boundaries between the units. For example, the U.S. car company Saturn, part of the General Motors Company, was restricted to selling 'compact' cars. Only recently was it allowed to produce mid-size cars and the popular Sport Utility Vehicles (SUVs). In the case of the major carriers, a domestic-international split might make the most sense. Certainly in the U.S., domestic service is increasingly seen as a commodity and price as the driver of consumer choice. International service demands larger aircraft and generates higher yields based on consumer desires (and willingness to pay) to receive higher levels of service on international flights. The battleground is likely to be the few high density, high yield domestic routes, although Robert Crandall has suggested that less than 500 of the roughly 6,000 routes in the U.S. might qualify for non-stop service (Crandall's Rx for Airlines, 2002).

If the 'carrier within a carrier' concept has not worked well, then another questionable concept is the ability of airlines to reposition themselves from high-cost, traditional carriers to low-cost competitors. Two bankruptcies did allow Continental Airlines to achieve lower input costs (primarily labor costs) than their major traditional competitors, but this is not the same as repositioning to achieve the cost structure of a Southwest (Oum and Yu, 1998). At the present time, America West and US Airways are attempting to lower costs through changes in labor costs or offering purchased meal options. There is no evidence yet that they can or will become true low-cost carriers. Most of the world's carriers are attempting to lower costs, but few of these carriers would appear to have a reasonable chance of competing against the 'true' low cost carriers.

Thinking the Unthinkable

The industry has tried cost-cutting before only to give back these advantages when times improved. They have tried some incremental shifts in market focus and marginal tinkering with revenue systems. These are all short-term solutions to longterm systemic problems. These issues have been addresses in more detail in the previous chapters in this section. Now it is time to consider what role, if any, the world's governments can play. Deregulation has been praised for the dramatic lowering of fares and damned for creating the destructive price competition that has been a part of the financial crisis experience by the industry in each of the last three decades. The truth is that the industry is still subject to a number of regulations; it is not regulation-free. The question becomes not whether you have regulation or not, but what you choose to regulate. The airline industry will never achieve the ideal of perfect competition extolled by economists, but how many competitors are necessary to insure 'workable' or 'contestable' markets. Should governments intervene to save failing carriers? Should the government act to change bankruptcy laws to allow the market to adjust overcapacity more quickly or will investors and lenders self-adjust to the realities of a failing market? Should the government change its position on consolidation, foreign ownership, and right-to-establishment in the industry?

There are as many answers to these questions as there are 'experts' in aviation and economics. Let's consider the following possibilities:

No Action at All

In almost any situation, one possible response is to 'do nothing'. Sometimes doing nothing turns out to be better than 'doing something wrong'. The problem is that governments generally want to be seen as 'doing something'. In the case of national airlines, there is also likely to be tremendous pressure from citizens' groups and other stakeholders to act. In the United States, the extent to which the current crisis is blamed on the terrorist acts of 9/11 may lead many to argue for action to prevent another victory for terrorism; politics and aviation have never been strangers. If governments choose to act, there is a range of actions that they could attempt.

Consolidation

The first type of intervention governments might consider would be allowing further consolidation to occur in domestic markets. This option has a long history in aviation. Weaker carriers can either be acquired outright or, as in the case of TWA, another carrier may acquire the assets (not the liabilities) of the failing company. This is a market solution that has the potential to save some jobs, airports/local communities, etc. It would reduce some of the overcapacity in domestic markets while saving, hopefully, the valuable assets of the failing companies. Given the current financial weakness in the industry overall, it is not clear how much of this consolidation could occur in many national markets; the resources are simply not there to acquire others, at least not within the airline industry itself. Even if possibilities exist, governments probably will not, and should not, approve 'any merger'. Mergers between very similar competitors would result in greater competitive losses than mergers between complementary carriers. The effect of mergers between carriers with very similar routes structures has the potential to severely reduce capacity (and competition) in certain markets, resulting in higher prices, fewer choices, and lower capacity. In almost any conceivable merger or consolidation, there is likely to be some loss of jobs, cutbacks on redundant service or unprofitable routes, and closure of redundant facilities. This is simply the nature of such transactions whose aims are lowering costs through economies of scale, elimination of redundancy or synergistic sharing between the units of the 'new company'. Consolidation, of course, does not guarantee that any of these things will occur. The proposed merger of United and US Airways would not have created a better, higher quality carrier; it would have combined two high cost, poorly managed carriers into a bigger higher cost carrier. The combined carrier might have been in a better position to control capacity in the short run, but other U.S. carriers could not have allowed the size difference to continue for long. Pressure would have built for the approval of further consolidation to create 'more equal' competitors.

Foreign Ownership

Changes to rules on foreign ownership could open up the pool of potential investors and bring new money into the industry, but only if these investors are allowed the control that goes with stock ownership. As Richard Branson has noted, only a fool would invest in a company without some assurances of control. As noted in the introduction to this book, governments have historically resisted this option for a number of reasons, most notably national defense, but it could be a reasonable option for governments as long as they feel that they are able to retain the right to approve the proposed merger and can create mechanisms to 'control' the actions of these companies. In a separate, but related area, governments could grant the right-of-establishment in domestic markets allowing foreign companies to establish operations in domestic markets and operate as domestic competitors with the same rights, privileges, and obligations as 'true' domestic firms. The first action could save airlines that cannot attract domestic investment, however, it would not increase the number of competitors in domestic markets. The second action has the potential to actually increase the number of competitors in domestic markets, although if these new competitors prove more efficient than existing domestic competitors, there could be long-term reductions in the number of competitors.

    If consolidation occurs in national markets either through merger or simple airline failure, there will be pressure to open up domestic markets to foreign ownership or foreign carrier operation to increase competition. In fact, these two concepts are different sides of the same coin. Either way, the influence of foreign nationals in domestic markets increases. Many of these issues were already discussed in Chapter 16 on liberalization and will not be repeated here, but it is possible to envision a situation where investment among alliance partners could result eventually in an international carrier, owned and managed, by individuals from multiple countries. In essence, sixty years after the Chicago Conference the Australian-New Zealand proposal could come to pass (Chapter 3). Domestic markets could be left to low-cost carriers. International service would become the province of large multinational entities. The European fear that such an entity would be dominated by the U.S. mega-carriers is growing less likely given the financial weakness of U.S. carriers and the fact that the U.S. market is expected to recover more slowly than the rest of the world in terms of passenger and cargo traffic. Historically, U.S. carriers were thought to gain power from the fact that they brought with them a large domestic network, but this too is becoming less important as the domestic market shifts toward low-cost carriers. Governments tend to follow rather than lead, but for such a transition to occur there would have to be substantial changes in the rules and regulations governing not only ownership, but safety, airworthiness, licensing, etc.

Government Loans, Guarantees, etc

Governments have already intervened post-9/11 to reimburse carriers for direct losses and provide insurance coverage. The U.S. Airline Stabilization Board has also provided loans to eligible airlines. The question becomes 'How far are governments willing to go?' Given the furor over Belgium intervention in the case of Sabena and criticism over the handling of the bankruptcy of Swissair, there will be pressure brought to bear by the EC to prevent major government interventions to save failing carriers. If the EC is successful in preventing government intervention in their market, they would likely push the U.S. and other governments to do the same in their markets. This may not stop some national governments from attempting to creatively aid their struggling carriers, but it should prevent major, overt bailouts. While the U.S. government has historically preferred to intervene in indirect ways to aid their national carriers, the debate over the extent of government intervention is already underway. United Air Lines will be a test of the willingness of the U.S. government to allow the free market to determine the fate of its second largest carrier. In its bankruptcy filing, United acknowledged that it was losing US$20 million a day. Worse still, the business plan that had failed to convince the ATSB to intervene also failed to convince the private lenders of capital that United could return to profitability in a reasonable timeframe. At present, United has until March to convince the firms that granted it debtor-in-possession financing that they should invest further in the future of United. If they are unconvinced, United faces liquidation, unless the U.S. government intervenes (McCartney, 2002).

The sudden and rapid fall of a carrier that is responsible for roughly 20% of the domestic flights in the U.S. would certainly be disruptive, but it is not clear how long this disruption would last. There is enough capacity in the U.S. system to adjust to the loss of United. Certainly, American Airlines would benefit in Chicago and a number of other major cities. Regional and low-cost carriers would also now be able to swim in the pond without fear of being eaten by a bigger fish.

Labor costs at other carriers would likely fall due to a general downward pressure from the bankrupt carriers as well as the new supply of labor in the market. The Star Alliance would be forced to seek a new U.S. partner to fill this niche, most likely Northwest or Continental (or both). Internationally, it might take longer to adjust capacity only because of the restrictive nature of some bilaterals, but given the decline in both Atlantic and Pacific traffic to the U.S. since 9/11 this may also not pose a pressing problem. In both the domestic and national context, a reduction in capacity would benefit existing carriers, many of whom are currently struggling under the combined effects of 9/11 and the economic slowdown as well as potential new entrants.

If the U.S. government intervenes in some way to save United, prolonging their period in bankruptcy, American Airlines would most likely be under tremendous pressure to file for bankruptcy. America West, already weak, might also follow. In fact, the virus could spread throughout the major carriers. Bankruptcy laws are 'designed to serve two fundamental purposes: (1) to relieve an honest debtor from overburdensome financial obligations and give him or her a fresh start, free of claims of former creditors, and (2) to provide for equitable treatment of creditors who are competing for the debtor's limited assets' (Roszkowski, 1989: 603). It is not intended to relieve a company's management from the responsibility for their own actions or inactions nor to save companies without the resources, assets, or abilities to achieve future success. At the present time, it is not clear that United can either reduce its costs to be more competitive in domestic markets or shrink to profitability by shedding losing routes, units, or operations. There is a further difficulty involved with bankruptcy that relates to the fact that in many cases the pre-bankruptcy management remains in place and the company becomes controlled by its major creditors. These two factors can create conflicts of interest because the new owners and old management have incentives to strip the company of valuable assets to recoup their costs. If this occurs, the company that emerges from bankruptcy may do so without the assets it most needs to be competitive.

Even if the U.S. government does not intervene to 'save' United, it could opt to intervene in some way to limit (or manage) the chaos that its sudden collapse would cause. While it is possible to speculate on the winners and losers in such a chaos, it is not entirely clear that government can manage the process in a way that is any fairer or more efficient than the market. For example, the collapse of United would appear to benefit their chief competitor in Chicago, American Airlines. American already has a presence at Chicago O'Hare Airport and presumably could ramp up in a reasonably quick manner to increase their presence, whereas the other major carriers might find this more difficult. Small regional carriers might be able to re-deploy their assets relatively quickly, but might not be able to increase the size of their operations fast enough to hold on to these gains in the face of major carrier competition. Cross-Pacific competitor, Northwest, would appear to be in a position to benefit from a United liquidation more so than other U.S. carriers because it is considered an incumbent carrier in the all-important Japanese market. Short-term, consumers holding United tickets stand to lose unless other carriers are willing to honor those tickets, although even in this case, there is likely to be some 'fee' attached. As noted above, bankruptcy tends to favor the major creditors that assume control and are thus in a position to recoup more of their losses. Smaller creditors will not have this advantage.

Re-regulation

It is possible that the current crisis will cause some governments to re-examine the question of deregulation itself. Joseph Stiglitz, the 2001 Nobel Prize winner in Economics, has pointed out that deregulation episodes tend to give rise to a bubble-and-bust cycle (Stiglitz, 2002). Moreover, he has suggested that the benefits of deregulation have been overestimated citing the recent problems in financial markets, telecommunications, and electricity trading. Questions are being asked about the airline industry and the benefits and costs of deregulation. The self-interest of airlines who focus on growing their companies in the good times works to benefit consumers, especially when economic downturn creates overcapacity; it does not benefit the airlines faced with excess capacity, the aircraft leasing companies facing returned aircraft, the investors holding stock in failing companies or the local communities facing service cutbacks. Where you stand on the issue of re-regulation depends on where you sit, as the saying goes. Even those who might favor some form of re-regulation will not necessarily agree on what form that regulation should take. Does the government set service level standards? Does it control entry into the industry, establishing a maximum number of carriers or market share limits? Does it intervene to establish minimum/maximum prices? Does it intervene in labor issues, financial practices, alliance arrangements? The list of possible interventions is legion and the pros and cons of each action can, and will, be debated. Whatever the outcome in various countries, an ultimate judgment must be made on whether air transportation is an essential service that can be provided in a safe, economical way by a free market.

A Buffet Ending?

It is difficult to imagine a near-term future without some form of commercial air transportation. Air transportation is simply too vital to the growth and prosperity of the world economy and the nations that make up our world. This is the good news for those who have loved this industry for so long. The bad news may be that the aviation world as we know it may be ending and what emerges may not be the industry we would wish for our predecessors. The tragedy is that unless the industry applies the same ingenuity and daring to recreating itself in the aftermath of 9/11 as it did in the early years of its development, then it seems doomed to fulfill Warren Buffet's prophesy of making zero long-term profit. The challenge facing the airline industry is to prove Buffet wrong through thinking outside of the box that has been its home for so long. This is a challenge worthy of the next generation. It is my hope that the students of today will take up this challenge, not forgetting the past but not bound to its old ways and conventional wisdom.

References

Air Transport Association (2002), *State of the U.S. Airline Industry: A Report on Recent Trends for U.S. Air Carriers, 2002-2003*, Air Transport Association, Washington, D.C.

Arndt, M. and Zellner, W. (2002), 'How to Keep United Flying', *Business Week*, December 23, pp. 34-35.

'Crandall's Rx for Airlines' (2002), *Aviation Week and Space Technology*, November 18, p. 54.

Haddad, C. and Zellner, W. (2002), 'Getting Down and Dirty with Discounters', *Business Week*, October 28, pp. 77-78.

Holmes, S. and Matlack, C. (2002), 'Caught in United's Downdraft: How will Boeing's Finance and Leasing Business be Affected?', *Business Week*, December 23, p. 35.

McCartney, S. (2002), 'For United, liquidation is a very real possibility', *The Middle Seat*, December 20.

Oum, T.H. and Yu, C. (1998), *Winning Airlines: Productivity and Cost Competitiveness of the World's Major Airlines*, Kluwer Academic Publishers, Boston.

Roszkowski, M.E. (1989), *Business Law: Principles, Cases, and Policy*, Harper-Collins, New York.

Stiglitz, J. (2002), 'The roaring nineties', *Atlantic Monthly*, October, pp. 76-89.

Taneja, N.K. (1988), *The International Airline Industry: Trends, Issues & Challenges*, Lexington Books, Lexington, MA.

Velocci, A.L. (2002a), 'Can Majors Shift Focus Fast Enough to Survive', *Aviation Week and Space Technology*, November 18, pp. 52-54.

Velocci, A.L. (2002a), 'No Silver Bullet Seen for Airlines' Dilemma', *Aviation Week and Space Technology*, November 18, pp. 52-54.

Index